Welcome to Digital Photography

MARCIA REIFMAN
Santa Fe Community College and Santa Fe Workshops

LABYRINTH
PUBLICATIONS®
El Sobrante, CA

President and Publisher:
Brian Favro

Editorial Director:
Ted Ricks

Developmental Editor/Series Editor:
Russel Stolins

Managing Editor:
Laura A. Lionello

Production Manager:
Rad Proctor

Editorial Team:
Amy Berk and Holly Haynes

Indexing:
Susan Edwards

Cover Design:
Huckdesign

LABYRINTH
PUBLICATIONS®
El Sobrante, CA

Welcome to Digital Photography
by Marcia Reifman

Labyrinth Publications
3314 Morningside Drive
El Sobrante, California 94803
800.522.9746
On the Web at labpub.com

ISBN 1-59136-065-X

Manufactured in the United States of America.

05 06 07 08 09 0 9 8 7 6 5 4 3 2 1

Welcome to
Digital Photography

Table of Contents

Index of Quick Reference Tables

General Tasks

Memory Cards

Resolution

Sharing Photos

Preface

Welcome to Digital Photography provides comprehensive coverage of purchasing and working with digital cameras. The book begins with an overview of choosing and evaluating digital cameras and compares them to standard film cameras. Students also learn how the instruction manual that comes with the camera can be an invaluable resource. Next, students learn about memory cards: how to transfer images, format the cards, back up photos, and care for storage media. Of course, effective composition is important, so students learn the basics of this as well as how to use various camera settings. Once students are familiar with these settings, they move on to learning about exposure, depth of field, resolution, white balance settings, and file compression and formats. Finally it's time to begin the process of editing and refining photographs, and students are introduced to Photoshop Elements. In the final lesson, students learn how to share their photos with others through printing, posting to the Web, and emailing.

Labyrinth has been writing and publishing Microsoft® Office courses for more than 10 years. We are now expanding our book list to include other application programs including Macromedia® Dreamweaver®, Intuit® QuickBooks®, digital photography, and more. Labyrinth has developed a unique instructional design that makes learning faster and easier for students at all skill levels. Teachers have found that the Labyrinth model provides effective learning for students in both self-paced and instructor-led environments. The material is carefully crafted and built around compelling case studies that demonstrate the relevance of the subject matter. Mastery of this subject matter is ensured through the use of multiple levels of carefully crafted exercises. This book includes Concepts Review quizzes, and Hands-On and Skill Builder exercises.

Welcome to Digital Photography is also supported on the Labyrinth Web site with a comprehensive instructor support package that includes a printable solutions guide, lecture notes, a course syllabus, and more.

We are grateful to the many instructors who have used Labyrinth titles and suggested improvements to us during the 10 years we have been writing and publishing various best-selling series of textbooks. *Welcome to Digital Photography* has benefited from the review and suggestions of Bonnie Quan, Salinas Adult Education Center (Salinas, CA) and David Walk, Walla Walla Community College (Walla Walla, WA).

About the Author

Marcia Reifman (MA, Photography and Education) heads the digital imaging program at Santa Fe Community College in Santa Fe, New Mexico. She also teaches digital photography at Santa Fe Workshops and serves as house manager for Photo New York, Photo LA, and Photo San Francisco. At SFCC, she has twice been honored with the Teacher Excellence Award. In addition, Marcia has been recognized with a place in Who's Who Among America's Teachers®. She brings more than 20 years of experience in the photography field as a commercial and fine art photographer and a teacher. Marcia divides her time between teaching, creating fine art photography, and private consulting. She is passionate and committed to bringing clarity and ease to the world of digital imaging.

Introduction

Welcome to Labyrinth Publications, where you'll find your course to success. Our real world, project-based approach to education helps students grasp concepts, not just read about them, and prepares them for success in the workplace. Our straightforward, easy-to-follow language is ideal for both instructor-led classes and self-paced labs. At Labyrinth, we're dedicated to one purpose: delivering quality courseware that is comprehensive yet concise, effective, and affordable. It's no wonder that Labyrinth is a recognized leader in Microsoft Office and operating system courseware.

More than a million users have learned Office our way. At Labyrinth, we believe that successful teaching begins with exceptional courseware. That's why we've made it our goal to develop innovative texts that empower both teachers and students. We give educators the necessary resources to deliver clear, relevant instruction and students the power to take their new skills far beyond the classroom.

Labyrinth Gives You More Choices

- ProStart™ Series—This new series of full-length, full-featured texts teach professional-level skills with popular programs by Macromedia and Intuit using Labyrinth's accessible and efficient methods. As they complete work projects, students learn how to create deliverables that are ready for primetime and to manage bookkeeping tasks for small businesses.
- Microsoft Office 2003 Series—These full-length, full-featured texts explore applications in the Office 2003 system. All application-specific books in

this series are Microsoft Office Specialist approved for the Microsoft Office 2003 certification exams, and the Word and Excel books are also approved for the Microsoft Office 2003 Expert certification exams.

- Silver™ Series—Designed especially for adult learners, seniors, and non-native English speakers, this series includes larger fonts and screens, our unmistakable straightforward design, and fun hands-on projects.
- Quick Courses—Designed for short classes, self-paced courses, and accelerated workshops, each lesson in these books is broken down into subtopics that provide quick access to key concepts.
- ProStart Foundations™ Series—These full-length, full-featured texts for operating systems and applications include new Microsoft Windows titles and are designed to lay a solid foundation for students.
- ProStart Series for Office XP—These full-length, full-featured texts walk students through the basic and advanced skills of the primary Office XP applications. Most are Microsoft Office Specialist approved. The Office XP Essentials and Comprehensive courses offer surveys of all the primary Office XP applications.
- Briefcase™ Series for Office XP—The popular and inexpensive choice for short classes, self-paced courses, and accelerated workshops (mix and match for longer classes), these concise texts provide quick access to key concepts. Most are Microsoft Office Specialist approved.

Silver Series Teaching Resources

Instructor Support Material

To help ensure success, Labyrinth provides a comprehensive instructor support package that includes the following:

- Lecture notes, including a list of topic presented and estimated time to complete each lesson
- Answer keys for the Concepts Review questions in each lesson
- Comprehensive classroom setup instructions
- A customizable sample syllabus

- A teacher-customizable background knowledge survey to gather information on student needs and experience at the beginning of the course
- Printer-friendly exercise solution guides and solution files for the Hands-On and Skill Builder exercises

These and more resources are available on our Web site at labpub.com and on our instructor support CD, which you can obtain by calling our customer service staff at 800.522.9746.

Web site

The Web site labpub.com/learn/silver/digphoto/ features content designed to support the lessons and provide additional learning resources for this book. This main page contains links to individual lesson pages, if applicable.

Labyrinth's Successful Instructional Design

In conjunction with the straightforward, easy to read and understand writing style, Labyrinth books feature a proven instructional design. The following pages demonstrate the carefully crafted design elements that build student confidence and ensure their success.

Lesson introductions present clear learning objectives.

LESSON 3

Choosing and Evaluating Digital Cameras

Digital cameras are no longer a thing of the future; they now outsell film cameras, and manufacturers are producing two to six new digital camera models each year. Digital camera owners can now easily share their photos on the Web and they do not even need computer access to get good quality, low-cost prints. Digital cameras are becoming more affordable and easier to use. It is now commonplace to see people holding digital cameras out in

KAIT
BRIAN

PAGE Meade (866-439-0989)

Case studies introduce a practical application that integrate topics presented in each lesson.

Case Study

Elisa is feeling confident about using her digital camera now that she has mastered its basic settings and features. She easily navigates through her instruction manual when she has a question or needs to learn more about a specific option or setting. It is now time to better understand the use of memory cards, how to transfer images from the memory card to the computer, where and how to store images, and how to back up images so they are well preserved for the future.

Taking pictures is Elisa's way of preserving memories and recording events in her life. She is committed to doing this in the best way possible by following a few key concepts pertaining to storing and caring for her images.

Concepts discussions are kept concise and use illustrations for added clarity and to help students understand the material introduced.

Quick Reference tables provide generic procedures for key tasks that will work outside the context of the lesson.

Working with Storage Media

Types, capacity, and care of digital memory cards were covered in Lesson 2, Working with Camera Manuals, Memory Cards, and Composition Basics. We will now explore the best way to use these cards in the camera and the choices available for transferring image files to the computer. In this section, you will learn how to replay, delete, and protect images, and how to format memory cards.

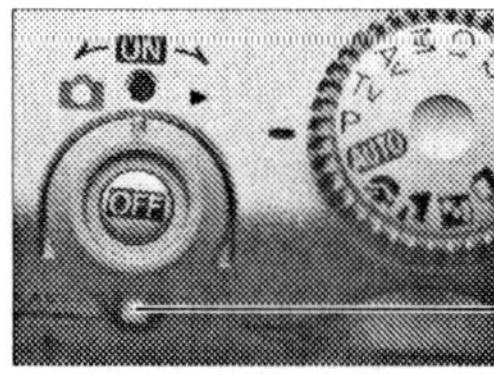

Replay lever on the Canon Power Shot

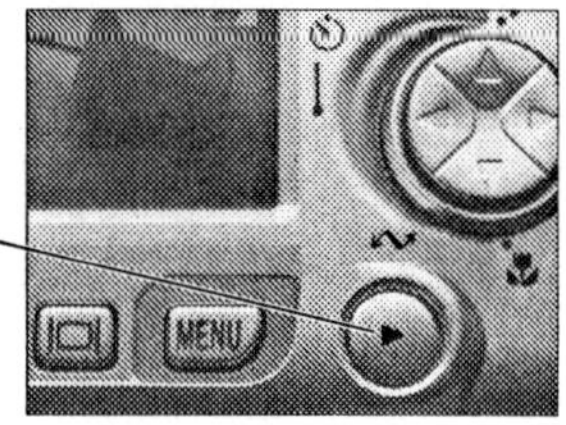

Replay button on the Nikon Coolpix

The following table illustrates the image replay options and when to use each.

QUICK REFERENCE: Using Replay Options

Image Replay Option	How It Looks	When to Use
Single View		To check exposure and composition or to show to others
Index		To edit or quickly locate specific images
Magnifying (Zoom Mode)		To check sharpness and focus

Hands-On exercises are detailed tutorials that help students master the skills introduced in the concepts discussions. The illustrations provide clear instructions and allow unparalleled ease of use.

HANDS-ON 3.1 **Edit a Photo**

In this exercise, you will crop the photo and use the Quick Fix panel to perform some automated color correction.

Before You Begin: The Anna010 file should still be open.

Crop the Photo

Now you will crop some unnecessary portions of the photo.

1. Follow these steps to crop the photo:

Ⓐ Click the Fit On Screen button near the top-left corner of the PE window to resize the photos to the proper proportion.

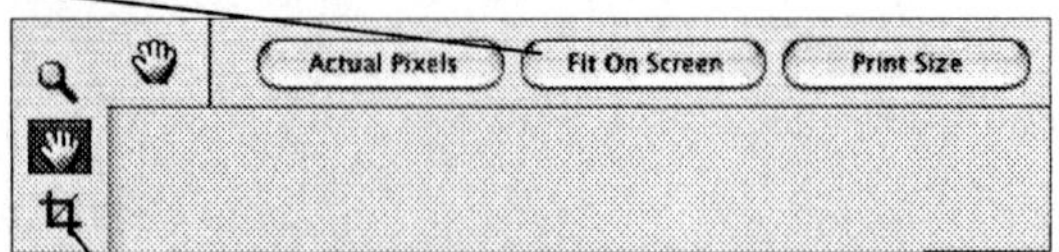

Ⓑ Choose the Crop tool.

Ⓒ In After (not Before) view, drag a selection box around the subject of the photo.

Ⓓ Double-click anywhere within the selection to complete the crop command.

The **Concepts Review section** at the end of each lesson includes both true/false and multiple choice questions.

Concepts Review

True/False Questions

			Page number
1. One of the major advantages of a larger compact digital camera is a larger LCD.	**true**	**false**	______
2. The LCD on SLR cameras may be used for composing and reviewing pictures.	**true**	**false**	______
3. A three megapixel camera will give you 11 × 14 inch prints.	**true**	**false**	______
4. Each type of memory card is made for a specific brand of camera.	**true**	**false**	______
5. A digital camera with a long shutter lag is not the best choice for action shots.	**true**	**false**	______

Multiple Choice Questions

1. Instead of film, digital cameras use ________.

   Page number: ______

   a. filters that let in red, green, and blue light
   b. a small plate covered with a grid of light sensors

3. What is the major difference between digital (electronic) viewfinder compacts and other midsize compacts?

   Page number: ______

   a. They have a swivel and tilt LCD viewing screen
   b. They have a larger optical viewfinder

Skill Builder exercises provide fun, hands-on projects with reduced levels of detailed instruction so students can develop and test their mastery of the material.

Skill Builders

SKILL BUILDER 3.1 Review Images for Sharpness

In this exercise, you will use the Replay features to check the sharpness and composition of your pictures.

Before You Begin: Make sure your camera is set on Automatic or Program so you can determine exposure settings.

Take Several Photos

1. Choose someone who is willing to spend about 20 minutes having his/her hands photographed.
   You will be practicing your skills with composition and using focus lock.
2. Pose the person so his/her hands are against a solid color background.
   You can use a piece of cloth, a sheet, a jacket, or a blank wall behind or under the hands.
3. Carefully frame the hands so they are not directly in the center of the photograph.
   This helps balance the composition and makes the photograph more interesting.
4. Using focus lock, take a picture that centers on the fingernails.
   This will give you a point of focus when checking for sharpness in Replay mode.
5. Repeat steps 1–4, selecting different parts of the hands on which to focus. Take five more pictures trying different angles and framing techniques. Remember to use focus lock.

Replay the Photos

6. Go inside or under the cover of shade and set your camera to Replay (or Review).
   Remember, it is always easier to see the LCD when you are not in bright ambient light.
7. Scroll through your pictures using the arrows on the omni dial.
   This will give you a quick review.
8. Choose your first picture and, using your zoom feature, magnify the picture as much as possible.
   As you increase the magnification you will see a smaller part of the picture.

How This Book Is Organized

The information in this book is presented so that you master the fundamental skills first, and then build on those skills as you work with the more comprehensive topics.

Visual Conventions

This book uses many visual and typographical cues to guide you through the lessons. This page provides examples and describes the functions of each cue.

`Type this text` Anything you should type at the keyboard is printed in this typeface.

Tips, Notes, and Warnings are used throughout the text to draw attention to certain topics.

Command→Command This convention indicates multiple selections to be made from a menu bar. For example, File→Save means to select File, and then to select Save.

Supplementary information available on the Web page for this book is highlighted with this icon. Visit the Web page periodically for helpful tips and content.

Windows XP
Macintosh OS X Exercises specific to the Windows platform or the Macintosh platform are clearly marked.

Hands-On exercises are introduced immediately after concept discussions. They provide detailed, step-by-step tutorials so you can master the skills presented.

The Concepts Review section includes both true/false and multiple choice questions designed to gauge your understanding of concepts.

Skill Builder exercises provide additional hands-on practice with moderate assistance.

Welcome to
Digital Photography

LESSON 1

Choosing and Evaluating Digital Cameras

Digital cameras are no longer a thing of the future; they now outsell film cameras, and manufacturers are producing two to six new digital camera models each year. Digital camera owners can now easily share their photos on the Web and they do not even need computer access to get good quality, low-cost prints. Digital cameras are becoming more affordable and easier to use. It is now commonplace to see people holding digital cameras out in front of them instead of up to their eyes. With digital cameras, photographers can immediately view their pictures—something that, until now, was only possible with Polaroid cameras.

In this lesson, you will learn about the advantages of using a digital camera, the types of digital cameras available, how digital cameras work, and how to choose and evaluate the right camera for you.

Additional learning resources are available at ***labpub.com/learn/silver/digphoto/***

Case Study

Barbara is planning a vacation. In the past she has always taken her trusty compact film camera with her on trips. She's decided to buy a digital camera but knows very little about them. She finds out all she can about how digital cameras differ from film cameras, the types of digital cameras available, what features to look for, and where to obtain objective information about the myriad models available. When Barbara completes her research, she determines her needs and goes out to explore and try out the cameras firsthand, knowing she is adequately prepared to make a well-informed choice.

There are many cameras to choose from. These are just a few examples.

Comparing Digital Cameras to Film Cameras

From the outside, film and digital cameras appear pretty much the same—except that digital cameras have a LCD (liquid crystal display) viewing screen. Both have a lens and a shutter button. It is on the inside where you see the differences.

Film is a roll of plastic coated with a gel, called emulsion. Color film has three layers of emulsion. Each layer has a dye that lets in only red, green or blue light through to the film. (All visible colors are combinations of red, green and blue light.) Each layer of emulsion is overlaid, one on another, and each has varying levels of exposure (depending on the color it allows through.) When the layers are combined the result is a full color image.

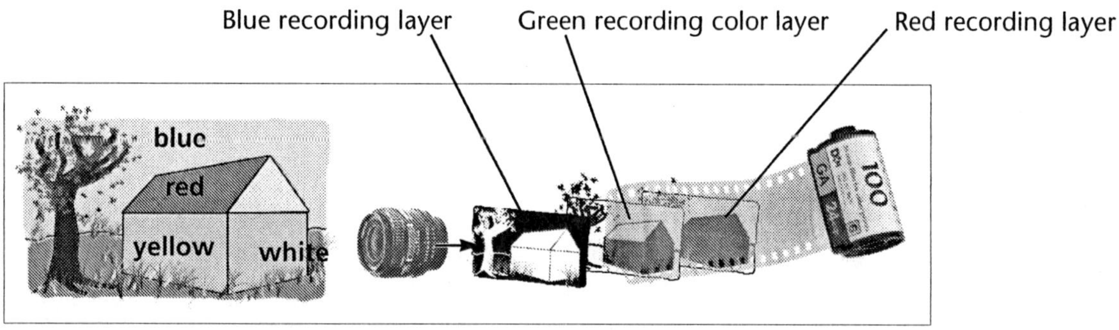

How film records color

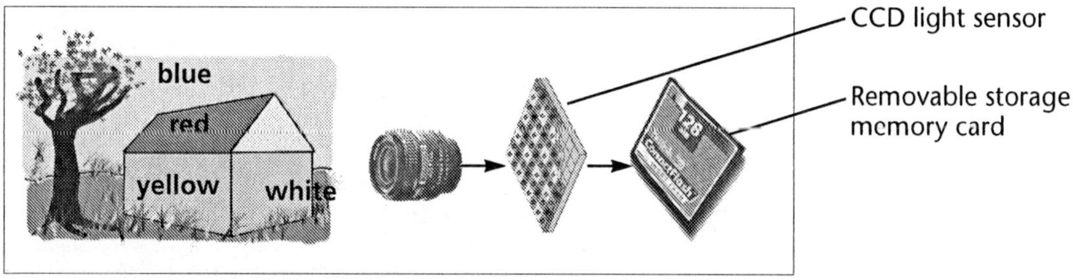

How digital cameras record color (see next topic)

The CCD

Digital cameras do not use film. Instead, there is a small plate, called a CCD (charge-coupled device) that is covered with a grid of light sensors. These sensors are called pixels, which is short for picture elements. Each sensor has a filter that lets in red, green, or blue light—just like the dyes on color film. The camera has a microprocessor (like a computer) that assembles the color information in a digital file and saves the file to a storage device (the memory card.) You will learn more about pixels and memory cards in Lesson 2, Working with Camera Manuals, Memory Cards, and Composition Basics.

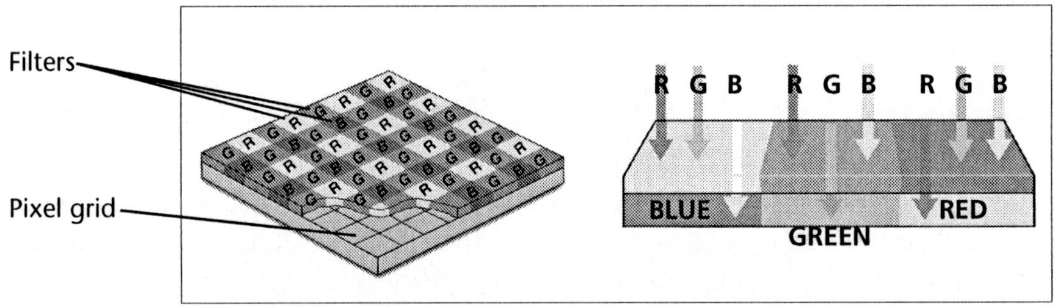

Sensor array with pixels and magnification of the filters on the pixel grid

Understanding the Types of Digital Cameras

There are hundreds of models of digital cameras on the market today. These models can be classified into three basic categories, as described in the following Quick Reference table. Knowing about these categories will enable you to make appropriate choices when purchasing a digital camera.

QUICK REFERENCE: Defining Digital Camera Types

Type of Digital Camera	When to Use	Price Range
Compact Point and Shoot	You want a light camera that you can easily take with you anywhere	\$100–\$700
Compact with Digital (Electronic) Viewfinders	You like the compactness of a point and shoot but want features similar to an SLR digital camera	\$600–\$1,000
Digital SLR	You are used to using a traditional SLR camera and would like a professional-level camera that allows you to change lenses	\$900–\$3,000

Compact Point and Shoot Cameras

Compact point and shoot cameras come in pocket size and midsize. The obvious advantage of the pocket size model is that you can easily take it anywhere you go. They can be as small as a credit card, easily fitting into a pocket or small bag, and very light. Midsize compacts are larger but still quite easy to carry. The advantage of the larger size is a larger LCD and more advanced features than with smaller cameras.

Point and shoot used to mean just that—you point the camera at your subject and click the shutter. With the advent of electronic film cameras, that changed. Zoom lenses and many shooting modes became available to the photographer. The development of digital cameras has made it possible to offer even more special settings and control features. Compact point and shoots are great entry cameras into digital photography and you may find it is the perfect type for you. The prices range from $100–$700.

Looking through the optical viewfinders on compact point and shoot cameras is similar to looking through a window.

Compact Cameras with Digital (Electronic) Viewfinders

Compacts with digital (electronic) viewfinders are very similar to midsize compacts except for one major feature: a digital viewfinder. The term "digital viewfinder" is often used interchangeably with the term "electronic viewfinder." Looking through a digital optical viewfinder is similar to looking at the LCD except that the image you see is smaller. You actually see a digitized version of what the camera sees. If a camera does not have a digital viewfinder, then looking through the optical viewfinder is similar to looking through a window. You cannot tell if your picture is in focus or exactly how much of the scene the camera is capturing. Compacts with digital viewfinders appeal most to those who want the same feel of a traditional film SLR (single lens reflex) camera without the cost of a digital SLR (explained in the next section). Compact digital cameras with digital viewfinders range in price from $600–$1,000.

This is an example of a compact camera with a digital viewfinder. It has the look and feel of a digital SLR camera but is lighter and cheaper. Looking through the viewfinder is like looking at the LCD.

This illustration shows how looking through the optical viewfinder on a compact point and shoot (left) differs from looking through a digital SLR (right). The difference in what you see and what the camera sees on a compact point and shoot is more noticeable when you are closer to your subject. Using the LCD instead of the optical viewfinder on a compact allows you to see what the camera lens sees.

Digital SLR Cameras

SLR stands for single lens reflex. Simply put, when you use an SLR, what you see is what you get. When you look through the optical viewfinder, you see what the camera sees via a mirror that reflects the image into the viewfinder (see the preceding illustration). With SLR cameras, you also have the ability to use many different lens sizes. Adapters are available for compacts and work well, but are not the same as a camera with interchangeable lenses. Most SLRs are made for those who want more manual control options, advanced features, and premium optics and materials. These cameras are much bigger and heavier than compacts and the LCD is used only for playing back (reviewing) images, not for composing pictures. In compact digital cameras the LCD is used for both composing and taking pictures. SLR cameras start at about $900 for just the camera body without the lens and go up to $2,000 or more, depending on the desired features. This is usually not an entry-level camera unless you are switching from a film SLR camera to a digital SLR camera. That said, lower priced, lighter digital SLR cameras are rapidly becoming a realistic option for many who would have previously chosen higher priced compacts.

These Nikons are considered professional-level cameras.

This Canon Rebel is considered a prosumer camera and is lighter and smaller than professional SLR cameras.

Buying a Digital Camera: Features to Look For

The following list shows more features to look for when choosing a digital camera.

- Comfort and ease of use
- Resolution
- LCD viewing area
- Lens Quality
- Shutter lag and processing time
- Shooting modes
- Batteries
- Memory cards

Comfort and Ease of Use

It is important to get a camera that fits your hands. Are you easily able to push all the buttons and turn the dials and are they located in easy-to-use positions? A camera may have every feature you want, but if it doesn't feel good in your hands or is too heavy and big you will probably not use it. It's a good idea to go to several stores and actually try out the cameras. Or, ask friends or family members with digital cameras if you can experiment with their cameras.

TIP! You should be able to pick up a camera and immediately sense if it is a comfortable fit. Trust your instincts.

Make sure your camera suits you.

Resolution

Resolution affects the size and quality of prints. The resolution is displayed as megapixels or as pixel width and pixel height; for example, 480 pixels by 640 pixels. Remember, the word pixel stands for picture element and these picture elements make up the picture, similar to a mosaic made of hundreds of tiles. A megapixel equals approximately one million pixels. The more megapixels, the bigger your print can be and the more detail it can show.

Megapixels and Print Size

A one megapixel camera gives you good quality 3 × 5 inch prints, a two megapixel camera gives you good quality 5 × 7 inch prints, a three megapixel camera gives you good quality 8 × 10 inch prints, and a six megapixel camera gives you nice 13 × 19 inch prints. You're probably wondering how this relates to the camera you should buy. Does it mean that if you want your pictures to be no larger than 5 × 7 inches you should buy a three maegapixel camera? Not necessarily. Since the cost of digital cameras keeps decreasing, it is best to buy one that has a high megapixel count, just in case you later change your mind about what size prints you want. When you buy a six megapixel camera you have the option to set the resolution to one through six megapixels to get the print size you need. The following Quick Reference table shows how megapixels, pixel width and height, and print size are related.

TIP! Resolution is important, but don't buy a camera based solely on this feature.

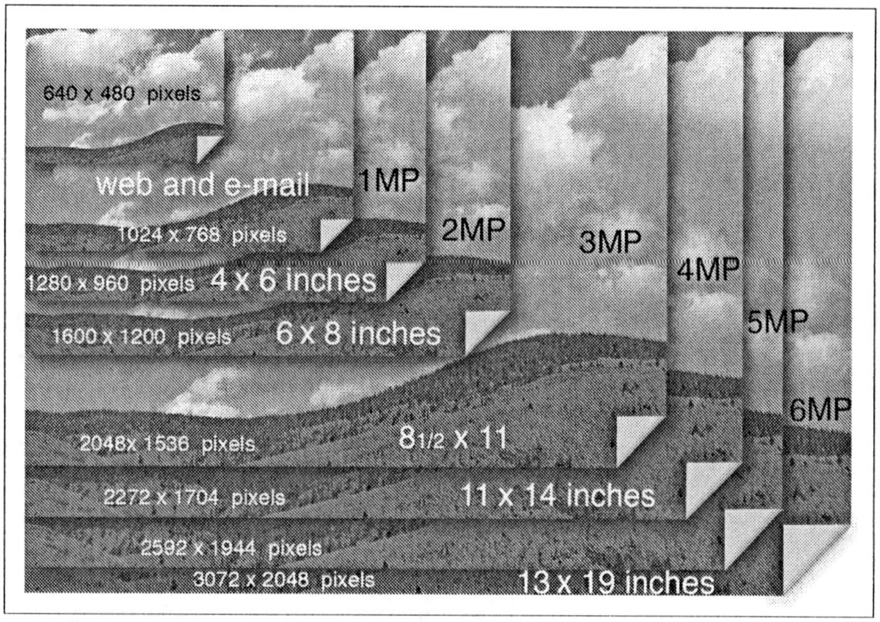

LCD

The LCD is where you compose and instantly review pictures. It is undoubtedly the most revolutionary and useful feature on digital cameras because it gives you instant feedback. LCDs come in different sizes and can have many features. Some swivel, rotate, or flip. Some might be difficult to see in bright light. If possible, test the LCD of a camera you are considering purchasing both in and out of the store. LCDs that swivel, rotate and flip are very useful for viewing images clearly in a variety of shooting situations. It is also important to see how readable the menu is in the LCD monitor.

TIP! The bigger and brighter the LCD, the better!

This camera features a very useful tilted LCD.

Lens

Image quality is directly related to lens quality. Better optics reduces image aberrations and improves color fidelity.

Zoom Capability Most of us are familiar with the zoom lens, a feature that allows you to move a lens in and out to change the perceived distance between the camera and the subject through magnification. This feature is an important consideration if you want a camera that can capture parts of a scene from very far away. Digital compact cameras have a built-in zoom. Digital SLR cameras can, of course, use any kind of lens.

Zoom Factor The zoom factor indicates the amount of zoom possible using a specific lens. The zoom factor is shown as 3X, 4X, etc. If a camera has a 4X zoom factor, the subject will be appear four times closer when the zoom lens is fully extended. You may also see the specifications shown in standard film camera equivalents such as 35 mm to 90 mm. A higher number converts to a greater zoom factor. You may also see the zoom factor expressed in numbers like 7 to 20. These are true digital camera specifications. Multiply by five to determine the approximate 35 mm film camera equivalent. For example, if a camera features an 8 to 15 digital zoom, the 35 mm equivalent is approximately 40 mm × 75 mm. On a traditional 35 mm camera, a 50 mm lens is considered "normal" or most similar to what our eyes see. Anything less than 50 mm is considered wide angle and anything more than 50 mm is considered telephoto. A zoom lens contains a range from wide angle to telephoto, and this makes them very convenient.

TIP! The larger the number—regardless of the mathematical method used—the greater the zoom capability.

Digital Zoom vs. Optical Zoom It is important to understand the difference between optical and digital zoom. Optical zoom moves the lens to actually magnify the image. Digital zoom selects a group of pixels in the scene and processes them to look larger, resulting in a magnified but blurry enlarged image. Most digital cameras have both optical and digital zoom features. The digital zoom feature is not very useful because it typically results in images with poor quality.

This photo was taken using optical zoom only.

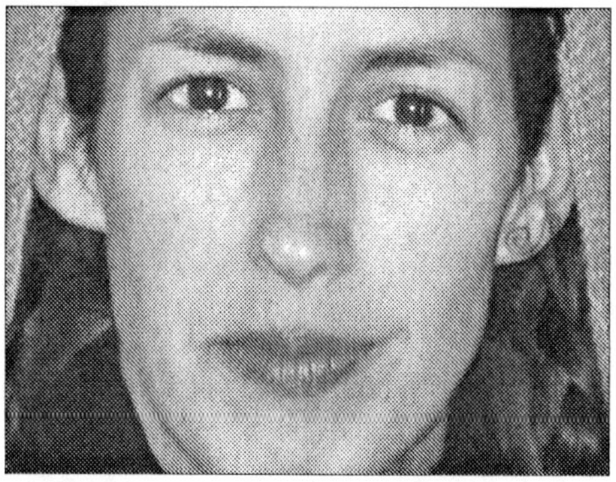

This photo was taken using digital zoom. Note that it is not as sharp as the photo taken with optical zoom.

Detail of the picture taken with optical zoom

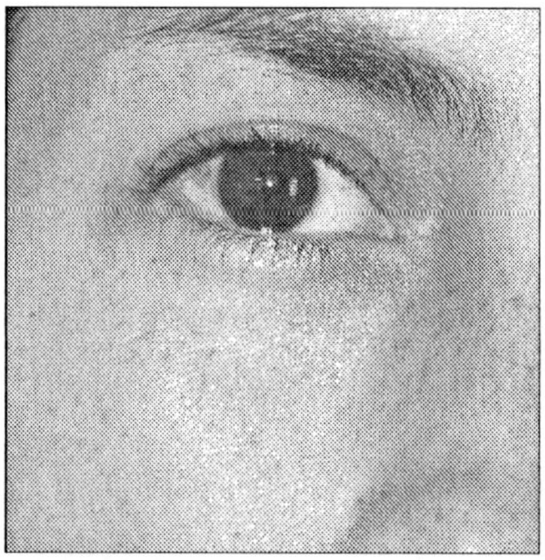

Detail of the picture taken with digital zoom

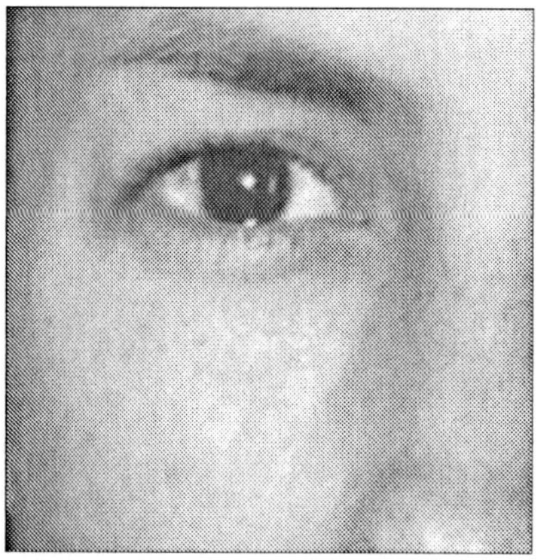

TIP! Pay attention to optical zoom ratings and ignore digital zoom ratings.

Shutter Lag and Image Processing Time

The shutter on film cameras fires the moment the shutter button is pressed. Most compact digital cameras take a split second to charge the sensor and perform exposure and focus operations before the shutter fires. This is called shutter lag. If you take a lot of action shots or want continuous shooting, this feature is important. Image processing time affects how quickly you can take the next picture. Remember, on a digital camera once the shutter has fired, the information recorded on the sensor plate must be transferred to the memory card. The amount of lag processing time varies with different cameras, camera settings, and memory cards.

TIP! Ask questions and read a lot of reviews to determine the best shutter lag and processing time available on the camera you are interested in.

Shooting Modes

Almost all compact and some SLR digital cameras come with specialized scene modes: landscape, portrait, sports, night, macro, etc. These features are especially useful to novice photographers. Once you are more familiar with your camera you can take advantage of more advanced shooting modes: shutter speed, aperture priority modes, and advanced customizable settings. Specialized scene modes are found on virtually every compact digital camera. Advanced modes are available on SLR models and many compacts. Shooting modes will be covered in detail in Lesson 4, Working with Customized Camera Settings.

QUICK REFERENCE: Defining Common Shooting Modes

Mode	Symbol	When to Use
Portrait		You want to blur the background to make the person stand out
Sports		You want to freeze action in sports or any moving subject, even waterfalls!
Landscape	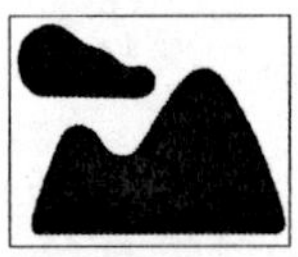	You want to capture wide scenic views with all elements of the picture sharp
Night Portrait Scene	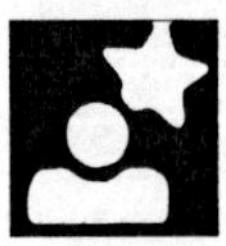	You want to take pictures of people at twilight or at night while keeping a natural exposure for the background
Macro (or close up)		You want to take close-up pictures of flowers, plants, insects, etc.; allows you to get within inches of the subject

TIP! If you are a beginner, be sure to find a camera with easy-to-use shooting modes.

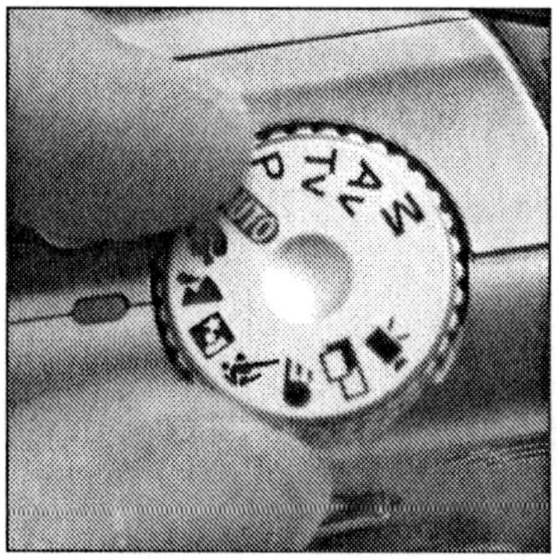

On these cameras, shooting modes are represented by pictures on the dial located on the top of the camera.

Shooting modes may also be found in the menu. Some cameras have a feature that shows you where to put your subject when composing the picture!

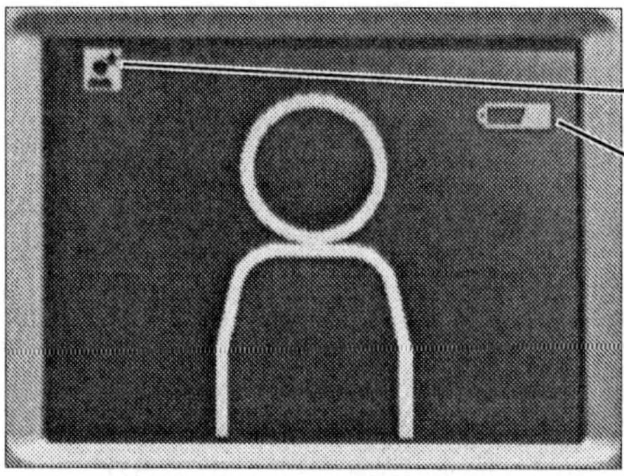

This icon shows that the camera is set in Portrait mode.

Note that the battery is not fully charged.

Batteries

All batteries are not equal, and not all digital cameras use the same type of battery. Some cameras come with non-rechargeable batteries, and these can be replaced with the rechargeable type. Some cameras do not come with a charger even though the batteries are rechargeable. Instead there is a power cord you plug into an AC wall socket and the camera. It's a good idea to buy a charger so you can use the camera while the batteries are being charged. There are several different types of batteries:

- **Alkaline** batteries are not rechargeable; instead, they put out less and less power until they are dead. They are the most common and the cheapest.
- **Lithium-ion** batteries offer a longer life but are more expensive than alkaline batteries. They are rechargeable and camera specific (manufactured to work with each brand and type of digital camera).

- **NiCad** (Nickel Cadmium) batteries are rechargeable. These economical cards must be completely drained before being recharged. This is important because they develop "memory." That is, if you recharge your battery while it is two-thirds full, it will always need to be recharged when two-thirds full and will only take a one-third charge. This could drastically decrease the usefulness of this battery.
- **NMH** (Nickel Metal Hydride) batteries provide greater power and endurance than NiCads. They are more expensive but do not develop memory. They can be recharged to full at any time, even if not completely drained.

TIP! Find out what type of battery comes with your camera and if it can take another type. Always have an extra charged battery ready to use.

Memory Cards

Memory cards are often equated with film, but they are so much better because they can be used over and over. Each camera uses a specific type of memory card, and some cameras can take more than one type. There are six different types of memory cards:

- **SmartMedia™** cards are the thinnest and lightest. You must be especially careful in handling these because the contacts are exposed and vulnerable to dust and dirt. They are becoming a discontinued product.
- **CompactFlash®** cards are the most widely used. They are thicker and less susceptible to damage than SmartMedia cards. Cameras using CompactFlash can also use the Super Drive, which has moving parts and is actually a tiny hard drive. (The Super Drive is less reliable because of the moving parts.)
- **Memory Stick™** and **Memory Stick PRO™** cards are used exclusively by Sony cameras and are longer and thinner than the other types of storage media. Several other companies also make Memory Sticks.
- **MultiMedia** cards are much smaller than the other memory cards.
- **Secure Digital** cards are the newest form of MultiMedia cards.
- **xD-Picture Card™** is used exclusively by Fuji and Olympus® cameras. They are expensive compared to CompactFlash and Memory Stick.

TIP! Most digital cameras come with a relatively small capacity memory card so be prepared to pick up a larger one (at least 128 megabytes) when you buy your camera.

The following Quick Reference table gives a general idea of how many quality pictures you can get from your memory card depending on the megapixel size you choose. For example, if you use one megapixel you will get a lot of pictures, but they will only be useful for Web posting, emailing, and creating small prints.

QUICK REFERENCE: Outlining Memory Card Storage Capacity

Print Size	Resolution	Megapixel Size*	128 MB Memory Card	256 MB Memory Card	512 MB Memory Card
4 × 6	1280 × 960	One	356 pictures	731 pictures	1464 pictures
6 × 8	1800 × 1200	Two	142 pictures	284 pictures	568 pictures
8 × 10	2048 × 1536	Three	106 pictures	213 pictures	428 pictures
11 × 14	2272 × 1704	Four	64 pictures	128 pictures	256 pictures
13 × 19	3072 × 2048	Six	49 pictures	102 pictures	206 pictures

*One megapixel is approximately one million pixels.

Researching Digital Cameras

Now that you know some of the major features to look for, it's time to do some research about which camera is best for you. Talk to friends and family members who have a digital camera and listen to what they have to say about their specific models.

Where to Look

There are many places you can look to obtain reliable information. Here are some suggestions:

- Computer and digital photography magazines and Web sites have excellent reviews and thorough comparisons of digital cameras. Check out PCPhoto (pcphotomag.com), eDigitalPhoto (edigitalphoto.com), and Popular Photography and Imaging (pop-photo.com).
- Search the Web for reviews of specific cameras. In your favorite search engine (like google.com), type in the name of the camera you are researching with the word "review" after it (for example, "nikon coolpix 8700 digital camera review").

TIP! If you want to learn more about how individuals feel about a camera, use Google Groups rather than the standard search. This searches Usenet, the world's largest bulletin board.

Finding the Best Camera for You

It is important to know how you will be using your camera and why you want one. To help you make the right decision, consider the following questions:

- What is my main reason for getting a digital camera?

  Emailing photos to friends and family

  Making small snapshots for friends and family

  Using in your business as a way to capture images for marketing purposes

  Manipulating photographs in the computer and printing high quality, large prints

  Photographing special subjects (landscapes, candid shots, posed shots, sports, close ups shots)

- How much money do I want to spend?

  Decide how much money you want to allocate for purchasing a digital camera

  Determine the features you must have and the features you are willing to do without

Probably the first question a salesperson will ask is what you want to use your camera for. Think of this process as similar to purchasing a car. You have many options to consider before making your final decision.

Matching the Camera to the User

The following Quick Reference table shows typical users and the digital cameras best suited for each.

QUICK REFERENCE: Choosing a Digital Camera

What You Want to Use the Camera For	Features to Look For	Cameras with These Features
Landscapes and scenic views	35 mm to 110 mm optical zoom lens (35 mm equivalent)	Digital SLRs and most compacts
Sports, action, and candid shots	Fast processing time, minimum shutter lag, and continuous (burst) shooting mode	Advanced compacts and digital SLRs
Portraits and people	Lens with optical zoom of at least 110 mm when zoomed out (35 mm equivalent)	Digital SLRs and most compacts
Web, email, and 4 × 6 prints	Three megapixels	Any compact
Large prints	Minimum five megapixels and a high-quality lens	Compacts and digital SLRs

Concepts Review

True/False Questions

			Page number
1. One of the major advantages of a larger compact digital camera is a larger LCD.	**true**	**false**	_______
2. The LCD on SLR cameras may be used for composing and reviewing pictures.	**true**	**false**	_______
3. A three megapixel camera will give you 11 × 14 inch prints.	**true**	**false**	_______
4. Each type of memory card is made for a specific brand of camera.	**true**	**false**	_______
5. A digital camera with a long shutter lag is not the best choice for action shots.	**true**	**false**	_______
6. It is best to use non-rechargeable batteries because you don't have to carry around extra equipment.	**true**	**false**	_______
7. Compact digital cameras are best if you want a very light and small camera.	**true**	**false**	_______
8. How many megapixels you choose affects the amount of pictures that can be stored on a memory card.	**true**	**false**	_______
9. Pixel means picture element.	**true**	**false**	_______
10. Compact digital cameras are not a good choice for taking pictures of landscapes.	**true**	**false**	_______

Multiple Choice Questions

1. Instead of film, digital cameras use ________.

   Page number: ______

   a. filters that let in red, green, and blue light

   b. a small plate covered with a grid of light sensors

   c. a postprocessor that converts light into an image

   d. memory cards

2. Which feature should you look for when choosing a digital camera?

   Page number: ______

   a. Comfort

   b. Ease of use

   c. Battery type

   d. All of the above

3. What is the major difference between digital (electronic) viewfinder compacts and other midsize compacts?

   Page number: ______

   a. They have a swivel and tilt LCD viewing screen

   b. They have a larger optical viewfinder

   c. They show colors more accurately

   d. They use the optical viewfinder or LCD to show exactly what the camera lens sees

4. The more megapixels a digital camera has, ________.

   Page number: ______

   a. the more colors a photograph will have

   b. the larger the photograph can be

   c. the faster the camera will take pictures

   d. All of the above

Skill Builders

SKILL BUILDER 1.1 Research Digital Cameras

In this exercise, you will use the knowledge gained in this lesson to help Barbara find the digital camera that best suits her needs.

Ask the Questions

1. Why do you want a digital camera?

   Barbara wants a camera that she can carry in her pocket.

2. What will you use your digital camera for most often?

   Barbara's primary use will be taking pictures of family and vacations.

3. What's the largest size print you will want?

   Barbara is pretty sure that she will want prints no larger than 8 × 10 inches.

4. How long do you want to keep this camera?

   Barbara would like to keep this camera for at least three years.

5. What type of pictures do you think you'll be taking?

   Barbara will concentrate on candid portraits and landscape pictures.

6. How much money do you want to spend?

   Barbara has put aside $400 for a digital camera.

Identify the Necessary Features

Based on Barbara's answers, you will now determine the major features that will satisfy her needs.

7. What type of resolution (megapixels) does Barbara need?

   To refresh your knowledge, see the Resolution section on page 8 and the Megapixels and Print Size section on page 8. Since Barbara wants 8 × 10 inch prints, a three megapixel camera should serve her purpose.

8. Will Barbara benefit more from a stationary or a movable LCD screen?

   This determines the angle from which you can take a picture. It is important to Barbara to have a movable LCD viewing screen.

9. What size zoom lens should Barbara get?

   This will determine how close you can get to subjects. The closer you want to zoom in, the longer the lens must be. Barbara wants a long zoom because she intends to take candid shots so a 35–110 mm lens is a good choice. She would like a longer one, but cannot afford it at this time.

10. How important is shutter lag and processing time?

The time it takes to press the shutter and transfer information to the memory card determines how quickly you can take several pictures, one after the other. Barbara knows this will be an important feature for the types of pictures she wants to capture.

11. What type of battery and memory card should Barbara get?

The type of battery determines how long a camera can be used before the battery needs to be recharged or replaced. Some memory cards are less expensive and more common than others. For Barbara, the battery type is important, but not the kind of memory card.

Do Some Research

Now you will help Barbara research the cameras currently available.

12. Go to the library or your favorite books store to find magazines that give reviews of different digital cameras.

13. Find stores that carry digital cameras.

Electronic superstores, discount chain stores, camera shops, and office supply stores are good places to start looking.

14. List in hand, go around to the stores and start looking at and handling cameras. Ask lots of questions and take notes.

This will be an informative experience because you might find different opinions and different information at each place you go. After you have visited one or two stores, you will better know how and what questions to ask.

15. Check out your friends' digital cameras, if applicable.

This is one of the best ways to get hands-on experience with digital cameras.

16. Make a new list based on the information you have gathered.

List the pros and cons of the cameras you have seen. Don't forget to record prices!

17. Compile a written report from the information you gathered and share it with the class.

LESSON 2

Working with Camera Manuals, Memory Cards, and Composition Basics

With so many affordable digital cameras available, they have become the first choice for many photographers—both to replace an older camera and as a new purchase. Although digital cameras may look almost identical to film cameras, learning how to use them may seem like a daunting task. In this lesson, you will familiarize yourself with the camera's instruction manual (which will be a great resource to you) and learn about memory cards (also called digital film). You will also learn the basics of dynamic composition and how to use these concepts so your photographs express what you saw and felt at the time you took them.

Additional learning resources are available at ***labpub.com/learn/silver/digphoto/***

Case Study

Frank has just purchased his first digital camera. Although he was diligent in researching the best camera for his needs, he is now faced with the daunting task of learning how to use what seems like a pretty complex piece of equipment. Even though he has had many film cameras before and is familiar with some basic photographic concepts, he feels somewhat intimidated by this new technology. He decides to take a simple approach and learn the basic skills, one step at a time. He starts by learning how to find his way around the camera manual, load the memory card, choose between the optical viewfinder and LCD, use focus lock, and compose great pictures.

Using the Instruction Manual

For some, using an instruction manual seems far too complex and confusing. However, as you begin learning more about your camera by reading the manual, you will find it a great resource and friend. You may find yourself using the instruction manual more than you ever imagined. Most instruction manuals come with both a table of contents and an index. The table of contents is valuable for finding major categories and subcategories.

CONTENTS

The table of contents can be very detailed with subcategories or simple with only main topics

CONTENTS

Same Idea, Different Words

One challenge in using an instruction manual is that different camera manufacturers use different names for the same category or topic. Throughout this book you will be given definitions of terms and several ways they are referred to, so it will be easier to find the item in your manual. For example, "formatting a memory card" may also be listed as "card set-up."

The index, found in the back of your instruction manual, is a great way to look up individual words. For example, to find out how to set the date and time you could search for "date."

Index

The index is detailed and specific. It also shows you all locations for the topic you are looking for.

HANDS-ON 2.1 Use the Table of Contents and Index

In this exercise, you will find information about inserting the memory card in the table of contents and index of your camera's instruction manual. Just complete the first part of this exercise if your instruction manual does not have an index.

Use the Table of Contents

1. Look in the table of contents for a major category called Getting Started.
   This topic may also be listed as Preparation, Preparing the Camera, or Camera Set-up.

Contents

2. Find a subcategory listed as Inserting a Memory Card.

   Turn back to the main category page if your manual does not have subcategories.

Use the Index

3. Look in the index for Memory Card. Turn to the page(s) indicated and you should find instructions for inserting a memory card.

   This topic may also be listed as the type of memory card (i.e., CompactFlash, Memory Stick, SmartMedia, etc.).

M

Macro 24
Manual exposure mode 45
Memory Stick 17, 119
  remaining indicator 124
Menu settings 39, 111

Memory card, 161
  approved cards, 159
  capacity of, 48
  formatting, 135
  insertion and removal of, 16
  reading images from, 44

As you use your manual, you will become familiar with the arrangement of information.

Dealing with Memory Cards

Memory cards are often equated with film. Unlike film, though, memory cards can be used over and over. They are essentially a mini storage device; you could even use them to copy and transfer files from one computer to another. As mentioned in Lesson 1, Choosing and Evaluating Digital Cameras, there are several types of memory cards and each digital camera requires a specific kind of card. Some memory cards can be used in more than one brand of camera. For example, Nikon™ cameras can use the CompactFlash card from Canon cameras.

It is essential to format (erase all pictures on) a card before using it in another camera. We will cover this topic in Lesson 3, Working with Memory Cards and Image Review. Memory cards come with different storage capacities and are priced accordingly. The following illustration shows the types of memory cards available.

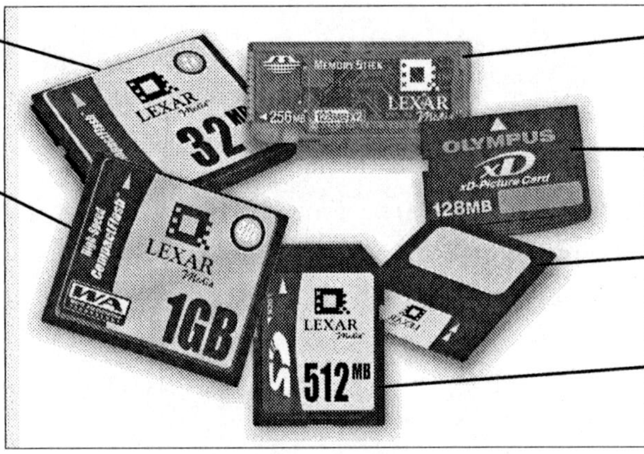

Storage Capacity

The storage capacity of memory cards is usually measured in megabytes (MB). There are approximately one million bytes of data in one megabyte. A byte is a single character of data (A, B, C, %, 4). One megabyte stores about three average-length novels or one, 3-inch, high resolution color photograph. As you can see, saving photographs uses a large amount of storage space. The card that comes with cameras usually has a small capacity—16 or 32 MB. The following Quick Reference table shows the storage capacity of a typical memory card included with most new digital cameras.

QUICK REFERENCE: Defining Memory Card Storage Capacity

Term	Description	Example
Bit	A single on-off switch in a computer circuit	0 or 1
Byte	A single character of data composed of eight bits strung together	A, B, C, $, @, %, or /
Kilobyte (KB)	Approximately one thousand bytes of data	About one single-spaced typed page of text
Megabyte (MB)	Approximately one million bytes of data	About three average-length novels
16 MB memory card	Small memory card included with many new digital cameras	25–50 standard quality 4 × 6 inch prints *Or* 150 high quality pictures for email *Or* 1 high quality 8 × 10 inch print

TIP! It's a good idea to buy an additional card with at least 128 MB of memory.

On the Web For information on purchasing additional memory cards, see the Web page for this book (labpub.com/learn/silver/digphoto/).

Proper Handling

Because memory cards are so small, portable, and fragile, it is easy to misplace or damage them. Here are some useful suggestions for taking care of your memory card:

- Don't write directly or put any kind of sticker on the card.
- Avoid putting the card in direct sunlight.
- Don't put the card in your pocket or other places where they can get crushed or laundered.
- Make sure the camera is turned off before inserting or removing the card.
- Insert the card with the label facing the proper direction. Look in your manual or quick-start guide for an illustration.
- Keep all cards in their plastic containers when not in use to protect them from dust and dirt. You can also buy memory card wallets, which organize and hold several cards.
- Be particularly careful with SmartMedia cards. They are susceptible to damage because they are so thin and the contacts are exposed.

HANDS-ON 2.2 Insert and Remove the Memory Card

In this exercise, you will insert and remove the memory card in your camera.

Before You Begin: Skip to step 4 if you have already inserted a memory card in your camera.

1. Make sure your camera is turned off. The on/off button or lever is often found on the top of the camera.

   Buttons, dials, and levers are located in different places on different cameras. The following figures illustrate some of the many positions of the power buttons and levers.

On/off lever on the Canon PowerShot G5

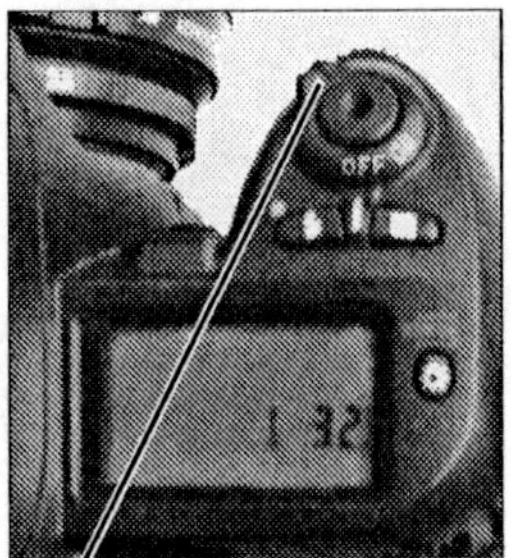

On/off switch on the Nikon D100 digital SLR

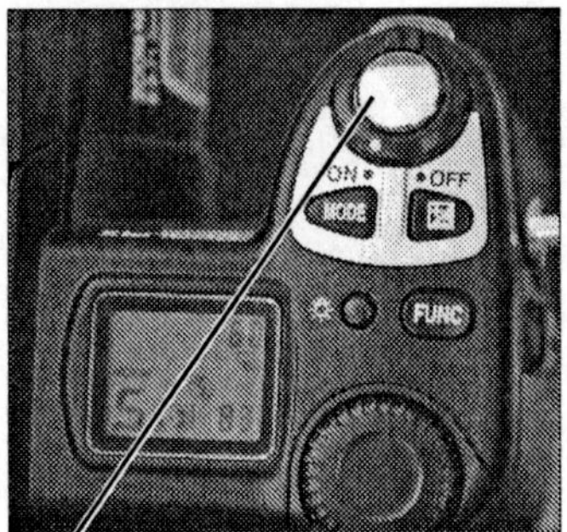

On/off switch on the Nikon Coolpix 5400

On/off button on the Sony Cybershot

2. Open the memory card door found on the back or side of your camera.

   WARNING! In the next step, take extra care to insert the memory card properly! Inserting the card upside down or backward could damage the card or the camera.

3. Insert the memory card firmly, with the contacts pointing down and the label facing in the proper direction. Refer to your manual for correct placement.

   You might hear a slight click as the card slides into place.

Be sure to check which way the label should face for your camera.

Contact points go into the camera first.

You may see a little projection next to where you placed the card. This is the eject button. If your camera does not have an eject button, just push in the card to make it pop out.

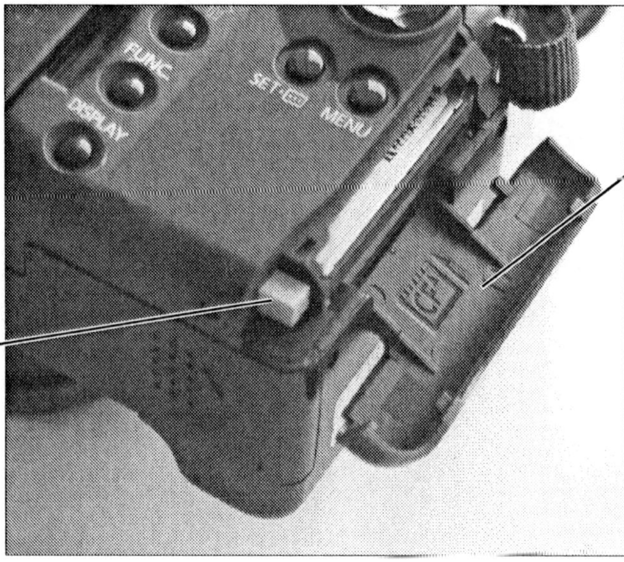

Memory card door

Eject button for ejecting a memory card

4. Press the card eject button or push the card in to eject it from the camera.

Using Optical Viewfinders and LCDs

As you know, there are two ways to compose your subject. You can look through the optical viewfinder as you would on a film camera or use the LCD. Both methods have their strengths and weaknesses.

On this camera, the LCD monitor is used to compose a picture.

The only way to compose pictures on this digital SLR is through the viewfinder. The LCD is used exclusively for reviewing pictures after they are taken.

Composing with the Optical Viewfinder

The optical viewfinder makes viewing easier in bright light but it actually captures only about 80–95% of what you see, depending on the camera model. Many digital cameras compensate for this by showing you less in the optical viewfinder then what is captured. This means that when you compose a picture with the subject touching the top and bottom of the frame, more of the scene is captured than what you see in the viewfinder. You actually have to get closer and crop part of the scene if you want to the subject to fill the frame. Essentially, the optical viewfinder is adjusted to show what the LCD sees. As you can see in the first of the following three illustrations, the optical viewfinder captures the same amount as the LCD. The following illustrations simulate how much you have to cut off to successfully fill the frame with the subject.

TIP! Be sure to check the LCD after you take a picture with the optical viewfinder to make sure you are capturing the subject the way you saw it.

Scene as it appears in the optical viewfinder.

Scene that is actually photographed using the optical viewfinder. Notice how much more of the scene is captured. This is also almost identical to what is seen and captured in the LCD.

How the scene must be seen in the optical viewfinder to capture what is in the first picture (to make the top and bottom of the door touch the frame).

Composing with the LCD

The LCD allows you to accurately see the picture you are taking. However, because it may be difficult to see the display in bright light, using the optical viewfinder may be a better choice in bright, ambient light. You may remember that some cameras come with digital (electronic) viewfinders. These are a smaller version of the LCD, though they show the same amount. The disadvantage of the electronic viewfinder is that it magnifies the digitized picture, revealing a potentially distracting pattern. As new models are released this feature is being greatly improved. You can also purchase LCD shades or hoods to block out the surrounding light. Refer to the Resources section on the Web page for this book (labpub.com/learn/silver/digphoto/) to learn about these accessories.

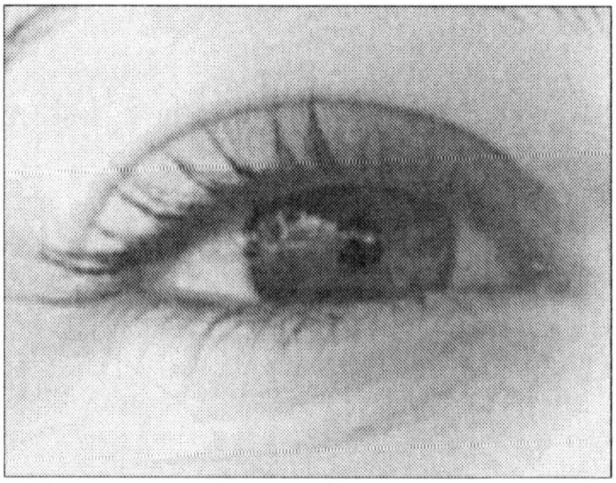

As seen through the LCD

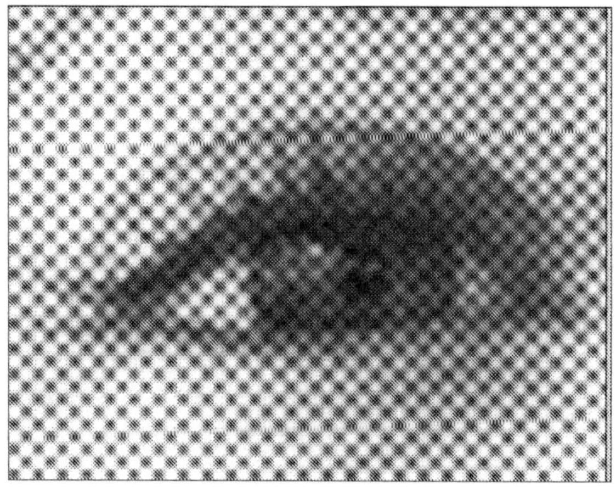

As seen through the digital viewfinder

Composing with Focus Lock

Have you ever taken a picture of two people standing side by side, only to find out when you viewed the picture that they were blurred, but what was right between them in the background was sharp and clear? To make sure this doesn't happen, digital cameras (and film cameras also) have a feature called focus lock. Using this feature enables you to point the camera at a subject and lock the focus, making sure the subject is sharply in focus.

How It Works An easy way to select a focus area on digital cameras is to use the shutter button to temporarily engage focus lock. Pressing and holding the shutter halfway down locks the focus on whatever the camera is focused on. This makes it easy to aim the camera at a subject, focus, hold the shutter button down halfway and then re-aim the camera, compose and press the shutter all the way down to take the picture.

Notice that the man in the background is perfectly in focus, even though the two girls in front were the intended subjects.

To ensure that the intended subjects are in focus, aiming and use focus lock on either woman, and then re-aim and compose.

TIP! Depth of field, which will be discussed in Lesson 5, Exploring Exposure, is also a factor in how much of a scene is in focus.

HANDS-ON 2.3 Use Focus Lock

In this exercise, you will use focus lock to ensure your subject is in focus.

Before You Begin: This is a group exercise. Choose three classmates to make up your group before beginning with step 1.

1. Set your camera's shooting mode to Automatic or Program. Remember, this setting is usually found on a dial on the top of the camera body.

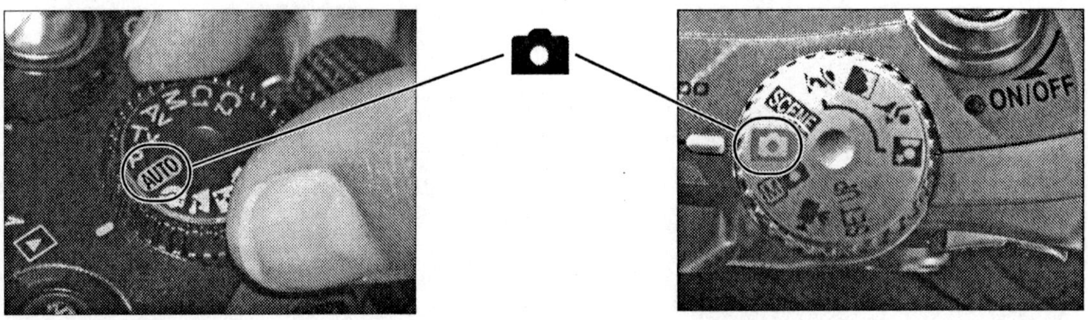

Focus lock will work with any shooting mode.

2. Have two group members stand about one foot apart and facing the camera. Have the third member stand three to five feet behind the others.
3. Look through the viewfinder or LCD and compose all three people so they are all in the frame.

4. Aim straight in front of you, at the middle person. Hold the shutter button down halfway to lock the focus, and then press down the shutter all the way to take the picture.

   Your point of focus will be the group member in the background. This middle person will be sharp because you aimed the camera on him or her, even though you had everybody framed.

5. Now, with the group still in position, point the camera at the person on the left and hold down the shutter button halfway. Keep the shutter depressed to lock the focus. **Don't take the picture yet!**

   This confirms the area of focus. Both group members in front will be in focus because they are standing the same distance from the camera.

6. Keep the shutter depressed halfway, swing the camera around to the group so all are once again in the frame, and then press down the shutter completely.

   Do not press too hard on the shutter button when setting focus lock or you will accidentally take a picture. If this happens, just try again.

7. Continue to switch roles from photographer to one of the people being photographed until everyone has taken the two pictures described in the preceding steps.

8. When everyone is finished, switch to Playback mode and view your pictures. In which of the two pictures are the group members in the foreground in focus?

   You may have to magnify the picture to see the difference.

Learning About Composition Basics

Composition describes how elements are placed and framed in a photograph. In this section, we will cover some basic concepts and techniques.

Organization

When we look at a scene we tend to only see the subject that interests us, blocking out anything that could distract from the main target of importance. Thus, it is helpful to be aware of everything else in the frame as you look through the viewfinder or in the LCD. The camera does not block out everything except your point of interest; it captures every detail, whether you want it to or not. At first, it may take a long time to look in the optical viewfinder or LCD and see every element in the frame. You are training yourself to see what the camera sees. After some practice, the process will come more naturally and easily.

How to Organize Your Shots Following are suggestions for successfully capturing your main area of interest in a photograph:

- In the viewfinder or LCD, locate your main area of interest and then look at everything else in the frame. Are the other elements distracting? Do they draw the eye toward or away from the subject? Do they help tell the story?
- Turn the camera vertically to see if this alignment better captures the subject.

Trying both horizontal and vertical compositions is a great way of exploring creative possibilities in your pictures. Notice the different perspectives.

- Try a different angle by changing the camera's viewpoint. This is particularly easy if your camera has an LCD that swivels.

Notice how the background items distract from the main subject.

This picture was taken by getting closer and using a different viewpoint (from above).

- Move around the subject to change your viewpoint. Take pictures from the back, top, and below. Don't be afraid to crouch or lie down and look up.
- Fill the frame with your subject by getting closer or zooming in. Don't be afraid to cut off part of the subject or surrounding area. Take your first shot the way you initially see the scene, then get closer, and then get even closer. By doing this, you are distilling the image down to its essential elements.

This picture was taken several feet from the main subject. Notice all the distracting elements. Can you tell that the bush is the main subject?

You can start seeing that the subject is the bush as you get a little closer.

Filling the frame in the viewfinder or LCD is a great way to improve composition and zero in on the subject.

Getting even closer allows you to capture detail and the essence of the leaves, which is the inspiration for the picture.

TIP! Getting closer is often thought to be the single best way to improve a photograph.

- Remember to look back after you have taken the picture and are moving on. See what it looks like from that viewpoint.
- Trust your own vision. Don't ignore a subject because you think it won't be interesting to anyone else.

Landscape Pictures

It is easy to stop and take a picture in the midst of a beautiful nature scene. Usually, we do this without really seeing what will be conveyed in the photograph. The result is typically a nice picture, but one that doesn't really reflect what we saw at the time. Following is a list of suggestions for capturing interesting and dynamic landscapes:

- **Intent:** Pay attention to what first attracted you to the scene. Was it a feeling of serenity, the colorful flowers, a faraway mountain, or a beautiful sunset? Choose what is important.
- **Position:** Change your position to better catch your point of focus. In the following illustration, notice how getting closer to the ground emphasizes the sculpture and not the distracting elements.

- **Emphasis:** Decide which part of the scene is most important and give more emphasis to it by placing it in the top two-thirds or the bottom two-thirds of the picture frame. Putting the horizon line higher gives more emphasis to what is below while putting the horizon line toward the bottom of the frame emphasizes what is above it.
- **Framing:** One way to create perspective and call attention to the subject is to frame the image. For example, show tree branches on either side of the frame. As you can see in the following illustrations, including the branches in the foreground leads your eye to the main subject and adds perspective and depth.

Without framing

Tree used to frame picture and create a stronger sense of depth

Pictures of People

Candid and posed pictures are two of the most popular forms of capturing images of our friends and family. Successful candid pictures are best achieved by using specific shooting modes, which we will cover in Lesson 4, Working with Customized Camera Settings. This section covers techniques for taking posed pictures of people.

An image of sitting in a studio might come to mind when you think of posing a subject. However, whenever we ask someone to smile we are preparing a posed photograph. Try the following techniques to make posed pictures go from stiff and posed to natural, relaxed, and flattering:

- Don't take pictures of people in bright sunlight. Cloudy and overcast days are great for taking people pictures because the light is soft and even and will eliminate harsh shadows. Take pictures in light shade if it is a sunny day.

Taken in bright sun

Taken in shade

TIP! Using fill flash is a great way of illuminating people in the shade without causing harsh shadows. Flash is covered in Lesson 4, Working with Customized Camera Settings.

QUICK REFERENCE: Taking Effective Portraits

Consideration	Explanation
Sun	Forget about having the sun behind you. The person being photographed is directly in the sun and squinting. Go into the shade and you will both feel better.
Distance	Get closer! This will almost always improve a picture. Don't be concerned if you cut off the top of someone's head or parts of arms or legs. This is called *cropping*. You will find that cropping allows you to effectively capture the person because there is nothing distracting around the subject.
Position	Have the person sit or lean against a wall instead of standing at attention. This will relax him/her and give you a more natural picture.
Comfort	Let your subject know it is okay to feel a little uncomfortable. It is normal. Tell them they don't have to smile while you are setting up the shot. Then, when you are ready, you can capture them in a more spontaneous mood.
Number of Shots	Take more than one picture. As you take more shots your subject will become less stiff and you will have a variety of poses to choose from.
Involving the Subject	Take advantage of using a digital camera by showing the images to your subject immediately. This will make the project more fun for both of you.

Concepts Review

True/False Questions

			Page number
1. Your instruction manual index is the best place to locate specific topics about your digital camera.	**true**	**false**	______
2. Always insert memory cards with the contacts facing toward the camera.	**true**	**false**	______
3. The best way to organize your memory cards is to label each one.	**true**	**false**	______
4. Always turn off the camera before inserting or removing a memory card.	**true**	**false**	______
5. Do not write on memory cards.	**true**	**false**	______
6. Framing your picture using the LCD allows you to accurately see the picture you are taking.	**true**	**false**	______
7. Composition is how elements in the picture are framed.	**true**	**false**	______
8. Pressing and holding the shutter halfway down locks the focus.	**true**	**false**	______
9. The best way to improve any photograph is to turn the camera vertical.	**true**	**false**	______
10. Always stand with the sun behind you when taking pictures so your subject is properly lit.	**true**	**false**	______

Multiple Choice Questions

1. The storage capacity of memory cards is usually measured in _______.

   Page number: ______

   a. megapixels

   b. bytes

   c. megabytes

   d. All of the above

2. Which of the following statements about using a digital (electronic) viewfinder is true?

   Page number: ______

   a. It makes viewing easier in bright light.

   b. You can see exactly what the camera lens sees.

   c. You can see if the subject is in focus.

   d. All of the above

3. The quickest and best way to improve a picture is to _______.

   Page number: ______

   a. try a different angle

   b. locate the main area of interest

   c. turn the camera vertical

   d. None of the above

4. Which of the following elements will help you take better landscape pictures?

   Page number: ______

   a. Emphasis

   b. Position

   c. Framing

   d. All of the above

Skill Builders

SKILL BUILDER 2.1 Frame a Scene

In this exercise, you will frame a scene in two ways and compare them in Playback mode. Photographers may use either method, depending on the scene and the ambient lighting.

NOTE! If you are using a digital SLR camera you will not be able to compose with the LCD. Instead, start about three feet from your subject and move backward about one foot at a time. Review the results to see if there was any distance where the subject was cut off.

1. Pick a subject to photograph. You may choose a person or a large object with a clear top and bottom (small tree, bush, chair, etc.).
   A person is the best choice because you can easily move him or her to the proper place.
2. Direct the person to stand, or place the object, about six feet from the camera. Move away from the subject if it is a stationary object until you are about six feet from it.
3. Set your camera to Automatic (A or 📷) or Program (P) mode, and then use the optical viewfinder to frame the subject so the top and bottom of the person or object are at the top and bottom of the frame in the viewfinder.
   You may have to move closer or step back to frame the subject to make both the top and the bottom fill the frame.
4. Take the picture. Then, without moving, use the LCD to frame the subject in the same way you did before. Make sure the top and bottom of the subject just touch the top and bottom of the frame.
5. Take another picture.
6. Move back from the subject about one foot and take two more pictures, one using the optical viewfinder and one using the LCD.
   Don't try to fill the frame, just take the pictures as they appear.
7. Step back another foot and repeat step 6.
   Repeat this process two more times, stepping back about one foot each time. Move the object further away if you are unable to step back.
8. Step into the shade or go indoors and set your camera in Playback or Review mode.

9. Scroll through your photos and see if the subject was cut off in any of the pictures you took using the optical viewfinder.

   The picture taken using the optical viewfinder will be the first in each pair as you moved further from the subject.

10. Once you have reviewed your photos, note how close you could get to your subject using the optical viewfinder without cutting off the top or bottom.

    This information is very valuable because you now know how close you can get to make sure you are capturing the entire subject. There will be times, usually in bright ambient light, when you will want or need to use the optical viewfinder.

SKILL BUILDER 2.2 Use Composition Techniques

In this exercise you, will use several techniques to improve the composition of your photographs.

Before You Begin: Make sure your camera is set to Automatic (A or [camera icon]) or Program (P) shooting mode.

Fill the Frame

1. Choose any subject: people, flowers, scenes, architecture, etc.
2. Using the optical viewfinder or the LCD, frame the subject the way you ordinarily would and take the picture.
3. Get closer to your subject by either stepping forward or using the zoom.

   IMPORTANT! Do not use the digital zoom.

4. Completely fill the frame with the subject so there is nothing else in the picture.

   Don't be afraid to cut off parts of your subject. In fact, you may have to in order to completely fill the frame.

5. Set the camera in Playback or Review mode and compare your results.

   Ask yourself and others which photograph better conveys your subject. **Remember, sometimes less is more!**

Frame Horizontally and Vertically

6. Choose another subject to photograph.
   Any subject or scene will work.
7. Using either the optical viewfinder or LCD, hold the camera horizontally, and then compose and take the picture.
   Usually, we tend to hold the camera horizontally when taking pictures.
8. Hold the camera vertically, compose and take a picture of the same subject or scene.
9. Take four more pictures of different subjects, repeating steps 7 and 8.
10. Review your pictures and note which pictures, if any, benefited from using vertical composition.
    It's always worth trying different compositions and viewpoints, especially since you are not using up rolls of film.

LESSON 3

Working with Memory Cards and Image Review

One of the major differences between film cameras and digital cameras is the way in which images are stored. Digital cameras use memory cards instead of film. Using memory cards offers many options for capturing pictures and using stored image files, whether it is printing them, posting them to the Web, emailing them, or creating slide shows. Because the images are stored on the memory card inside the digital camera, they can be replayed (reviewed) at any time. This is one of the most exciting features of owning a digital camera. Because you can see what you have just taken, you can immediately recompose or delete an image while it is still "in" the camera. There are several types of memory cards and more than one way to transfer the images from the card to a computer, printer, or other device. In this lesson, you will learn how to replay images in the camera, format your memory card, transfer images from the camera to the computer, and organize and back up your photos.

*Additional learning resources are available at **labpub.com/learn/silver/digphoto/***

Case Study

Elisa is feeling confident about using her digital camera now that she has mastered its basic settings and features. She easily navigates through her instruction manual when she has a question or needs to learn more about a specific option or setting. It is now time to better understand the use of memory cards, how to transfer images from the memory card to the computer, where and how to store images, and how to back up images so they are well preserved for the future.

Taking pictures is Elisa's way of preserving memories and recording events in her life. She is committed to doing this in the best way possible by following a few key concepts pertaining to storing and caring for her images.

Working with Storage Media

Types, capacity, and care of digital memory cards were covered in Lesson 2, Working with Camera Manuals, Memory Cards, and Composition Basics. We will now explore the best way to use these cards in the camera and the choices available for transferring image files to the computer. In this section, you will learn how to replay, delete, and protect images, and how to format memory cards.

Image Replay

The ability to review your pictures as soon as you've taken them is one of the most attractive features of digital cameras. Unfortunately, it is difficult to see the pictures in bright light. Monitor hoods are a valuable aid for viewing LCDs in bright light. A monitor hood is a rubber or plastic device that attaches directly to the LCD on the camera. Sources for buying hoods are found in the Resources section on the Web page for this book (labpub.com/learn/silver/digphoto/).

Other than with Polaroid cameras, instant review has previously been unavailable. Instant review is the ultimate instant gratification for photographers and is a great aid to ensuring correct exposure and great composition. The options for replaying (or reviewing) images include viewing them one at a time, in Index mode (several thumbnail pictures at once), as a slide show, and magnified. The LCD is used for image replay and, as noted, uses a lot of battery power. Most of us would agree, however, it is difficult to resist taking a look at the pictures you just made.

Playback Mode Accessing Playback mode differs with each brand and model of camera. Some cameras have a specific button or lever while others just require pushing the display button. Most cameras use the omni dial (the one with the four arrows) to scroll forward and backward through images.

Replay lever on the Canon Power Shot

Replay button on the Nikon Coolpix

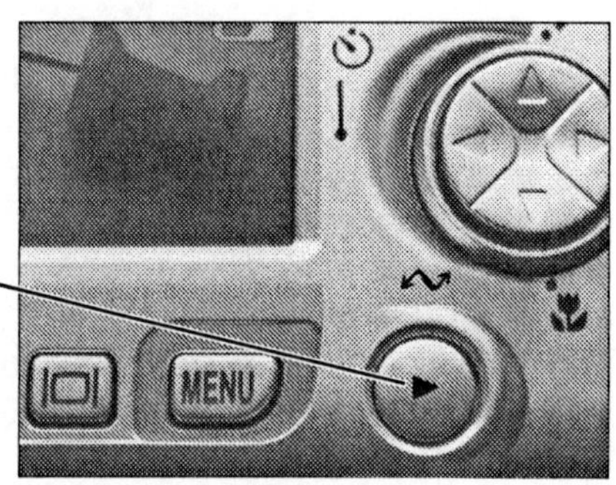

The following table illustrates the image replay options and when to use each.

QUICK REFERENCE: Using Replay Options

Image Replay Option	How It Looks	When to Use
Single View		To check exposure and composition or to show to others
Index	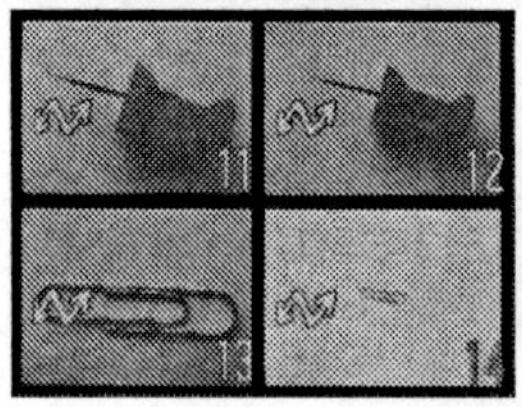 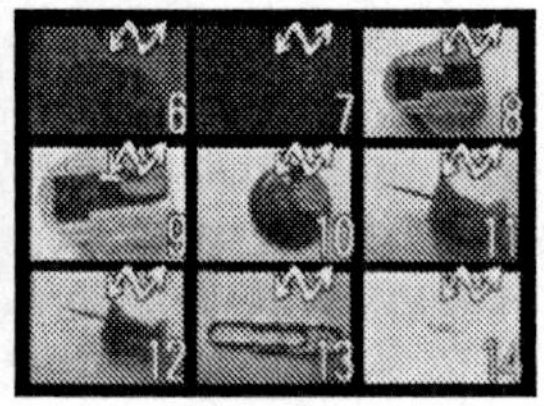	To edit or quickly locate specific images
Magnifying (Zoom Mode)		To check sharpness and focus
Slide Show	Looks just like Single View, but images scroll automatically	To quickly review all images; good for showing others; uses the most battery power

HANDS-ON 3.1 Review Pictures with the LCD

In this exercise, you will review photos in your camera.

1. Take ten pictures with your camera. Choose any subject you like, inside or outdoors.

   You will use these pictures to practice using the replay feature.

2. Look in your instruction manual for the section on Playback. Try the index first. If your manual doesn't have one, look in the table of contents.

   Try looking up words such as Playback, Image Review, Image Playback, Viewing Still Images, Still Image Editing, or Playing Back Images. Or, look for a setting or switch on the camera that appears similar to the familiar Play button.

3. Set your camera for Image Playback. Select one image using the Single View, and then use the arrows on the omni dial to scroll through the images.

   TIP! Each camera differs in the way the arrows work. On some cameras, you use the up and down arrows to scroll; on others you use the right and left arrows.

   It's easy to review all of your photos rapidly with the Replay feature.

4. If your camera has this feature, set the Image Playback to Index mode so you can see thumbnail pictures of several images. Skip to step 6 if your camera doesn't have this feature.

   You might be able to set it for different sets: 9 images, 12 images, etc. Try all of the options your camera has.

5. Practice scrolling through each set. Select an image and then go back to Single View mode.

Use the Zoom View

6. Look in your instruction manual for guidance and set the viewing mode to Magnify (zoom) to see one of your pictures magnified in Playback mode. Skip to step 9 if your camera does not have the zoom view feature.

   Using Zoom mode allows you to see the image very enlarged. This will help you see if your picture is in focus.

   TIP! The zoom lever used for zooming in when taking a picture is also often used to zoom in Replay mode. Look for the magnifying glass on the camera body. This indicates the Zoom feature.

7. Zoom in step by step until you have magnified as much as possible. Scroll up and down and side to side using the arrows on the omni dial. Find the area that should be the center of focus and determine if it is sharp enough.

   Use this feature if you are not sure your picture is sharply and properly focused.

8. When you finish, zoom out so the image is in Single View.

9. Switch back to Record mode so you are ready to take more pictures.

Locking Photos

To make sure you do not accidentally delete images, you can lock (or protect) them through the use of a button or switch often represented by a key. The picture you want to save is selected and locked by pressing the key button.

WARNING! If you format the memory card, all locked image(s) are deleted.

This figure shows how to access the lock feature on the Nikon Coolpix using the menu in the LCD. Notice that it is called Protect instead of Lock.

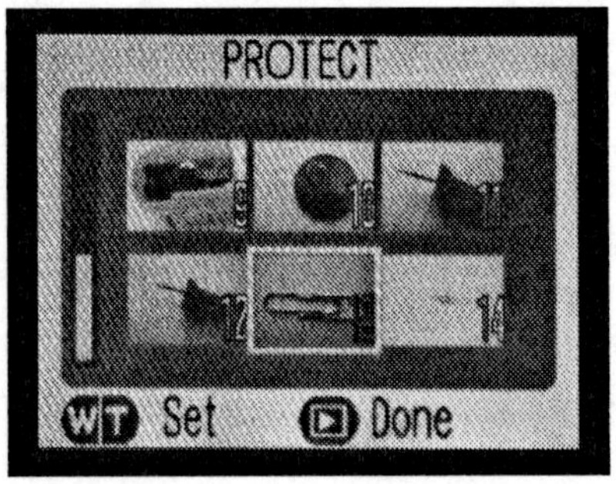

This figure shows the display that appears after selecting Protect. Now the selected image can be protected (locked).

This icon represents the Playback menu, which is where the lock feature is found (called Protect).

This figure shows the window as it appears when Protect is selected. Notice the key icon.

This icon shows that the picture is locked.

Press this key to lock the picture.

Deleting Photos

You may want to eliminate one or more images because you don't like them, because you took one when you intended to just lock the focus, or for some other reason. Deleting frees up space on your memory card. The process is pretty straightforward on most cameras and the button or switch used to delete is often be represented by a trashcan. You will get a message asking if you really want to delete before the actual process is engaged. On many models you have the option to delete all pictures or just individual images.

A trashcan icon is the symbol most often used to represent the delete button.

HANDS-ON 3.2 Lock and Delete Photos in the Camera

In this exercise, you will locate and carry out the locking and deleting functions.

1. Find the directions for locking (protecting) an image and lock the picture that currently shows in Playback mode.

   A locked picture remains locked until you unlock it or reformat the memory card. Reformatting will be covered later in this lesson.

2. Display another photo, lock it, and then try to delete it using the instructions in your manual.

   The delete command will not work and the camera may display a prompt that the photo is locked.

3. Display the locked picture, and then unlock it using the same button and procedure you used to lock it.

   This is called toggling. It means you use the same command or control to both turn on and turn off the same feature.

4. Try deleting the unlocked photo.

   This time, the command works.

Transferring Images

Once you have reviewed and edited your images in the camera it is important to transfer them to the computer, save them, and back them up. Your pictures will be safely stored in two locations. Transferring images is also referred to as downloading.

Transfer Methods

There are three primary methods of transferring images from your digital camera to a computer:

- **Via Direct Cable Connection:** You can connect your camera directly to the computer with a USB cable that comes with it. Your camera features software (found on the CD that also comes with your camera) for transferring and editing images.
- **Via a Memory Card Reader:** You can eject the memory card and insert it into a card reader that connects to your computer with a USB cable.
- **Via a Docking Station:** Some cameras come with a docking station used to transfer pictures from the camera to the computer, recharge batteries, and print.

USB cable connected from the camera to the computer

USB Cable connected to the camera

Correct end of USB Cable to insert in camera

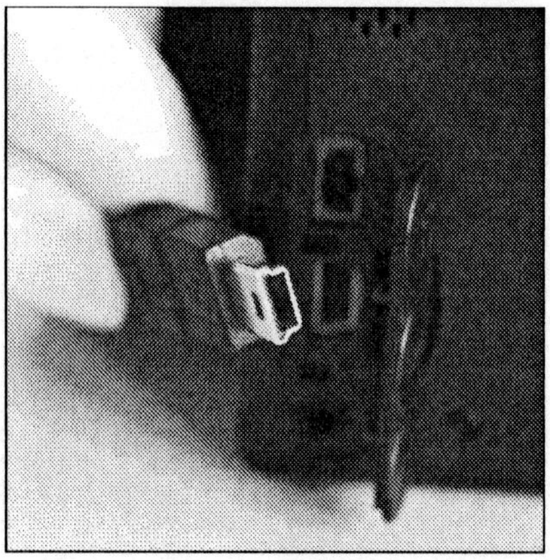

USB cable and USB port on the computer

Memory Card Readers

A memory card reader is a small device in which you insert your memory card and then transfer your photos to any drive or folder in your computer. Most memory card readers connect to your computer with a USB cable. Memory card readers are simple and easy to use, and eliminate the need to connect your camera to the computer.

Types of Memory Card Readers Memory card readers come in many sizes, shapes, and brands. They are relatively inexpensive and may come with one slot for a specific type of memory card or with many slots to accommodate different types of cards. These are referred to as universal or six-in-one card readers.

TIP! USB 2.0 card readers transfer photos many times faster than USB 1.0 card readers.

This memory card reader only accepts Compact Flash cards.

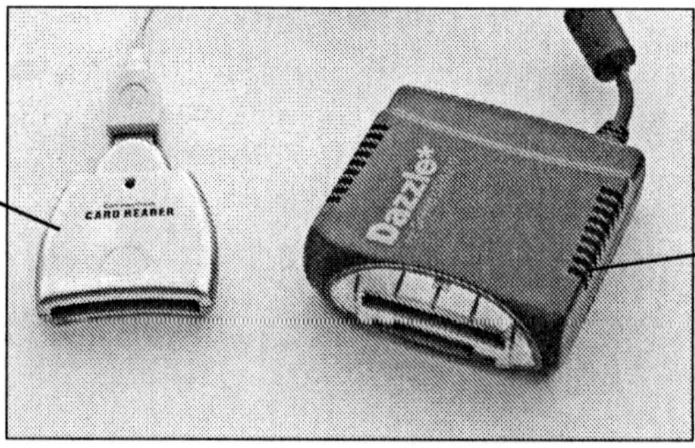

This memory card reader has several slots and will accept most types of memory cards.

Recognizing a Memory Card Reader on the Computer Most new computers that run Windows XP or Macintosh OS X recognize your memory card reader automatically when you connect it to the computer. On Macintosh computers the card reader appears as a device icon on the Desktop. On Windows computers it appears as another drive in the My Computer folder. Memory card readers also come with software that enables older computers to recognize the card reader as a drive. Try installing the software that came with the card reader if the computer does not recognize it automatically.

Why Use a Memory Card Reader? There are distinct advantages for using a memory card reader:

- Battery power is preserved because the camera isn't used to transfer the images to the computer.
- It usually transfers photos faster than a direct cable connection from the camera to the computer.
- You can bypass the camera transfer software and download image files directly to the computer.

TIP! Some card readers will not work with a USB hub (a device for connecting several USB devices to the computer simultaneously.) Make sure the card reader is connected directly to the computer. If it still doesn't work, install the card reader software. If this doesn't help, the card reader may be damaged or just not compatible with your computer system. Exchange it or try a different brand.

Docking Station Some digital cameras come with their own docking stations. Docking stations connect the camera directly to the computer without the need to plug in a cable to the camera separately. They act much like memory card readers. To use, place the camera in the dock and press a download button. The image files are automatically transferred to the computer.

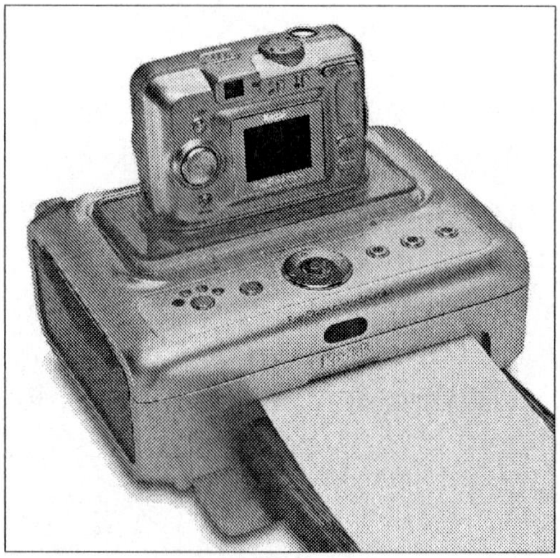

Kodak Easy Share digital camera on an Easy Share Kodak docking station

About the Next Hands-On Exercise Although the downloading software that came with your camera is very functional, the method you will use in the next exercise does not involve using it or any bundled software that came with your computer. (Examples of bundled software would be iPhoto on Macintosh computers and Photoshop Elements on Windows computers.) Your camera comes with instructions for using the bundled software. However, the following exercise will work on most computers, even if they do not contain special software.

Storing Your Exercise Files Throughout this course you will be referred to files in your "file storage location." You can store your exercise files on various media, such as a USB flash drive, the My Documents folder, the My Pictures folder, or to a network drive at a school or company. See Appendix A, Using File Storage Media, for additional information on alternative file storage media.

QUICK REFERENCE: Transferring Photos to the Computer

Task	Procedure
Connect using a memory card reader	• Attach the memory card reader to an available USB port on the computer. • Carefully eject the memory card from your camera. • Gently insert the memory card into the memory card reader (usually with the label side of the memory card facing up).
Connect using a cable to your camera	• Switch off the power on your camera. • Connect the cable between your camera and an available USB port. • (Optional) Start the software that came with your camera. • Switch on the power to your camera. • If necessary, set your camera to Playback mode. (Some camera models require this setting in order to connect to the computer.)
Manually transfer photos after making a connection	• Navigate to the folder containing the photos. • Choose Edit→Select All from the menu bar. • Choose Edit→Copy from the menu bar. • Navigate to the destination on the computer for the photos. If desired, you can create a new folder at the destination. • Choose Edit→Paste at the destination folder.

HANDS-ON 3.3A Transfer Images from the Camera to the Computer (Windows XP)

If you running Macintosh OS X, skip to Hands-On 3.3B on page 62.

In this exercise, you will learn a universal method for bringing your images into the computer.

Navigate to Your Photos

The method used in this exercise will work with computers that run Windows XP. Another program may open when you attach a camera or memory card to the computer if you installed software that came with your camera or have other photo editing software. Close this application if it opens.

First, you will connect the camera or memory card. Then, you will navigate to the photos.

1. Follow the steps for the type of connection you are using:

External Memory Card Reader

- Attach the memory card reader to an available USB port on the computer.
- Choose Cancel if Windows displays a prompt to perform an action or displays a wizard.
- Eject the memory card from the camera.
- Slide the memory card into the card reader, label side up.

- Choose Cancel if Windows displays a prompt to perform an action or displays a wizard.

Memory Card Reader Built In to the Computer

- Eject the memory card from the camera.
- Slide the memory card into the card reader, label side up.
- Choose Cancel if Windows displays a prompt to perform an action or displays a wizard.

Cable Connection to Camera

- Switch off the power on your camera.
- Connect the USB cable between the camera and an available USB port on the computer.
- Switch on the power to your camera.
- Choose Cancel if Windows displays a prompt to perform an action or displays a wizard.

These methods will work with any Windows XP computer. This is why you are told to cancel any prompt or wizard window.

2. Click the Start button, and then choose My Computer.

   Windows displays all of the available drives, including your card reader or camera.

3. Double-click to open the camera or memory card drive. The drive letter and icon you see may not match the following illustration.

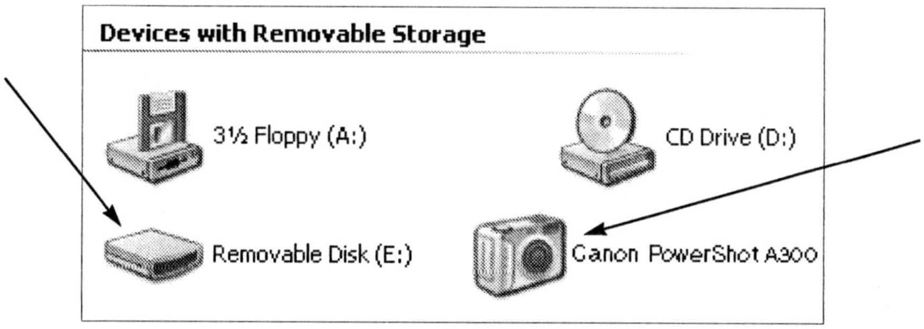

Windows displays the contents of your camera (removable disk) or memory card reader. Depending on your camera model, you may have to open one or more folders to see your photos. If you are transferring directly from the camera, you will see a camera icon.

4. Double-click the folder icon(s) within your camera or memory card reader until you see your photos. (Depending on the speed of your computer, it may take a few moments for the photos to appear.)

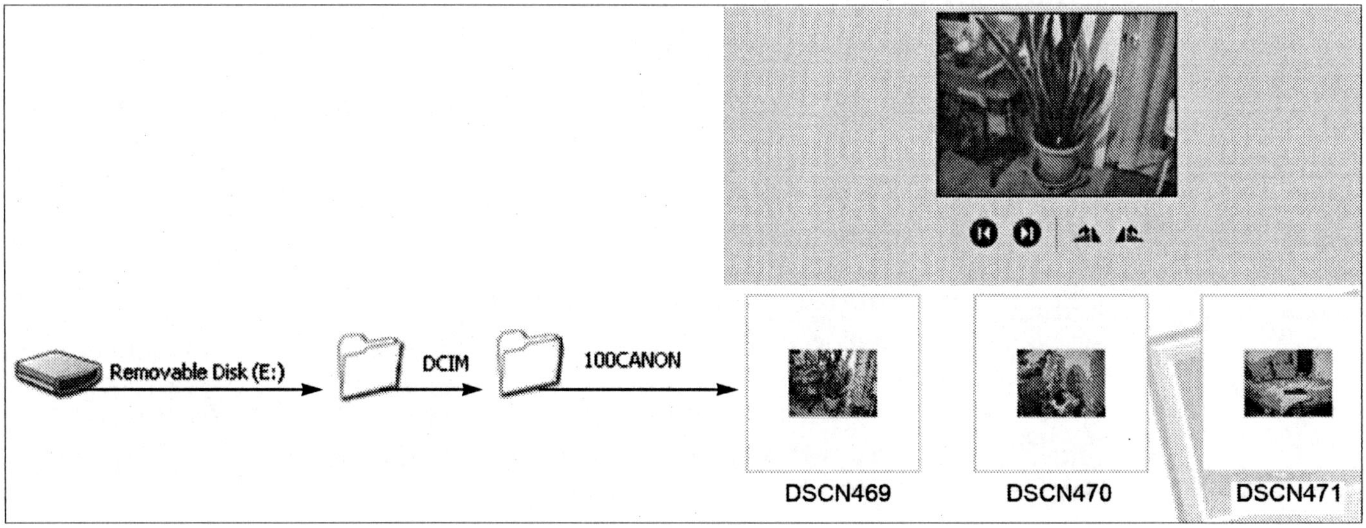

After a pause, Windows displays your photos in Thumbnail or Filmstrip view.

Select Photos to Transfer

Now you will transfer the photos to a folder on your computer.

5. Follow these steps to select all of the photos:

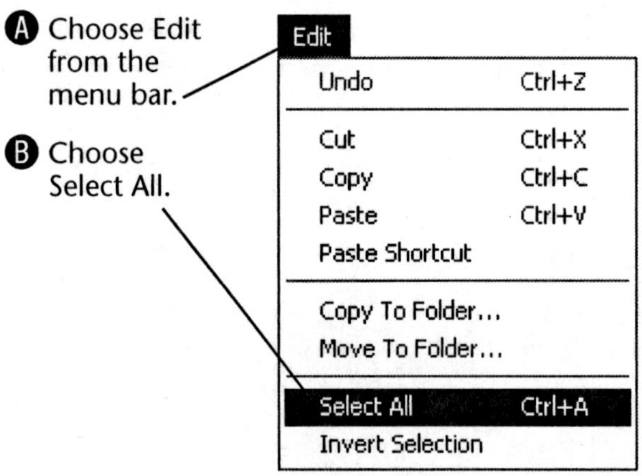

Windows highlights all of your photos to indicate that they are selected for your next command.

NOTE! In future instructions, menu bar commands will be written like this: Choose Edit→Select All from the menu bar.

6. Choose Edit→Copy from the menu bar.

   Nothing changes on the screen, but Windows knows that it should paste all of these files when you give that command.

Create a New Folder in My Pictures

7. Click the My Pictures shortcut in the Other Places section on the left side of the card reader files window.

   You can also choose your preferred file storage location, such as the My Documents folder or a USB flash drive.

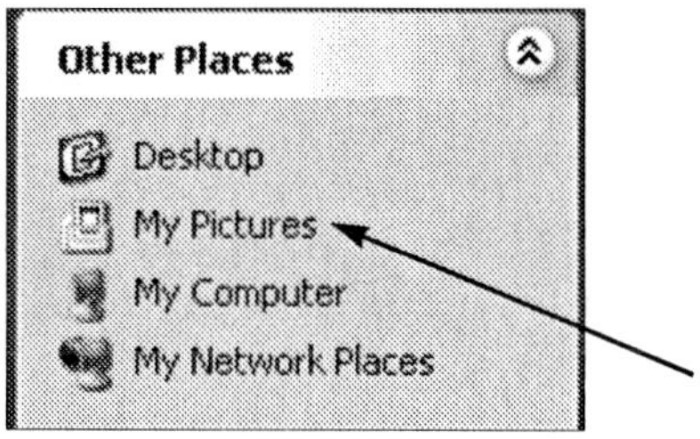

   Windows displays the My Pictures folder.

8. Choose File→New→Folder from the menu bar.

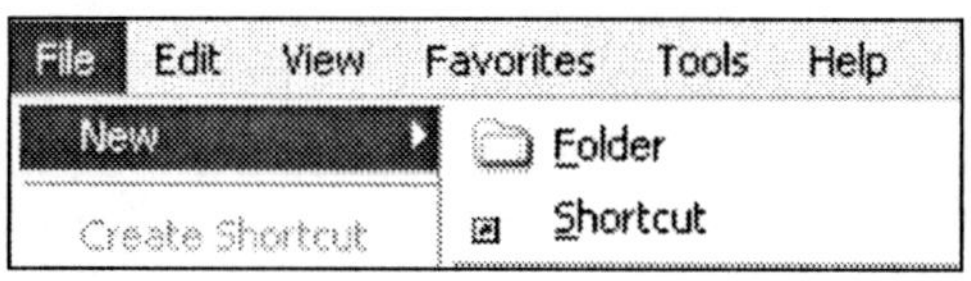

   Windows creates a new folder and highlights the name so you can rename it.

9. Type **`Lesson 3 Photos`** as the new folder name, and then tap [Enter].

   NOTE! Right-click the folder name and choose Rename from the context (pop-up) menu if the highlight disappears before you begin typing the new name.

Transfer the Photos

10. Open the new Lesson 3 Photos folder.

    Since you just created it, the folder is empty, of course.

11. Choose Edit→Paste from the menu bar.

    Windows displays the progress of copying your photos. Depending on the size and number of photos, this process can take a minute or more.

12. Close [X] the Lesson 3 Photos folder.

13. Follow the appropriate step to disconnect the camera or memory card reader:
    - **Camera and Cable:** Shut off the camera, and then disconnect the cable from the computer and the camera.
    - **Memory Card Reader:** Remove the card from the card reader, and then disconnect the card reader from the computer. Make sure your camera is switched off, and then insert the card back into the camera.

Congratulations! You have successfully copied images from your camera and saved them to a folder on your computer.

Skip the next exercise and continue reading the Formatting Memory Cards section on page 68.

HANDS-ON 3.3B Transfer Images from the Camera to the Computer (Macintosh OS X)

If you running Windows XP, follow Hands-On 3.3A on page 58.

In this exercise, you will learn a universal method for bringing your images into the computer.

Navigate to Your Photos

The method used in this exercise will work with any Macintosh OS X computer. Another program may open when you attach a camera or memory card to the computer if you installed software that came with your camera or have other photo editing software. Close this application if it opens.

First, you will connect the camera or memory card. Then, you will navigate to the photos.

1. Follow the steps for the type of connection you are going to use:

External Memory Card Reader

- Attach the memory card reader to an available USB port on your computer.
- Eject the memory card from the camera.
- Slide the memory card into the card reader, label side up. Try inserting the memory card upside down in the memory card reader if the icon does not show on the Desktop. Usually the card will go in with the label facing up, but some are inserted with the label facing down.

- Click the Choose Later button if you see a Welcome to iPhoto window, Quit Image Capture, or any other program that launches by choosing File→Quit.

The name of your memory card should appear on the Desktop.

Memory Card Reader Built In to the Computer

- Eject the memory card from the camera.
- Slide the memory card into the card reader, label side up. Try inserting the memory card upside down in the memory card reader if the icon does not show on the Desktop. Usually the card will go in with the label facing up, but some are inserted with the label facing down.
- Click the Choose Later button if you see a Welcome to iPhoto window, Quit Image Capture, or any other program that launches by choosing File→Quit.

The name of your memory card should appear on the Desktop.

Cable Connection to Camera

- Switch off the power to your camera.
- Connect the cable between your camera and an available USB port on the computer.
- Switch on the power to your camera.
- Click the Choose Later button if you see a Welcome to iPhoto window, Quit Image Capture, or any other program that launches by choosing File→Quit.

The name of your memory card should appear on the Desktop.

2. Double-click the memory card reader icon on the Desktop. The name of the icon you see will probably not match the following illustration.

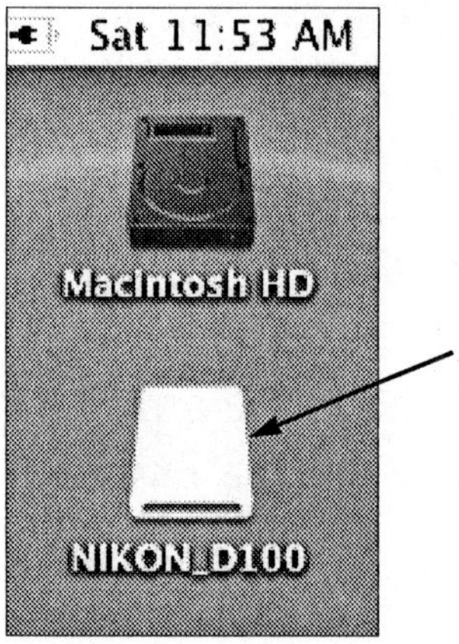

The Mac displays the contents of your camera or memory card reader. Depending on your camera model, you may have to open one or more folders to see your photos.

3. Follow these steps to view your photos:

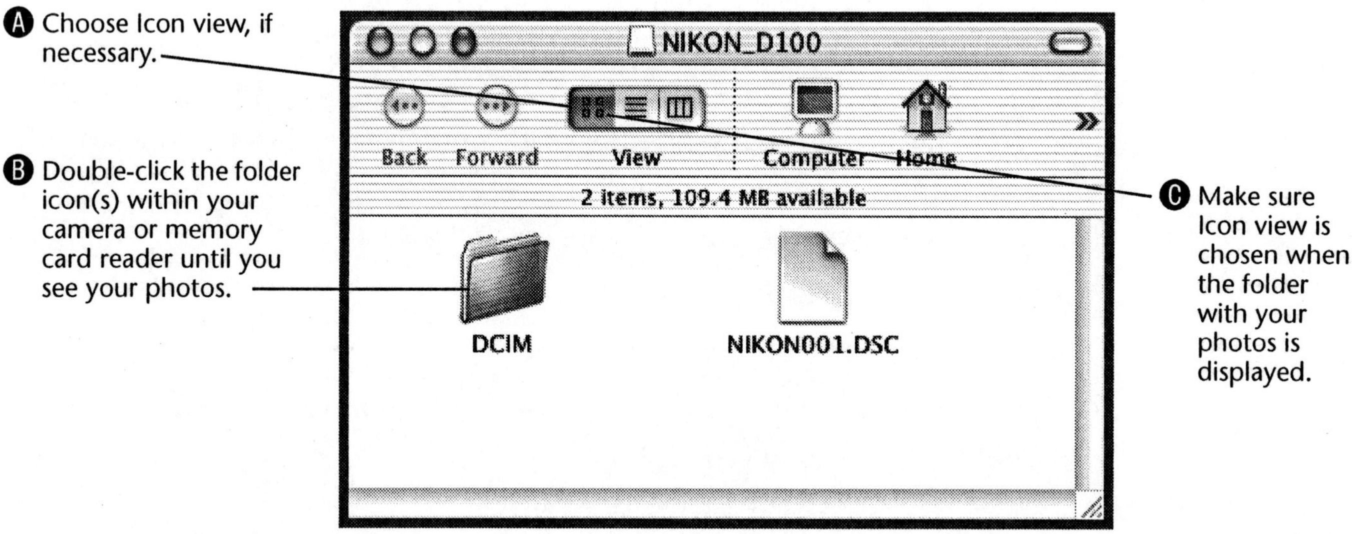

Depending on the speed of your computer, it may take a few moments for thumbnails of the photos to appear.

Select the Photos to Transfer

Now you will select all of the photos on the memory card to transfer to a folder on your computer.

4. Follow these steps to select all of the photos:

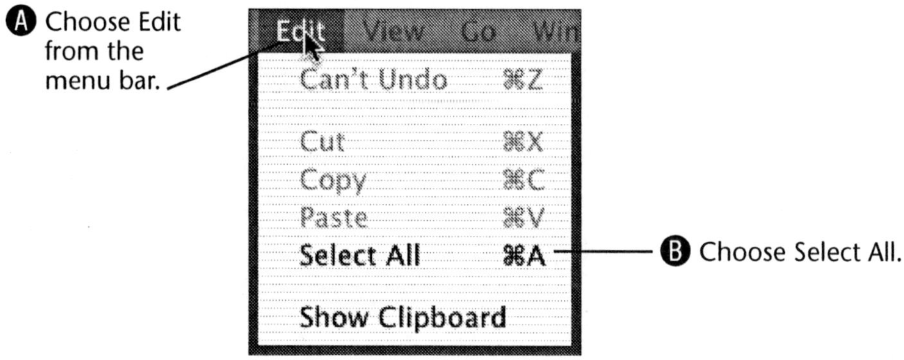

All of your photos are highlighted to indicate that they are selected for your next command.

NOTE! In future instructions, menu bar commands will be written like this: Choose Edit→Select All from the menu bar.

5. Choose Edit→Copy from the menu bar.

   Nothing changes on the screen, but Macintosh OS X knows that it should paste all of these files when you give that command.

6. Close  the pictures window.

Navigate to the Destination and Create a New Folder

7. Double-click the Macintosh HD icon, and then follow these steps to navigate to the Pictures folder:

   The Pictures folder is a standard folder created for your Macintosh OS X. You can also choose to save your images to another file storage location.

A Choose Icon view. (Switching to icon view makes folder navigation easier.)

B Scroll down the sidebar panel on the left side of the window and choose the Pictures folder.

C Choose File→New→Folder from the menu bar. A new folder is created and the name is highlighted so you can rename it.

D Type **`Lesson 3 Photos`** as the new folder name and tap [Return].

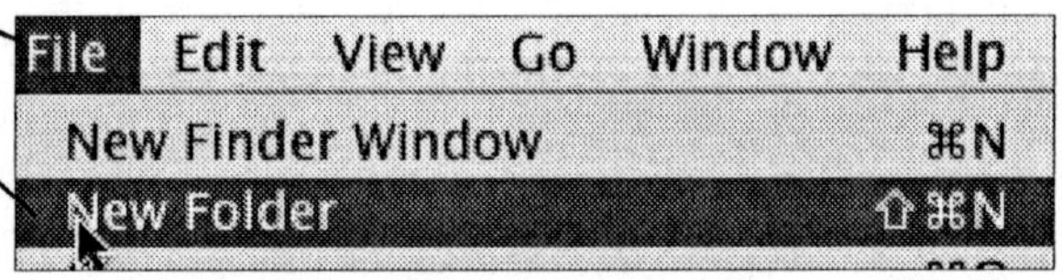

NOTE! Slowly click twice on the untitled folder and type in the name if the highlight disappears before you start typing the new name. You may have to do this more than once. Be patient with yourself.

8. Double-click the Lesson 3 Photos folder.

   The Macintosh displays the Lesson 3 Photos folder. It is still empty at the moment.

Transfer the Photos

9. Choose Edit→Paste Item from the menu bar.

   Macintosh OS X displays the progress of copying your photos. Depending on the size and number of photos, this process can take a minute or more.

10. Close the Lesson 3 Photos window.

    Now that you have transferred your photos, you will disconnect the memory card reader or camera from the computer. Pay close attention to the following warning and follow the instructions in step 11 with care.

    WARNING! Disconnecting the camera from the computer before ejecting the camera or memory card icon can damage the memory card.

11. Hold down the mouse button and drag the camera or card reader icon to the trashcan. As you get closer, the trashcan turns into an arrow to indicate eject. Continue dragging until the arrow turns dark grey, and then release the mouse.

    It is now safe to disconnect the camera from the computer.

12. Follow the appropriate steps to disconnect the camera or memory card reader:

    - **Camera and Cable:** Shut off the camera, and then disconnect the cable from the computer and the camera icon.
    - **Memory Card Reader:** Remove the card from the card reader, and then disconnect the card reader from the computer. Make sure your camera is switched off, and then insert the card back into the camera.

    Congratulations! You have successfully downloaded images and saved them to a folder on your computer.

Formatting Memory Cards

Formatting a memory card is different from merely deleting all the images from the card. It does accomplish this task, but it also does a clean sweep of the card so that new photos may be stored to it efficiently. When you delete files from a memory card, the files are removed but the old image data is not physically erased from the card. When you format a card, it completely erases old image data and allows all the space on the card to be used in the most efficient way. It is important to format a digital memory card in the following instances:

- After digital files have been transferred and saved to the computer or other storage media
- When installing a new memory card for the first time
- When using a memory card from another camera
- If you experience a problem downloading images from a memory card

WARNING! Formatting a memory card erases all photos stored on it! Make sure you have transferred all photos you wish to keep before you format a memory card.

Formatting a Memory Card in Your Camera

Formatting a memory card while it is in the camera is usually done through the menu or by using one or two buttons on the camera. Usually a message will be displayed to inform you that formatting the memory card erases all of the photos on it. To continue, just click whatever button the message prompts you to (OK, Enter, etc.).

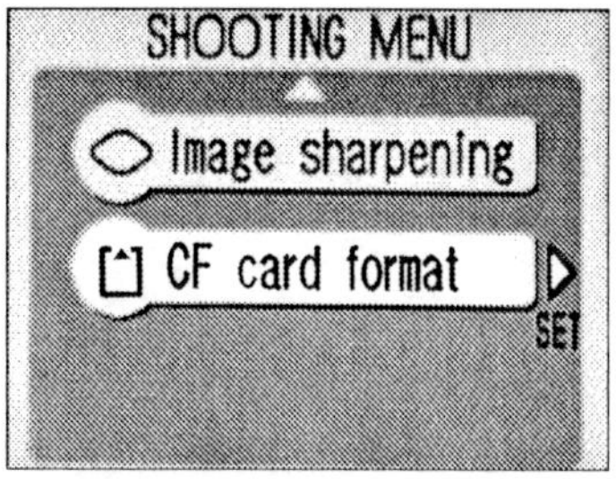

Notice that the format setting is located in the Shooting Menu on this digital camera.

Card Format is selected and a warning box is displayed before the memory card is actually formatted.

This illustration shows the Card Format setting on a Canon digital camera. The way the information is displayed will vary from camera to camera.

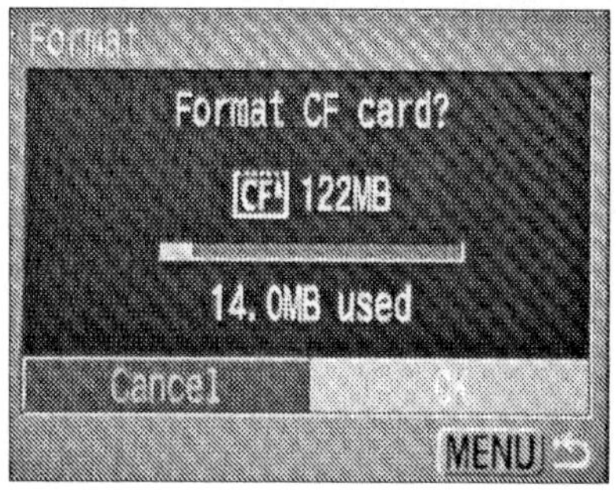

Before formatting a memory card, you have a chance to cancel the command. As you can see, not all cameras display a warning signal.

IMPORTANT! Make sure you know that you have transferred all photos you wish to keep to the computer. Once you format the card, all photos on it are lost and cannot be recovered.

QUICK REFERENCE: Formatting a Memory Card

Task	Procedure
Format a memory card in the camera	• If necessary, switch on the camera. • Display the camera's menu in the LCD. • Locate the Format command in the camera's general menu. • Execute the Format command and confirm that you wish to erase the memory card when prompted.

HANDS-ON 3.4 Format the Memory Card

In this exercise, you will format the memory card while it is inside the camera.

IMPORTANT! Do *not* perform this exercise in class if you want to keep any photos on this memory card. Perform this exercise at home after you have transferred the photos to your own computer.

1. *Important!* Make sure that all the photos on the memory card have already been downloaded to the computer.

   Remember, formatting a memory card *erases everything* on it, so transfer your pictures first.

2. Locate the instructions for formatting a memory card and format the card presently in your camera.

   When this process is finished your card should be empty.

Organizing Photographs

Some of the most important but often neglected aspects of digital photography are sorting, deleting, saving, and archiving your photographs. You want to be able to easily locate your photographs so you can print, email, etc. them later.

How to Organize Photos

How many times have you thrown all of your prints from film photography in a shoebox, only to find that you could not remember how or where you stored them? The same thing can happen with digital photographs unless you have an organized system. It is helpful to organize your files with keywords (subject, date, locale, event) so you can find them easily. Remember, you are collecting hundreds of digital photos that you will probably want for future use. Although it may seem tedious, if you get into the habit of organizing your image files when you first start using your camera, you will save hours of frustration and work later. The first tasks are to choose a storage location and to create folders.

TIP! Store all of your images in sets of folders inside one main folder instead of folders spread out over your hard drive or Desktop. You already began this process when you transferred your photos to the My Pictures folder (Windows XP) or the Pictures folder (Macintosh OS X).

On the Web For information on programs designed to organize your photos, see the Web page for this book (labpub.com/learn/silver/digphoto/).

Backing Up Your Digital Photos

Once you have stored your photographs in folders it is best to save a copy on an external storage disc like a CD or DVD. To do this you must have a CD or DVD burner, a device that allows you to burn (save) your files to a recordable CD or DVD. CD burners are included in most computers sold today. You can also buy a separate, external CD burner.

Backing up your photographs guarantees that you will not permanently lose your images due to a hard drive crash, by accidentally deleting folders, or because of any computer glitch. Backing up your digital photo files takes time, but is well worth the effort. Just like creating an image management system, developing good habits early on is a wise practice.

TIP! External hard drives are also an excellent ways to back up your digital files.

On the Web For information on the pros and cons of working with CD burners, DVD burners, and external hard drives, see the Web page for this book (labpub.com/learn/silver/digphoto/).

CD Burners

A CD burner is a device that enables you to record (also called "burn" and "write") data from your computer to individual writable CD-ROMs. The discs must be made for recording, called writable discs. Many computers today come with built-in CD burners. These are called internal CD burners. External CD burners are also available and can be connected to the computer via a USB or Firewire connection. The external CD burner is a standalone device, often called a peripheral because it is not built into the computer.

TIP! Many professional photographers keep backup discs of their files in fire-proof safes or safety deposit boxes.

Choosing CD Storage Media There are two types of writable CD discs:

- **CD-R**—These are write-once discs that cannot be erased.
- **CD-RW**—These rewriteable discs may be erased and used again if you wish.

A CD-R disc can record many sessions, which means you do not have to fill it up at one time. The term session refers to each time you add (burn) files on a CD-R disc that already contains saved files. You can record files at different times until it is full. Once full, it is considered an archived disc and can only be viewed. A CD-RW disc can also be recorded in sessions. Once full, you can erase it and use it again, much like you can with floppy and Zip disks. This sounds like a better alternative, but CD-RW disks are not as stable as CD-Rs and they are known to cause occasional problems when opened on different computer systems.

TIP! Never rely on a CD-RW disk for long-term storage of your photographs. Unlike CD-Rs, which can last 30 or more years, a CD-RW disk may go bad after just a year or two.

HANDS-ON 3.5A Burn Photos to a CD-R (Windows XP)

If you are running Macintosh OS X, skip to Hands-On 3.5B on page 75.

In this exercise, you will burn image files to a CD-R disc.

Before You Begin: Skip this exercise if your computer is not equipped with a CD-RW, DVD-R/CD-RW, or a DVD-RW drive.

Select the Files

There are many CD burning software programs. You may already be using one that works well for you. The one used here is the CD burning software bundled with your computer.

1. Choose Start→My Documents to open a My Documents window.
2. Point to the My Pictures folder or your file storage location, and then double click on the Lesson 3 Photos folder to open it. (You can open a different photos folder if you wish.)

   Windows displays the photos you transferred to the computer in Hands-On 3.3A or Hands-On 3.3B.
3. Choose Edit→Select All from the menu bar or use [Ctrl]+[A] from the keyboard.

   Windows highlights all of the photos for your next command.
4. Click the Copy to CD shortcut in the left panel.

   Windows displays the progress of saving your photos for burning to CD. You could also have copied the files to the CD drive with Copy and Paste, but this method's even easier.

   Windows also displays a balloon prompt indicating that you have files ready to write to CD.

5. Close [X] the Lesson 3 Photos window.

   The photos will remain ready to burn to CD indefinitely. You could also navigate to other folders and add additional files and/or folders to be burned to CD.

Start the Burn

6. Open the CD-RW drive, insert a blank CD-R (or CD-RW) disc, and then close the drive door.

   Windows opens a drive window for your CD-RW drive. Notice that the files you sent to CD in step 4 are displayed with dimmed icons. The small down arrow at the lower-left corner of the icons indicate that they are not yet burned to the CD.

7. Click the Write These Files to CD command in the task panel on the left side of the window.

The CD Writing Wizard window appears ready to help you start the burn. Notice the default CD name with the current date. You can replace it with a name of up to 16 characters, including spaces, commas, and other non-restricted punctuation.

8. Follow these steps to start the burn:

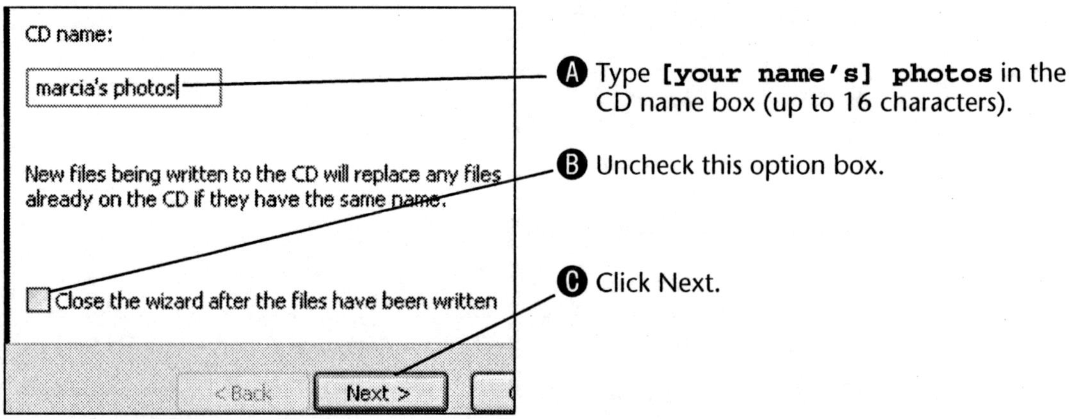

Depending on your hardware, Windows may display a prompt to create a HighMAT-compatible CD. There is no need to do this.

9. Leave the HighMAT-compatible CD box unchecked if Windows displays this prompt and click Next. Otherwise, continue to the next step.

The CD burner automatically begins writing your file to the recordable CD in the drive and displays the progress of the burn.

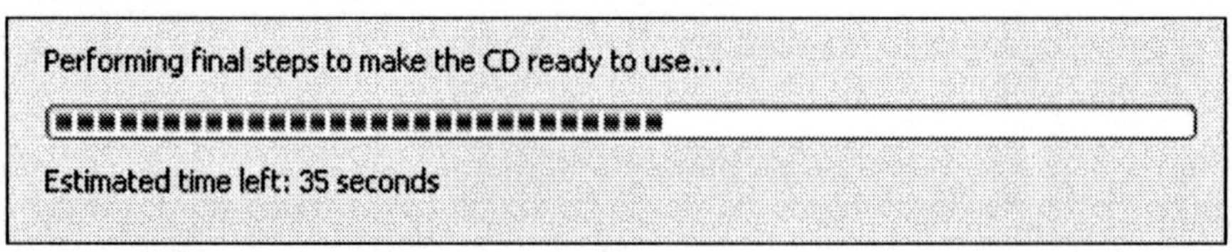

Windows ejects the CD when the burn is finished. Notice that the wizard window now asks if you wish to create another CD with the same files. This option is handy if you want to create multiple CDs. In this case, you will simply close the window.

10. Click the Finish button.

    Windows closes the CD Writing Wizard window. Notice that the drive window is still open, but empty. This is because the disc was ejected.

11. Leaving the newly burned CD in the drawer, close the CD-RW drive drawer.

    After a pause, your newly burned photos appear in the drive window.

12. Click the My Computer shortcut in the task panel on the left side of the drive window.

    Notice that the name of your disc appears beside the drive icon.

13. Follow these steps to eject the disc:

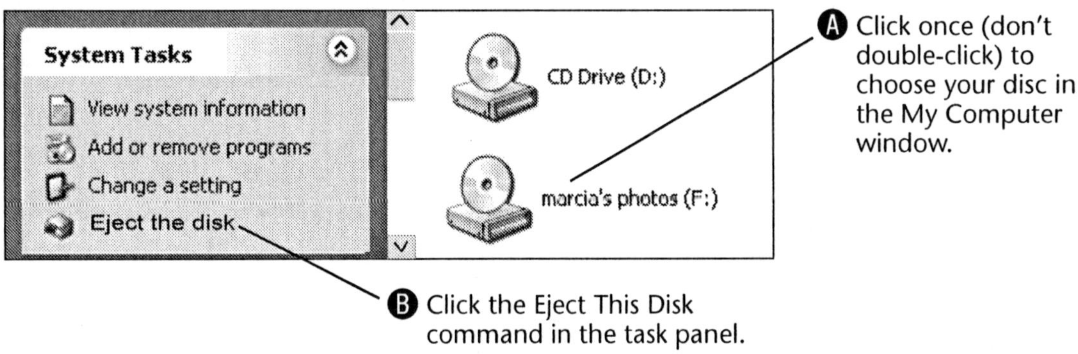

    Windows ejects your disc.

14. Carefully remove the disc from the drive drawer, and then gently close the drawer.

    Congratulations! You have successfully backed up your original files.

    Skip the next exercise and continue reading the Caring for and Handling CDs section on page 78.

HANDS-ON 3.5B Burn Photos to a CD-R (Macintosh OS X)

If you are running Windows XP, follow Hands-On 3.5A on page 72.

In this exercise, you will burn image files to a CD-R disc.

Before You Begin: Skip this exercise if your computer is not equipped with a CD-RW, DVD-R/CD-RW, or a DVD-RW drive.

Select the Files

There are many CD burning software programs. You may already be using one that works well for you. The one shown here is the CD burning software bundled with your computer.

1. Insert a blank CD-R disc in the CD drive.

If your Macintosh computer is a later model G4 or G5 model, open the CD drive by pressing the top right key on your keyboard. On any earlier model, open the CD drive by pressing the button on the CD tray in the CPU.

2. Macintosh OS X may display a prompt. If it does, jump to step 3. Otherwise, an untitled CD icon will appear on the Desktop. Follow these steps, and then jump to step 4:

   - Single-click on Untitled CD to select the folder name.
   - Rename the CD **`[Your Name's] Photos`**, and then tap Return.

   Click again in the title if you accidentally deselect while trying to rename the folder. It is just like selecting and changing a word in any program, for example, Microsoft Word.

3. When the Macintosh OS X displays a prompt, follow these steps:

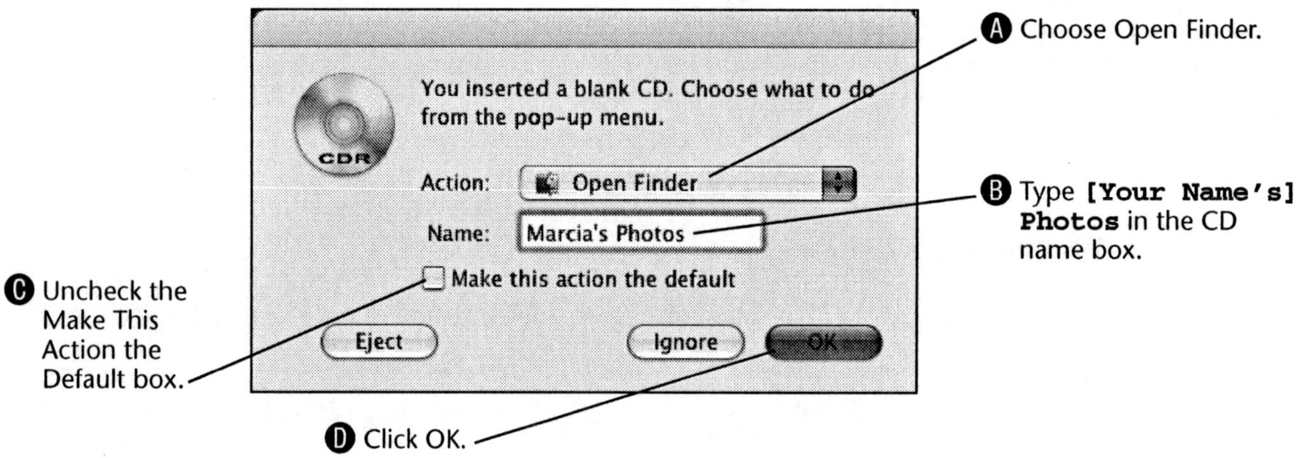

An icon of a CD is displayed on the Desktop.

4. Double-click the Macintosh HD icon, which displays the contents of the hard drive, and then follow these steps:

Ⓐ Scroll down and choose Pictures (or your file storage location) in the sidebar.

Ⓑ Choose View→As List from the menu bar.

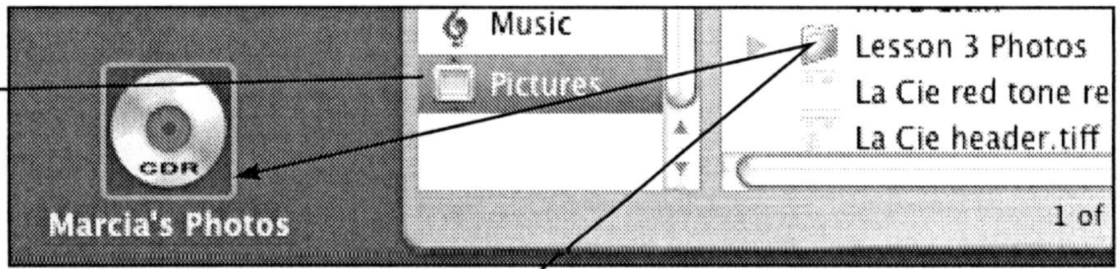

Ⓒ Scroll and choose the Lesson 3 Photos folder from the list, and then drag the Lesson 3 Photos folder into the [Your Name's] Photos CD.

The contents of the Lesson 3 Photos folder are copied into the CD. You will not see anything happen.

5. Drag the CD-R to the trashcan on the dock. The trashcan temporarily changes to a burn symbol as the CD-R nears it. Burn Disk will be displayed and the burning process will begin.

6. Follow these steps to start the burn:

Ⓐ Set the burn speed to Maximum.

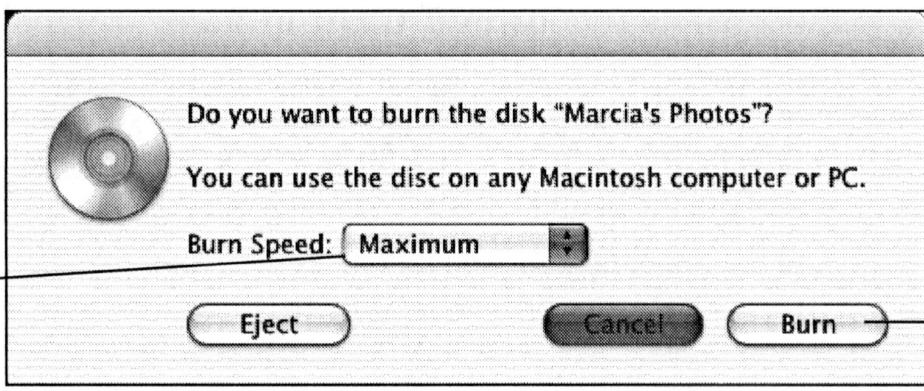

Ⓑ Click Burn.

The CD-R temporarily disappears from the Desktop and Macintosh OS X displays the progress of the burn. Depending on the size and number of photos, this process can take a minute or more.

7. The CD-R appears on the Desktop when the burning process is complete. Click and drag the disc to the trashcan to eject it.

   Congratulations! You have just backed up and archived your first set of photographs.

Caring for and Handling CDs

Establishing a reliable and easy-to-use file management system and backing up these digital photo files to CDs ensures the longevity of your digital pictures. How you care for your CDs is just as important as backing up your files. They are susceptible to damage if not cared for properly.

Tips for Long-Lasting CDs

The following tips will help ensure that your photo archives last as long as you can use present technology to maintain it:

- **Buy good quality discs:** Not all discs are created equal. In general, recognized brands are better than generic so it is worth the extra cost to buy name brand discs. Silver and gold discs are the most stable and longest lasting (find them online at dsgi.com).
- **Keep discs free from dust and scratches:** Always keep discs in envelopes or jewel cases. It doesn't take much damage to make a disc unreadable. Clean discs with a soft microfiber cloth.
- **Use CD marking pens to label discs:** Regular markers and ballpoint pens are not safe for use on CDs because they may penetrate through to the recorded layer. Electronic and office supply stores carry pens specifically made for writing on discs.
- **Store CDs in a dry and cool space:** Humidity and heat can cause damage to CDs.

- **Be aware of new storage technology:** Eventually CDs will be replaced with another, better storage technology, so keep abreast of new systems. You don't want to find yourself unable to access old discs because of outdated technology.
- **Back up your backups:** It's a good idea to transfer your backups to new discs every few years.

TIP! All longevity tests for CDs are done in laboratories. The technology has not been around long enough to know exactly how long discs will last.

Concepts Review

True/False Questions

			Page number
1. A locked image is not deleted when you format a memory card.	**true**	**false**	______
2. Magnifying (zooming) an image in Playback mode is a good method of determining if a picture is sharply focused.	**true**	**false**	______
3. Downloading is another term for transferring images to a computer.	**true**	**false**	______
4. It is not necessary to format brand new memory cards.	**true**	**false**	______
5. CD-Rs have a larger storage capacity then CD-RWs.	**true**	**false**	______
6. CD-RWs are the only discs that support multiple burning sessions.	**true**	**false**	______
7. In general, recognized brand name CDs are more reliable than generic CDs.	**true**	**false**	______
8. CD-RWs are the best choice for backing up image files because they can be used over and over again and cause fewer problems than CD-Rs.	**true**	**false**	______
9. Deleting all images in the computer is the same as formatting the memory card in the camera.	**true**	**false**	______
10. Using keywords when you store your image files makes finding them later very easy.	**true**	**false**	______

Multiple Choice Questions

1. Which of the following is an advantage of using a memory card reader over connecting the camera directly to the computer to transfer photos?

   Page number: ______

   a. It is faster

   b. Battery power is preserved

   c. The card reader is more compact and easier to carry around

   d. Both a and b

2. Burning a CD means ________.

   Page number: ______

   a. writing files from the computer to a CD

   b. recording data from the computer to a CD

   c. using a writable CD to back up your image files

   d. All of the above

3. What can you can do to make sure your archived discs last a long time?

   Page number: ______

   a. Use marking pens specifically made for writing on CDs

   b. Store the discs in a dry, cool place

   c. Transfer your backups to new discs every few years

   d. All of the above

4. Which of the following tasks can you perform in Playback mode?

   Page number: ______

   a. Magnify your picture using Zoom view

   b. Crop the picture

   c. Change the picture from color to black and white

   d. None of the above

Skill Builders

SKILL BUILDER 3.1 Review Images for Sharpness

In this exercise, you will use the Replay features to check the sharpness and composition of your pictures.

Before You Begin: Make sure your camera is set on Automatic or Program so you can determine exposure settings.

Take Several Photos

1. Choose someone who is willing to spend about 20 minutes having his/her hands photographed.

   You will be practicing your skills with composition and using focus lock.

2. Pose the person so his/her hands are against a solid color background.

   You can use a piece of cloth, a sheet, a jacket, or a blank wall behind or under the hands.

3. Carefully frame the hands so they are not directly in the center of the photograph.

   This helps balance the composition and makes the photograph more interesting.

4. Using focus lock, take a picture that centers on the fingernails.

   This will give you a point of focus when checking for sharpness in Replay mode.

5. Repeat steps 1–4, selecting different parts of the hands on which to focus. Take five more pictures trying different angles and framing techniques. Remember to use focus lock.

Replay the Photos

6. Go inside or under the cover of shade and set your camera to Replay (or Review).

   Remember, it is always easier to see the LCD when you are not in bright ambient light.

7. Scroll through your pictures using the arrows on the omni dial.

   This will give you a quick review.

8. Choose your first picture and, using your zoom feature, magnify the picture as much as possible.

   As you increase the magnification you will see a smaller part of the picture.

9. Scroll around the picture using the arrows on the omni dial. Stop when you see the fingernails.

   This is the place you focused on in your first picture.

10. Look carefully to determine if the picture is sharp and in focus.

11. Examine the remaining pictures. Are they sharp and in focus?

Re-Shoot and Review

12. Re-shoot the pictures if they do not look sharp, paying attention to how you use the focus lock.
    Focus lock is very helpful for achieving sharpness in the area you want in focus.

13. Review the pictures again and check for sharpness, using the zoom feature in the playback mode.

14. Save your pictures in the camera. You will use them again in Skill Builder 3.3.

SKILL BUILDER 3.2 Review Images to Evaluate Composition

In this exercise, you will use Image Replay to check the composition of your photographs.

Before You Begin: Make sure you are still in Automatic or Program mode.

1. Take a picture of something in nature (a tree or bush, flowers, etc.).
   As you look through the optical viewfinder or LCD to compose your picture, pay attention to what surrounds your main subject.

2. Take another picture of the same subject from a different angle, and then take three more pictures from more angles while getting closer to the subject.
   If necessary, refer to Lesson 2.

3. Once again, go in the shade or indoors to review your pictures using Image Replay.
   Look at the overall composition and evaluate the placement of your main subject. Does it look the way you saw it when you took the picture? What could you have done differently?

4. Take several more pictures using the same subject. Try holding the camera vertically, get closer, and try different angles. Don't be afraid to crop some of the subject.

5. Review your pictures again using Image Replay. Have you done a better job of capturing the subject the way you want to?
   Keep your pictures in the camera for use in the next exercise.

SKILL BUILDER 3.3 Transfer Your Images to the Computer

In this exercise, you will download your pictures to a new folder within your pictures folder.

1. Turn off the camera before you remove the memory card or connect it to the computer with a cable.

   TIP! If using a cable connection, you will have to turn the camera back on and possibly set it to Playback mode to complete the connection.

2. Transfer your pictures to your computer using a memory card reader or a cable connection.

   Remember to turn off the camera before removing the memory card and before connecting the cable to the camera.

3. Follow the directions for the operating system to locate your pictures folder on the hard drive and create a new folder within it:

   - **Windows XP:** Choose Start→My Documents→My Pictures. Double-click the Pictures folder to open it, and then create a new folder named **`Skill Builder 3.3`**.
   - **Macintosh OS X:** Double-click the HD icon on the Desktop and select the Pictures folder in the left pane. Single-click anywhere in the white area of the right pane. Then, choose File→New Folder from the menu and name it **`Skill Builder 3.3`**.

4. Follow the directions for your computer to find the memory card icon:

   - **Windows XP:** Choose Start→My Computer→Removable Drive.
   - **Macintosh OS X:** The memory card is located on the Desktop.

5. Double-click the memory card icon several times until you see individual image file icons, and then choose Edit→Select All.

   All of your images will be selected so you can move them to your new folder. You can also use a keyboard shortcut to select all the files in a folder by tapping [Ctrl]+[A] (Windows) or [⌘]+[A] (Macintosh).

6. Single-click any of the selected files, and then hold and drag (don't let go of the mouse) the files to the Skill Builder 3.3 folder.

   The files will be copied into the new folder.

7. Remove the memory card from the card reader or disconnect the cable from the computer and the camera. Remember to turn the camera off before disconnecting the cable from the camera and computer.

Macintosh Users: Remember to drag the memory card drive to the trashcan to eject it before removing the card from the card reader.

You now have all your images from these exercises in your computer to use any time you wish!

LESSON 4

Working with Customized Camera Settings

Digital cameras offer many ways of capturing pictures. The easiest setting, and the one most commonly used, is Fully Automatic. Although excellent photographs can be achieved using this fully automatic setting, other automatic modes allow you to make better pictures of specific subjects. Try these modes so you can make informed choices when using your camera. By utilizing these other settings, you are also gaining important knowledge about how your camera works.

Auto modes include Scene Assist and perhaps "creative" settings that allow you to alter the photograph's color and intensity, and to add special effects while you are taking the picture. This is a distinct difference from film cameras, in which you can only creatively change a picture after the film has been developed. In this lesson, you will use Scene Assist modes, flash settings, and the self-timer; shoot continuous pictures, one after the other; and create special photo effects.

*Additional learning resources are available at **labpub.com/learn/silver/digphoto/***

Case Study

Bruce is taking his digital camera with him on his summer vacation to different national parks, where he knows scenic vistas abound. He also has tickets for a baseball game in Los Angeles and wants to be prepared to capture the action. In addition, he has many other destinations planned: the beach, botanical gardens, museums, and visits with relatives and friends. He is ready to take his camera off Fully Automatic mode so he can better capture the variety of subjects he encounters.

Bruce knows that learning how to customize the automatic settings will allow him freedom and flexibility that simply cannot be achieved using Fully Automatic mode. He begins by looking in his instruction manual to see what automatic custom settings are available. He finds that with his particular model, he not only has Scene Assist modes but also creative modes that allow him to create unique and interesting photographs. After two weeks of fun and relaxation—and lots of picture taking—Bruce arrives home with a myriad of successful and creative photographic memories from his vacation.

Introducing Shooting Modes

Many settings are available in shooting mode. It is a good idea to start with the basics: Fully Automatic, in which the camera chooses all the settings; Scene Assist, in which the settings are determined according to the type of subject matter; and Program mode, which is a flexible version of Fully Automatic (you can choose and change some settings that you cannot in Fully Automatic).

Fully Automatic Mode

AUTO In Fully Automatic mode, all you do is press the shutter button. The camera does the rest. It is meant to be easy, and it is. This mode is often represented by the word "auto" encircled in green, and in it you take pictures using no special functions or manual adjustments. The camera sets the optimal focusing and exposure settings. Professional SLR digital cameras do not come with Fully Automatic mode. Instead, they feature Program mode that determines exposure settings automatically but also allows you to make certain manual adjustments, like ISO, which is a variable setting selected by the amount of available light. For example, you can set it so pictures can be taken in low light conditions without using the flash. Remember that shooting modes are often found on a dial on top of the camera. In some smaller compact cameras these modes are found in the menu options in the LCD. Check your instruction manual to find out where settings for your model are located.

Fully Automatic mode on the Canon Power Shot G5 digital camera

Fully Automatic mode on the Nikon Coolpix 3100 digital camera

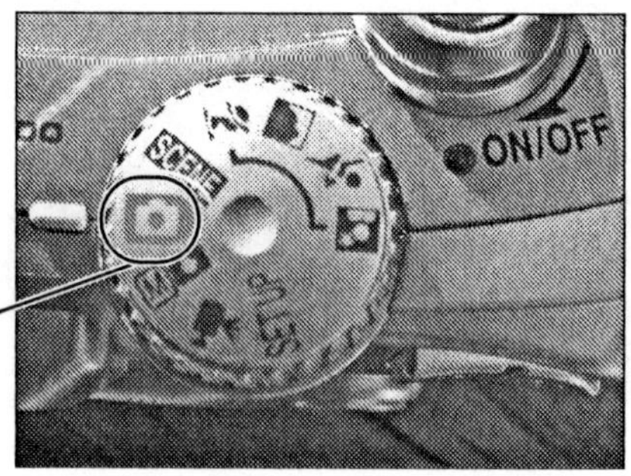

TIP! Pressing and holding down the shutter button halfway in any shooting mode activates and sets auto focus. Pressing all the way down and taking the picture or releasing the shutter button disengages the setting.

Introducing Scene Assist Modes

Scene Assist modes are found in the menu accessed through the LCD or on the dial on the top of the camera. Not all cameras, like advanced SLRs, have Scene Assist modes. Instead, they feature options that achieve the same effect but that are not automatic. Advanced modes are covered in Lesson 5, Exploring Exposure.

The following table shows the most common Scene Assist modes, their use, and a common symbol associated with each.

QUICK REFERENCE: Using Scene Assist Modes

Mode	Symbol	When to Use
Portrait		You want to blur the background to make the person stand out
Sports		You want to freeze action in sports or any moving subject, even waterfalls!
Landscape		You want to capture wide scenic views while keeping all elements sharp
Night Portrait Scene		You want to take pictures of people at twilight or night while keeping a natural exposure for the background (so it is not completely dark)
Macro (or close-up)		You want to take close-up pictures of flowers, plants, insects, etc. You are able to get within inches of the subject

Portrait Mode

Portrait mode blurs the background to make subjects stand out. Using a telephoto lens or extending the zoom lens to bring the subject close to you will blur the background even more. You can also have the subject stand further away from the background—be it a wall or bushes, or anything else—and the background will become less distinct.

Sports Mode

Sports mode may also be called Action mode. It is used to freeze fast-moving subjects. Usually we think of freezing action in sports, but Sports mode can also be effective when taking pictures of waterfalls, moving cars, or running animals.

Landscape Mode

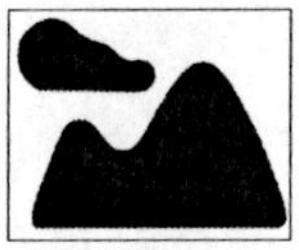

Landscape mode is used for wide scenic views. If you want everything in your picture to look very sharp, this is the mode to use. Using a wide-angle lens will further enhance the sense of depth. A wide-angle lens allows you to capture more in your picture than you can with other lenses. If you have a zoom lens, zoom out until you see more of the scene.

Night Portrait Scene

Night Portrait Scene mode is for photographs of subjects taken at twilight or at night. The flash illuminates the subject and gives the background a natural-looking exposure. This means the subjects is illuminated and the background is not completely dark.

NOTE! It is important that the camera and your subject remain still even after the flash fires. Using a tripod is helpful, but not mandatory, to keep the camera steady.

Macro (Close-Up)

Macro mode is used to take close-up pictures of flowers, insects, etc. You have to focus very close to your subject to make the most of this mode.

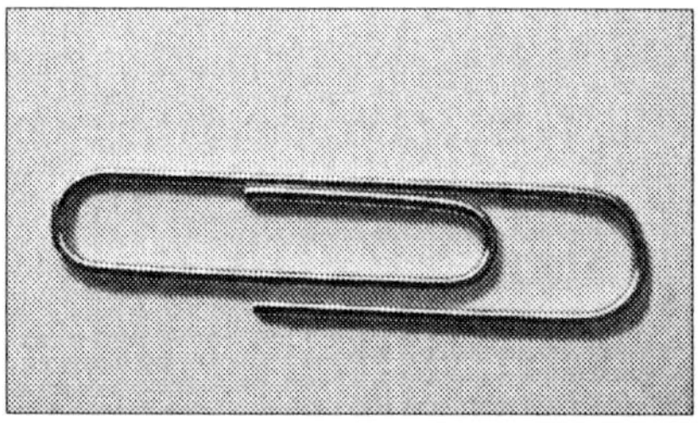

Picture taken in Macro mode, full frame, no cropping

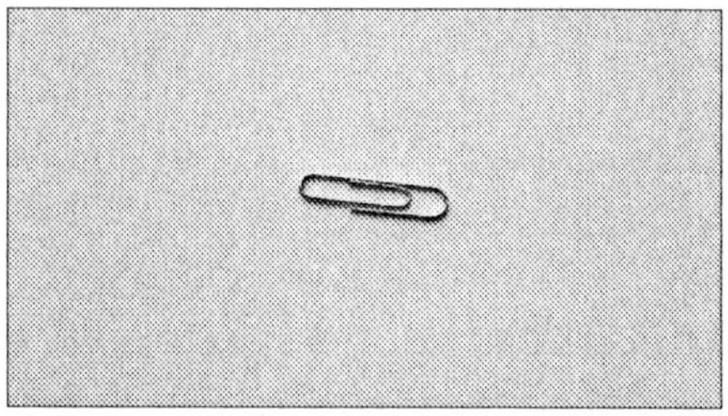

Picture taken in Normal mode, as close as possible to retain focus

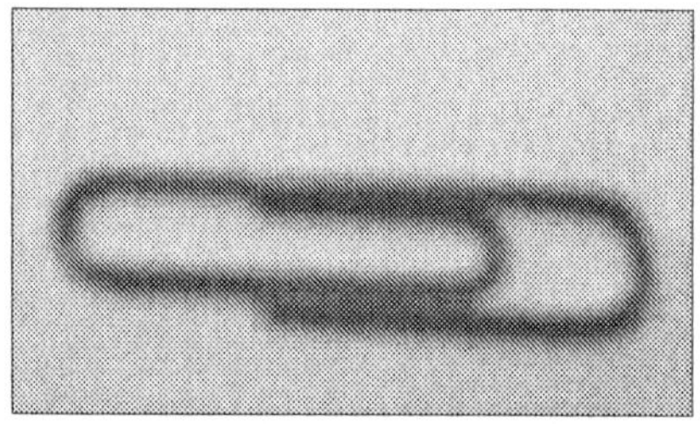

Picture taken in Normal mode but from the same distance as the Macro mode picture

HANDS-ON 4.1 Use Scene Assist Modes

In this exercise, you will find subjects for each Scene Assist mode and photograph them using the corresponding mode on your camera.

Before You Begin: Locate Scene Assist modes in your instruction manual. Your camera may have only some of the Scene Assist modes we have discussed. Practice this exercise with the modes available on your camera. Practice with any you have but that are not addressed here after you have completed this exercise.

TIP! Scene Assist modes may be listed in the index of your instruction manual under Shooting Modes, Auto Modes, or other names.

1. Set your camera to Portrait mode. Place your subject about five feet in front of a wall, bush, fence, or tree. Stand close enough or zoom in so your subject fills most of the frame, and then take the picture.

   In Portrait mode, the subject is the emphasis, and anything behind will be less sharp.

2. Now switch your camera to Sports mode. Set yourself up so you are ready when your subject passes. Have your subject run past you so that he/she is perpendicular to where you are standing. Take several pictures, and then check your LCD in Playback mode to ensure you caught the action.

   When you take pictures in Sports mode, the action is "frozen" and should not be blurred.

3. Switch your camera to Landscape mode and choose an outdoor subject such as a city skyline, a row of trees, or a field. If you have a zoom lens, zoom out until you see the most area of the landscape in your viewfinder or LCD. Take several pictures in this mode.

   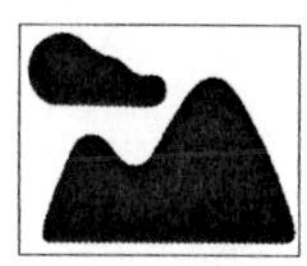

   In Landscape mode, everything in the picture is sharp and in focus.

4. Make sure your camera lens is not zoomed. That is, you should see the largest area of your subject.

   Macro mode (the next mode you will try) does not work well, and may not work at all, if your lens is zoomed.

5. Check your instruction manual to see how close you can get to an object in Macro (Close-Up) mode. It varies with each camera.

   This knowledge will help you perform the next step effectively.

6. Switch your camera to Macro or Close-Up mode. Find a flower, plant, or any small object. Get within six inches of your subject and focus carefully on one part of it. Take the picture and review it in your LCD. If it looks out of focus, get a little further away from the subject and take another picture. Repeat this until you have a sharp close-up image.

   It is best to take your pictures outdoors so the flash does not fire. The picture may be washed out (too light) if the flash is used at such a close distance.

7. Download your images to your computer and note if you achieved what you wanted with Scene Assist modes. Repeat this exercise if you did not get the results you hoped for.

   If you need a reminder on how to download files, see Lesson 3.

Exploring Flash

The built-in flash on your digital camera is extremely helpful when taking pictures in low light (indoors, night, shade, etc.) and has settings to control flash intensity, reduce red-eye, and determine how the flash synchronizes with the shutter speed (so it fires at the correct time.) The built-in flash may be a pop-up device on top of the camera or part of the camera body to the top and side of the lens.

The way the flash operates is very simple. A flash sensor reads the amount of light available to the subject and determines how much flash power must be used based on distance and available light. All of this happens in less than one second!

Flash located in the body of the Canon Power Shot G5

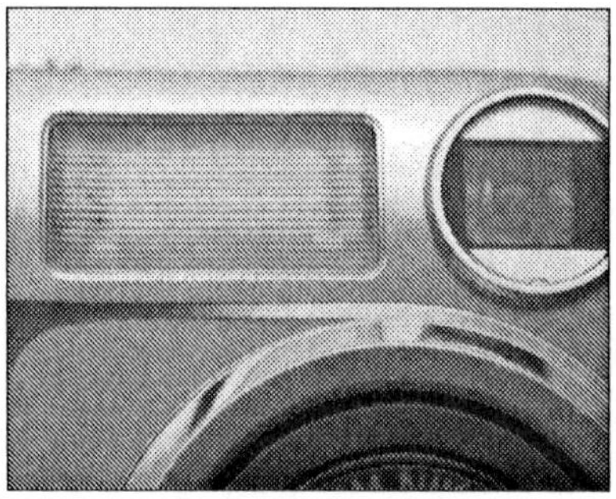

Flash located in the body of the Nikon Coolpix 3100

Pop-up flash in a Nikon digital SLR camera

TIP! Using the flash consumes a lot of battery power. Be sure to have an extra set or two of batteries available when you know you will be using the flash for long periods of time.

QUICK REFERENCE: Using Flash Settings

Setting	Symbol	When to Use
Auto		You want the flash to fire automatically, as required by the ambient lighting level
Auto Red-Eye Reduction		You are taking pictures of people or animals and want to avoid red-eye (The red-eye reduction lamp fires each time the main flash fires)
Always On		You want the flash to fire regardless of ambient light conditions; use when you want to have more light on your subject, even if it is not completely dark *Tip!* This is called fill flash, and is often used when taking pictures in deep shadow.
Always Off		You do not want the flash to fire, for instance in Macro mode, or you do not want to add extra light to the ambient lighting conditions

Canon Powershot G5

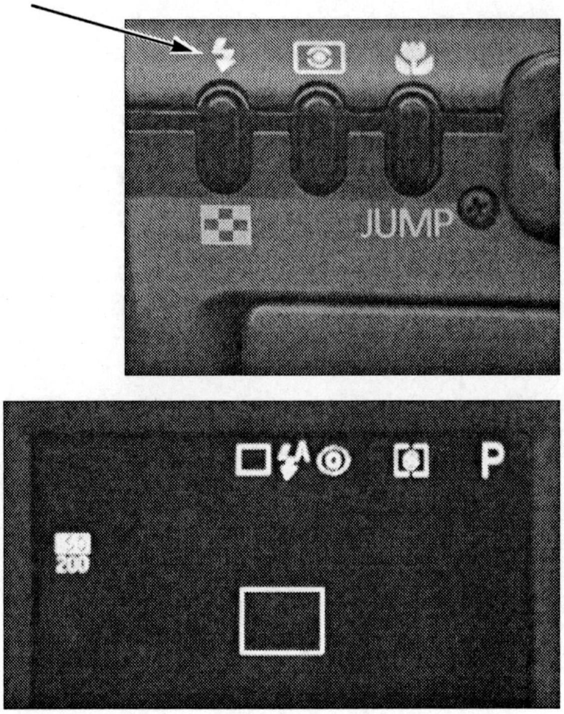

Nikon Coolpix 3100

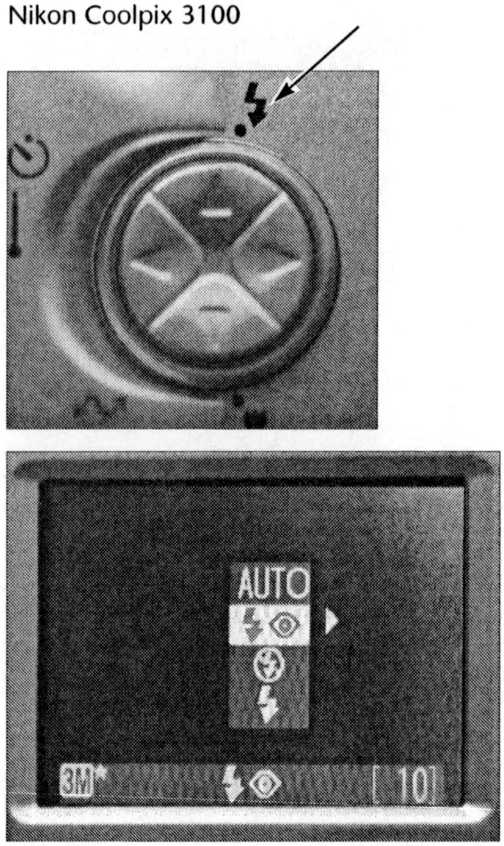

Location of flash settings

Fully Automatic Flash Mode

As mentioned, when you are using Automatic mode the camera's exposure system determines when to trigger the flash. This comes in handy if you're indoors and in low light conditions photographing social events like parties, receptions, and special ceremonies. If you have a pop-up flash, it will automatically activate when needed.

NOTE! Your built-in flash will only extend about 6–10 feet from the camera, so check your LCD to make sure your subject is within flash range. Your instruction manual will specify the flash range of your camera.

This picture was taken close to subject and well within the flash range (up to 10 feet).

This picture was taken further back using a zoom lens. It is not as bright but still shows detail.

This picture was taken outside the flash range using a zoom lens. When you step back past the flash range, the flash loses intensity.

Fill Flash Mode

You use Fill Flash mode when your subject is in the shade or in front of a very bright background (for example, the beach, snow, or a bright window). This mode "fills" in the dark area with light so the subject is not a dark silhouette. The subject becomes lighter to reveal detail. The background remains the same or will get lighter. If you don't use fill flash, the exposure meter in your camera is fooled by all the bright light in the scene and determines the exposure based on the brightness. Thus, your subject in front will appear too dark. When used in the shade, it brings out detail that would otherwise be lost in darkness.

TIP! Do not use the flash if you wish to create a silhouette effect.

Triggering the Flash

On professional SLR digital cameras, you trigger the flash by turning it on manually. On compact and non-professional SLR cameras the automatic flash feature must be disabled so you can control the flash. Sometimes the setting is called Always On or Flash Anytime. (Since you have been consistently using your instruction manual, you should be able to locate this section easily.)

The term Always On means the flash will always go off—even if lighting conditions do not warrant it. Use this setting when you want to use Fill Flash outdoors during the day. It is also possible to set the flash so it is always off. This means the flash will never fire no matter what the situation. This can be helpful if you want the scene to look natural and not washed out or if you want to take pictures indoors without a flash.

This picture was taken without Fill Flash.

This picture was taken with Fill Flash.

Red-Eye Reduction

Red-eye occurs when the subject's eyes become dilated because of being in the dark. The dilation is a result of the eyes adjusting to the dark. When the flash is fired the light reflects off the retina in the back of the eye. The reflected light is picked up by the camera and what you actually see is the reflection of blood in the eye. Animals and humans are susceptible to this phenomenon. Most cameras have a red-eye reduction setting. There are two versions of this setting:

- **Pre-Flash:** The camera fires one or more pre-flash bursts before the shutter releases.
- **Bright Light:** The camera shines a bright light in the subject's eyes before the flash fires.

The objective of these settings is to reduce the size of the pupils to prevent red-eye as much as possible. Note that it is not one hundred percent effective. Fortunately, most image editing programs, like Adobe® Photoshop® Elements, have tools to easily fix red-eye.

TIP! Be careful not to put your fingers in front of the flash or the flash sensor!

HANDS-ON 4.2 Use Flash Mode

In this exercise, you will locate and use the flash settings on your camera.

Before You Begin: In your instruction manual, find the section about using the flash. You should be able to use the index to find flash options.

1. In a semi-dark hallway or room, have your subject stand about six feet from the camera. Compose and take the picture using automatic flash in Automatic or Program mode. Remember, you have to manually pop up the flash on professional SLR cameras. You may also have to manually pop up the flash on non-professional digital SLR cameras.

   The flash should fire automatically if you are using a compact digital camera. The flash will usually pop up on digital SLR cameras if you are using Automatic or Scene Assist mode.

2. Move back another six feet from your subject so you are about twelve feet away. Compose and take another picture using the automatic flash.

3. Check your results in the LCD. If necessary, briefly go into Playback mode to take a longer look. Make sure to exit Playback mode when you are finished.

   Notice that your subject is darker in the second picture than in the first picture. The flash on your camera has a specific range of use.

4. Now, have your subject stand in deep shade or in front of a bright window. Set your flash so it will not fire, and then compose and take the picture. (The setting may be called Always Off or Flash/Cancel.)

   The flash will not fire and the subject will appear very dark.

5. Leave your subject in the same place, and set the flash setting to Always On, Fill Flash, or Forced Flash. Compose and take the picture.

   The flash will fire and "fill in" your subject with light, thereby revealing more detail in the areas that were too dark.

6. Check your results in Playback mode in the LCD.

   Notice that your pictures are distinctly different, and may be similar to the figures on page 98. Your results are influenced by lighting conditions and how your camera's flash works.

7. Take some more pictures in different lighting conditions, with and without the flash, and then check your results in Playback mode.

Introducing the Self-Timer

When the self-timer is on, pictures are taken several seconds after the shutter button is released. Many cameras also come with a remote, which is used for the same purpose. The self-timer setting is usually on a button or dial on the body of the camera. It is represented by a clock symbol.

Why Use the Self-Timer?

Most of us use the self-timer when we would like to include ourselves in the picture. When using the self-timer for this purpose, set the camera on a tripod or on a flat, stable surface. Preventing blurred images caused by camera shake can also be reduced if you use the self-timer, as you will see in the following exercise.

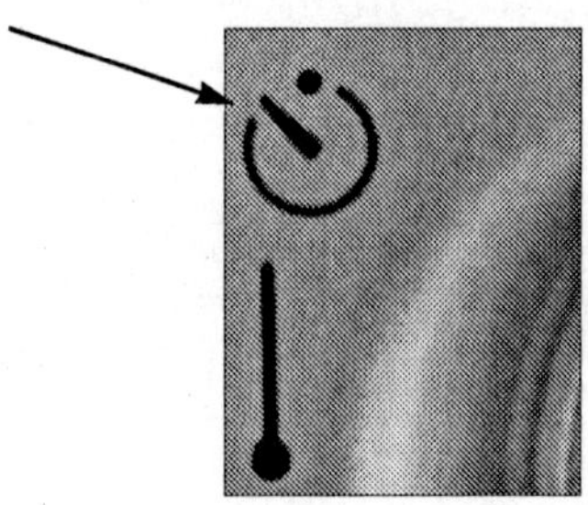

HANDS-ON 4.3 Use the Self-Timer to Become a Human Tripod!

If your photos are coming out a little blurry due to camera shake, here is a great way to keep the camera more stable without using a tripod. In this exercise, you will use the self-timer to help you hold the camera steady.

1. **Look in your camera's manual for directions on setting the self-timer.**

   You may want to change how long the self-timer waits before the shutter is released. Many cameras have this feature.

2. **If desired, use the camera's menu to set how many seconds must elapse before the shutter is released.**

   Once the self-timer is set, it will remain that way until you change it again.

3. **Get a general idea of how you want the picture composed by looking through the viewfinder or LCD.**

   It is important to set up your picture before you actually take it so you know what should be in focus.

4. **Turn on the self-timer by pressing the self-timer button on the camera body or by activating the setting in the LCD menu.**

   Your camera may beep while the self-timer is working, or you may just hear the shutter click when the time is up.

5. **Compose the picture, press the shutter button all the way down, and then release the button.**

   You will not hear the shutter release sound because the picture will not be taken until the time is up on the self-timer.

6. **Stand as still as possible while waiting for the shutter to sound.**

   Because you are not pressing down on the camera at the moment the picture is taken, camera shake is reduced, thereby resulting in sharper pictures!

Exploring Drive Modes

Have you wondered why you just missed the "perfect" picture in candid shots? Perhaps you were just a moment too late when trying to capture the wonderful expressions of children as they played. Part of the problem, especially with digital compact cameras, is the time lag between when you press the shutter and when the camera processes the picture and transfers it to the memory card (called shutter lag). The time it takes for these operations varies with each model of digital camera.

Shutter Lag

Your camera features special drive modes that affect shutter lag. You can choose from two drive modes depending on your shooting needs.

QUICK REFERENCE: Using Drive Modes

Drive Mode	Symbol	When to Use
Single	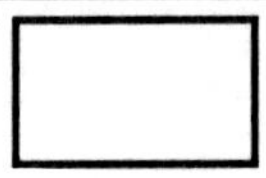	You want to take pictures one at a time, as you will in most conditions
Continuous (Burst, Sequential)	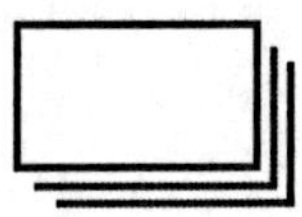	You want to take several pictures, one after the other, without any wait between shots; useful when photographing sports or any action

In Single mode, the camera takes and processes pictures one at time. In Continuous mode, as long as the shutter button is held down, pictures are taken one after the other without a time lag. Digital cameras have memory buffers (internal memory) that hold picture information until all pictures in a sequence have been taken. The pictures are transferred to the memory card when the sequence is complete. Usually one in the sequence of pictures taken will be the one you want.

TIP! The buffer, which is where the images are stored before being transferred to the memory card, can only hold a certain amount of pictures. Once full, the pictures must be transferred to the memory card before you can resume shooting.

You set drive modes by pressing a button on the camera or by using the menu or function displayed in the LCD menu.

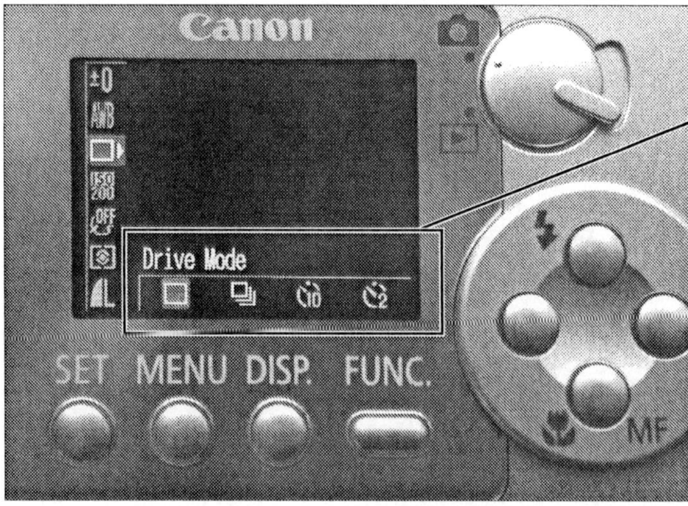

These are the drive mode settings in the menu of a Canon digital camera.

HANDS-ON 4.4 Use Single and Continuous Drive Modes

In this exercise, you will use drive modes to capture candid shots.

1. Look in the index of your instruction manual for Single Drive Mode or look in the table of contents for Drive Modes. Following the directions in your manual, set your camera to Single drive mode.

2. Find at least three people who are willing to be your subjects. Take turns with others in your class. It is important to have movement in these shots, so direct your subjects to engage in lively conversation and gesture.

   This exercise will work best if you do not have to use the flash so go outdoors or in a room with a lot of light.

3. Take six pictures, trying to capture the gestures and expressions of your subjects.

4. Switch to Continuous drive mode via the directions in your manual.

5. Repeal steps 3 and 4 using the Continuous drive setting. Make sure your subjects are moving, and take the photos under conditions that do not require the flash.

6. When finished, return to Single mode so you will be ready to take pictures one at a time.

   This is the normal (default) mode most users expect. Even if you switch it off and then on again, the camera will remain in the most recently set drive mode until you change the setting.

7. Download your pictures to the computer and compare your results.

   The pictures taken using Continuous drive mode should reveal more of the action caught from one picture to another, almost like movie stills.

Concepts Review

True/False Questions

			Page number
1. Using Sports mode evokes a feeling of action by blurring anything that moves.	**true**	**false**	______
2. The flash range of most built-in flash units is 6–10 feet from the camera.	**true**	**false**	______
3. Using Fill Flash lightens a subject in front of a bright window.	**true**	**false**	______
4. An easy way to increase flash intensity is to step farther away from your subject.	**true**	**false**	______
5. When using Single drive mode, the camera takes and processes pictures one at a time.	**true**	**false**	______
6. In Portrait shooting mode, everything, including the subject, is sharply in focus.	**true**	**false**	______
7. You use Night Portrait mode when you want everything in the picture to be sharp and in focus.	**true**	**false**	______
8. Continuous mode is used for capturing a sequence of pictures without shutter lag.	**true**	**false**	______
9. Using the flash consumes a lot of battery power.	**true**	**false**	______
10. Landscape mode is the best setting to use for subjects that should appear entirely sharp and in focus.	**true**	**false**	______

Multiple Choice Questions

1. When should you use fill flash?
   Page number: ______
   a. If you take pictures on the beach
   b. If you take pictures in the snow
   c. If the subject is in the shade
   d. All of the above

2. Using fill flash _______.
   Page number: ______
   a. consumes a lot of battery power
   b. slows down the time between pictures taken in Continuous mode
   c. helps bring out detail when taking pictures in low light or shade
   d. All of the above

3. How many feet from your subject should you be when taking pictures in Portrait mode?
   Page number: ______
   a. Four feet
   b. Six feet
   c. Ten feet
   d. None of the above

4. Which of the following is considered a shooting mode?
   Page number: ______
   a. Scene Assist
   b. Automatic
   c. Program
   d. All of the above

Skill Builders

SKILL BUILDER 4.1 Compare Modes

In this exercise, you will use Automatic mode and Scene Assist modes to take pictures of several different subjects. Then you will compare your results.

Before You Begin: Determine if your camera has Automatic mode and Scene Assist modes. Use Program mode (if available) if you do not have Automatic mode.

Take a Photo in Macro Mode

1. Find an object you can get very close to. If possible, go outside for this picture.
2. Set your zoom so it shows as much of the subject as possible.
   Macro mode is most effective without using zoom.
3. Set your camera to Automatic mode and get as close to your subject as possible.
4. Aim, focus, and shoot. Use the LCD to compose so you know that the picture is in focus.
5. Set your camera to Macro mode by following the directions in your manual. Then, take the same picture you took in step 3. Try to frame it as closely as possible to the one you took in Automatic mode.

Take a Landscape Picture

6. Find a location outdoors that gives you a long view of a landscape or cityscape. You should be able to see at least 30 feet.
7. Set your camera to Automatic mode and then aim, focus, and shoot.
   You can use either the optical viewfinder or the LCD to take this picture because your subject is far away from where you are standing and the chances of cutting something out of the picture are slim.
8. Set your camera to Landscape mode and take the same picture you took in step 2. Frame it as closely as possible to the one taken in Automatic mode.

Take an Action Shot

9. Find a subject that is moving: a person, a flag waving in the wind, etc.
10. Consider the following tips before you take the photo:
    - Use the optical viewfinder so you can follow the action better.
    - Lock in the focus first (focus lock) and then take the picture to prevent shutter lag. To do this, press the shutter button down halfway, focus, and take the picture.
11. Set your camera to Automatic and then aim, focus, and shoot.
12. Set your camera to Action (Sports) mode and take the same picture you took in step 11. Locking in the focus will also help in this picture.

Compare Your Results

13. Download and review your pictures. Can you see differences between photographs taken in each of the modes?

    This will help you determine when to use Automatic mode versus when to use Scene Assist modes.
14. Compare your results with others in the class who used different cameras.

    You might find that Scene Assist modes on different cameras produce different results.

LESSON 5

Exploring Exposure

One of the most important features on all cameras is exposure. Exposure means allowing just the right amount of light in the camera so the picture shows proper detail in the dark areas, middle tones, and lightest areas. Determining the correct amount of light is calculated by a built-in light meter. Most light meters do a great job in Automatic mode; however, you will sometimes want to control exposure modes to make sure the photograph comes out the way you want it to.

You already learned to use the automatic exposure settings known as Scene Assist modes. Manual and semi-automatic exposure modes and settings are just as easy to use and can aid in successful picture making. In this lesson, you will learn how, when, and why to use shutter speed priority, aperture priority, exposure lock, exposure compensation, and bracketing exposures.

Additional learning resources are available at ***labpub.com/learn/silver/digphoto/***

Case Study

Esmeralda has been successfully using Scene Assist modes, but she finds that sometimes they are not exactly what she needs. She is ready to take more control over her choices when it comes to exposure modes, and wants to know how and why they work. One of her upcoming photographic projects involves taking pictures of her daughter's relay race. Another is photographing scenery for her local nature club. She also will be taking pictures of her family on their annual ski trip and she knows she will need to understand how to get the correct exposure for this type of scene. Esmeralda learns what determines correct exposure and when to choose aperture and shutter speed priority. She also learns three great features—exposure bracketing, exposure compensation, and exposure lock—that enable her to take more than one picture of the same subject with slightly different exposure values. Later on, when viewing in the computer, she can choose which works best. This ensures that she will get the best possible exposure.

Learning About Exposure

Overexposure refers to too much light entering the camera, and it results in a washed out picture. Underexposure refers to too little light entering the camera, and it results in a picture that is too dark. Even experts who use image editing software like Photoshop Elements know that if a picture is overexposed, the very lightest areas of the photo will appear pure white and there is nothing they can do about it. Conversely, if a picture is underexposed, the darkest areas will appear pure black and with no detail in these areas. The best exposure shows detail in both the dark and light areas of the scene.

In this overexposed picture, these areas are considered "blown out" because they look pure white.

This is the same picture with the correct exposure. Note the detail in the lightest parts of the clouds.

In this underexposed picture, the dark areas did not get enough light and show little detail. The middle tones are properly exposed, though, and show detail.

This picture is properly exposed for the darkest areas but not for the lightest areas, which are almost pure white. You have to make choices about which part of the picture is most important.

TIP! It's usually best to take several exposures of the same picture when you are not sure which part you want properly exposed.

The Built-In Light Meter

To calculate exposure, the built-in light meter in your camera takes several considerations into account:

- The amount of light in the scene that hits the sensor
- The sensitivity of the sensor
- The length of time the sensor is exposed to light

On a bright, sunny day lots of light will hit the sensor in the camera. However, if your subject is in shadow, less light will come into the camera. What the light meter does with this light is determined by two main settings: aperture and shutter speed. When the camera is in Auto Exposure mode it has full control over these settings. You will now learn what these settings are, and how and when to use them in semi-automatic and manual modes.

How the Camera Chooses Settings So, how does the camera know what to choose for aperture and shutter speed settings? It uses the fastest possible shutter speed available to minimize camera shake so moving objects will not look blurry.

This camera displays Aperture Priority as A and Shutter Speed Priority as S.

This camera displays Aperture Priority as Av (aperture value) and Shutter Speed Priority as Tv (time value).

TIP! Lighting conditions affect how the shooting modes work, since they depend on the amount and type of ambient lighting conditions that exist.

Introducing Aperture

The aperture is the opening in a lens that emits the light that strikes the sensor. Basically, aperture means opening. The aperture can be set to let more or less light in the camera. You have no control over these settings in Automatic and Scene Assist modes. Using aperture priority, a semi-automatic mode, allows you to manually change the aperture settings. These settings are called f-stops.

Depth of field refers to how much of a scene will be sharp and in focus, and is determined mainly by the aperture (f-stop) setting.

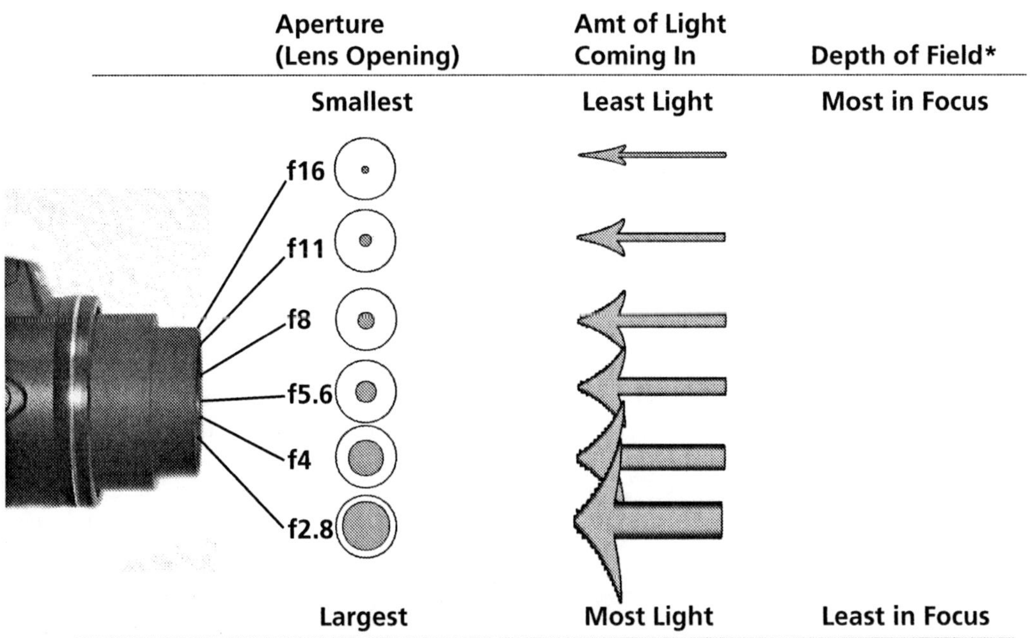

*Depth of Field is how much of the picture is in focus

What Is an F-Stop?

The f-stops correspond to how large or small the diameter of the aperture opens and closes. The opening and closing is often referred to as "opening up" and "stopping down." There is a standard range of f-stops numbers, as shown in the previous illustration. Every time you change the f-stop, the amount of light entering the lens halves or doubles depending on whether you are opening up or stopping down. As the f-stop number increases, the opening of the aperture decreases. It may sound a little confusing but, as you will see in the next section, memorizing all of the numbers is not necessary.

What F-Stops Mean All you need to know is that the aperture in a lens opens and closes, letting in more or less light. The f–stop number you choose determines how much light is let in. The larger the f-stop number, the less light enters the camera. The smaller the f-stop number, the more light enters the camera.

F-Stop Functions F-stop numbers have two functions:

1. To control the amount of light entering the camera
2. To control how much of the area of the photograph is in sharp focus (depth of field)

NOTE! Your camera may not correspond exactly to the numbers in the following table because f-stops are determined by lens type. Your camera should fall somewhere within these ranges.

QUICK REFERENCE: Using F-Stops

F-Stop Setting (Digital Compacts)	F-Stop Setting (Digital SLRs)	Equivalent Scene Assist Mode	When to Use
f2.0, f2.2, f2.5, f2.8, f3.0, f3.2, f3.5, f4.0, f5.0, f5.6	f2.8, f4, f5.6		You want your subject sharply in focus and the background less distinct or blurry; portraits benefit from the smaller f-stops
f6.3	f8, f11	none	You want the subject sharp and the background just slightly out of focus
f7.1, f8.0	f16, f22, f32	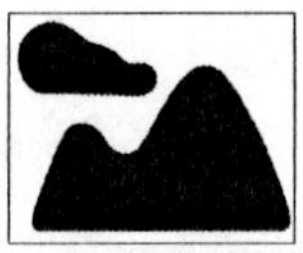	You take pictures of vistas and want everything sharply in focus

HANDS-ON 5.1A Set F-Stops (For Cameras with Adjustable F-Stop Settings)

This exercise is for cameras that have specific f-stop settings. Use this version if your camera has an A or Av setting on the shooting mode dial. Skip to Hands-On 5.1B on page 115 if your camera only has shooting mode symbols on the shooting mode dial or if the scene modes are located in the menu.

In this exercise, you set the f-stop numbers on your camera.

1. Look in the instruction manual for Aperture.

   Remember, f-stops correspond to aperture, the diameter of the opening in the lens that lets in light.

2. Locate the dial on your camera body that sets the aperture, known as aperture priority.

   Your camera may refer to aperture priority as Av or A.

3. Practice changing the f-stop number, following the directions in your manual. Turning the knob to A or Av, and then using one of the main dials to change the numbers will usually accomplish this.

   You will use the aperture priority feature in Hands-On 5.2A or Hands-On 5.2B, after you read about depth of field.

   Skip the next exercise and continue reading the Introducing Depth of Field section on page 116.

HANDS-ON 5.1B Use Scene Modes (For Cameras with No Adjustable F-Stop Settings)

This exercise is for cameras that only have shooting mode symbols on the shooting mode dial or if the scene modes are located in the menu. Go back to exercise Hands-On 5.1A on page 114 if your camera has specific f-stop settings or your camera has an A or Av setting on the shooting mode dial.

1. Look in your instruction manual and locate directions for choosing scene modes.

   Remember to look in the index first, if your manual has one. You will find scene modes listed under individual modes (Portrait, Landscape) or under Shooting Modes, Shooting According to Scene Conditions, etc.

2. Set the scene mode to Portrait.

   Using Portrait mode is equivalent to using a low f-stop number: more light will enter the camera and less will be in focus behind the subject.

3. Set the scene mode to Landscape.

   Using Landscape mode is equivalent to using a large f-stop number: less light will enter the camera and more of the scene behind the subject will be in focus.

4. Practice setting the scene modes until it becomes easy to use them.

   You will use these modes in Hands-On 5.2A or Hands-On 5.2B.

Introducing Depth of Field

Many people interested in photography have heard the term depth of field. It is often thought to be a complicated subject. As you will soon find out, though, depth of field is easy to comprehend and a breeze to control.

What Is Depth of Field?

Depth of field simply refers to how much of a scene is sharply in focus. If you are outside taking a picture of unending scenic glory you probably want everything to be sharply in focus. You want a wide or large depth of field. If you are making a portrait of your friends or family you probably don't want the background to be too sharp or it will distract from your main subject. You want a narrow or small depth of field.

How Much Will Be in Focus? Depth of field encompasses the distance in front of and behind what you are focusing on.

- Use a large depth of field to ensure that more in front of and behind the subject is sharply in focus.
- Use a small depth of field to ensure that less in front of and behind the subject is in focus.

The following illustration shows how much of a scene will be in focus. Because depth of field is controlled by f-stop settings, the amount in focus in front of and behind your subject is determined by your f-stop choice. It will always be one-third in front and two-thirds behind, but the actual distance will change with different f-stop settings.

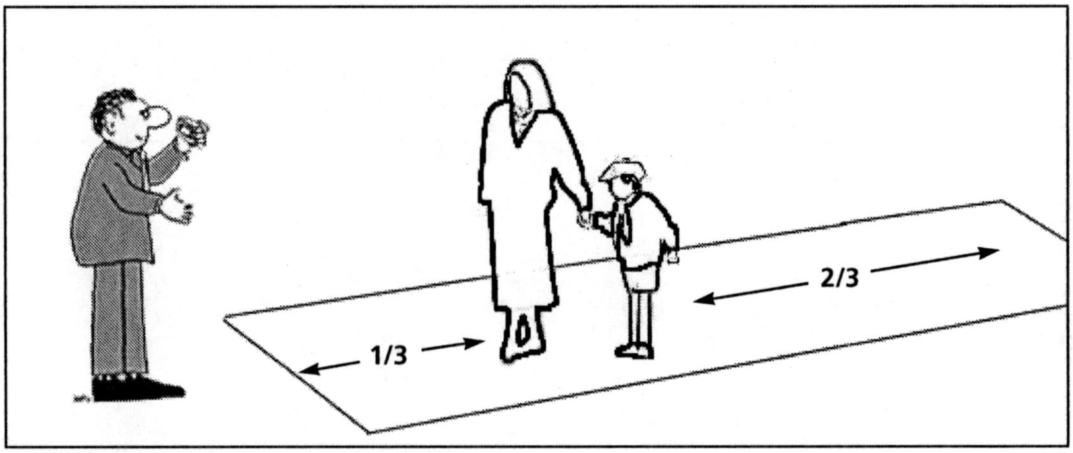

The amount of a picture in focus (depth of field) is one-third in front of and two-thirds behind the subject.

F-Stops on Film and Digital Cameras Digital compact cameras do not have f-stops larger than f8.0 because the sensor is smaller than in digital SLRS or traditional 35 mm film cameras. Using a small f-stop setting on a digital compact camera will not give you the same results you would get with a digital SLR: the background behind the subject will not be as blurred as you might like. Instead, try standing back further and zooming in to get the blurred effect.

Aperture Priority Mode

Aperture Priority mode is a semi-automatic setting. As you have learned, f-stops affect the size of the aperture and the size of the aperture affects depth of field. In Aperture Priority mode, you can select any f-stop and the camera will automatically select the shutter speed for correct exposure. Aperture Priority may be represented by Av or A, and is usually found on the shooting mode dial on top of the camera. Sometimes it is found in the menu in the LCD on the back of your camera. Choose Aperture Priority mode when how much is in focus is the most important element of the picture.

TIP! A smaller f-stop equals less depth of field and a larger number f-stop equals more depth of field. Use a small f-stop when you want the background to blur. Use a large f-stop number when you want everything in the scene to be sharp and in focus.

This photograph was taken using a small f-stop number. The cactus is in focus but the background is not.

This photograph shows detail from the same picture.

This is the same photograph taken with a large f-stop number. Everything in the picture is in focus and sharp.

This photograph shows detail from the same picture.

HANDS-ON 5.2A Use Aperture Priority Mode (For Cameras with Adjustable F-Stop Settings)

This exercise is for cameras that have specific f-stop settings. Use this version if your camera has an A or Av setting on the shooting mode dial. Skip to Hands-On 5.2B on page 119 if your camera only has shooting mode symbols on the shooting mode dial or if the scene modes are located in the menu.

In this exercise, you will use Aperture Priority settings to take pictures with a small and a large depth of field.

Before You Begin: Perform this exercise outside and do not use the flash.

1. Set your camera aperture to A or Av, as appropriate.
2. Change the f-stop to the lowest number available.

   Depending on the camera, this will be between f2 and f8 and should cause the background behind your subject to blur. The camera automatically sets the shutter speed as you change the aperture, ensuring proper exposure.
3. Have someone stand about four to five feet from the camera and make sure there is at least ten feet in the scene behind the subject. Focus your camera on the subject, using the eyes as a focal point, and then compose and take the picture.
4. Now set your camera to the largest f-stop number available and take the same picture.

   The range for the largest f-stop numbers is f7 to f32. Using this f-stop will make everything in the picture sharp and in focus.

5. Keep your camera set to the largest f-stop and take a picture of a landscape or a large expanse in a city. Focus on something about five feet from the camera.

   The entire scene should be sharp and in focus. You will check this later on the computer.

6. Change the setting back to the smallest f-stop, and then take the same picture you took in step 5.

   Everything in the scene behind the subject should be somewhat blurry.

7. Download your test images to the computer and compare them to see how sharp or blurry they are. You may have to zoom in to see the differences clearly.

   Congratulations! You now have your own aperture test, showing how different f-stops affect clarity and focus. Try other f-stops if you like to see how they compare to the largest and smallest f-steps.

Skip the rest of this exercise and continue reading the Setting Shutter Speed section on page 120.

HANDS-ON 5.2B Use Scene Modes (For Cameras with No F-Stop Settings)

This exercise is for cameras that only have shooting mode symbols on the shooting mode dial or if the scene modes are located in the menu. Follow exercise Hands-On 5.2A on page 118 if your camera has specific f-stop settings or your camera has an A or Av setting on the shooting mode dial.

Before You Begin: Perform this exercise outside and do not use the flash.

1. Set your camera to Portrait mode.

   This is the equivalent of a small f-stop, which will somewhat blur the background behind the subject.

2. Have someone stand about four to five feet from the camera and make sure there is at least ten feet in the scene behind the subject. Be sure to focus your camera on the subject, using the eyes as a focal point, and then compose and take the picture.

3. Now set your camera to Landscape mode, and take the same picture.

   This is the equivalent of a large f-stop, which should keep the entire scene sharply in focus.

4. Keep your camera on Landscape mode and take a picture of a landscape or a large expanse in a city. Focus on something about five feet from the camera.

   The equivalent f-stop is large and the entire scene should be sharp and in focus.

5. Change the setting to Portrait, and then take the same picture you took in step 4.

   This is like a small f-stop number, and the scene behind the subject should be somewhat blurry.

6. Download your test images to the computer and compare them to see how sharp or blurry they are. You may have to zoom in to see the differences clearly.

Setting Shutter Speed

The other component for correct exposure is shutter speed. While f-stops control the size of the aperture, shutter speed controls how long the aperture is open. Together they equal correct exposure. Shutter speed determines how motion will be captured. Will action be blurred or frozen? Shutter speeds are measured in very small fractions of a second up to several seconds or even minutes.

Shutter speeds are referred to in two ways:

- **Fractions:** Displayed as 1/60 (called one sixtieth), 1/500 (called one five hundredth), etc.
- **Whole numbers:** Displayed as 60 (called a sixtieth), 500 (called five hundredth), etc.

NOTE! If the shutter speed is one or more seconds you will see what looks like inch marks (") next to the number. As such, 2"5 means two-and-a-half seconds.

QUICK REFERENCE: Working with Shutter Speeds

Shutter Speed Setting	Equivalent Scene Assist Mode	When to Use
1/1000, 1/500		You want to freeze action in sports or other kind of activity
1/250, 1/125, 1/60	none	You want to reduce blur as a result of camera shake; also good for taking candid shots
1/30, 1/15	none	You want to show blur in sports and other activities or running water
1/8 and smaller		You want to take pictures in low light without a flash; requires use of a tripod

NOTE! These shutter speeds may not correspond exactly with what you see on your camera, but they will be similar.

Shutter Speed Priority Mode

Shutter Speed Priority mode is another semi-automatic setting. Use it to control how action is portrayed (frozen or blurred). In this mode, you can select any shutter speed and the camera will automatically select the correct f-stop. Shutter speed priority may be listed as Tv or S. Like the aperture setting, this setting is found on the shooting mode dial or the LCD menu.

This picture was taken with a fast shutter speed of 1/250 of a second.

This picture was taken with a slow shutter speed of 1/30 of a second.

TIP! The faster the shutter speed the smaller the fraction. This is good for freezing action. The slower the shutter speed the larger the fraction. This is good for blurring action.

HANDS-ON 5.3A Set Shutter Speeds (For Cameras with Adjustable Shutter Speed Settings)

Follow this exercise for cameras that have specific shutter speed settings. Use this version if your camera has an A or Av setting on the shooting mode dial. Hands-On 5.3B on page 123 is for cameras that do not have specific shutter speed settings. Use that version if your camera does not have an A or Av setting on the shooting mode dial or if the scene modes are located in the menu.

In this exercise, you will locate and set shutter speeds on your camera.

1. Look in the instruction manual for Shutter Speed.

   Remember, shutter speed determines how long the aperture stays open to allow in light.

2. Locate the dial on your camera body that sets the shutter speed.

   Your camera will refer to shutter speed priority as either S or Tv.

   The camera automatically sets the aperture as you change the shutter speed to ensure proper exposure.

3. Practice changing the shutter speed, following the directions in your manual, and then:
   - Turn the shooting mode knob to S or Tv and use the main dial to select different shutter speeds.
   - Set the shutter speed to 1/250 or larger (1/500, etc.).

   You may not be able to set the shutter speed exactly to 1/250 or 1/500; just use whatever setting is the closest.

4. Now you will set up a scene in which someone or something is moving. Choose one of the following:
   - Pair up with a classmate so you each have a turn being photographer and subject.
   - Find something that is moving in the wind if you are doing this exercise alone.

5. Before you take the picture, practice focusing on the moving subject. Find a spot next to the anticipated movement, hold the shutter halfway down to engage the focus lock, and then take the picture.

   You may have to take several pictures before capturing the motion just the way you want it. You should be able to see if the motion was frozen. The beauty of using a digital camera is that you can immediately see if you captured the picture properly.

6. Change the shutter speed to 1/30, and then repeat steps 4 and 5.

   When you review your pictures you will see that the motion is blurred. The faster the motion, the more it will blur.

7. Download your pictures to the computer and compare your results.

   Skip the rest of this exercise and continue reading the Adjusting Exposure section on page 124.

HANDS-ON 5.3B Use Scene Modes (For Cameras with No Shutter Speed Settings)

Follow this exercise for cameras that do not have specific shutter speed settings. Use this version if your camera does not have an A or Av setting on the shooting mode dial or if the scene modes are located in the menu. Hands-On 5.3A on page 122 is for cameras that have specific shutter speed settings.

1. Look in your instruction manual and locate directions for choosing scene modes.

   Look in the index first, if your manual has one. You will find scene modes listed under individual modes (Sports, etc.) or under Shooting Modes, Shooting According to Scene Conditions, etc.

2. Choose Sports mode.

   Using Sports mode is equivalent to using a fast shutter speed. It freezes the movement.

3. Now you will set up a scene in which someone or something or someone is moving. Choose one of the following:

   - Pair up with a classmate so you each have a turn being photographer and subject.
   - Find something that is moving in the wind if you are doing this exercise alone.

4. Before you take the picture, practice focusing on the moving subject. Find a spot next to the anticipated movement, hold the shutter halfway down to engage the focus lock, and then take the picture.

   You may have to take several pictures before capturing the motion just the way you want it. You should be able to see if the motion was frozen. The beauty of using a digital camera is that you can immediately see if you captured the picture properly.

   Sports mode should show the subject frozen in motion. There is not a specific shooting mode for blurring motion, but try the other modes. If one works, make a note of it.

Adjusting Exposure

Achieving correct exposure is one of the most important factors in obtaining good quality photographs. The exposure setting is what regulates how much light is used to create the image. As you have seen, exposure is regulated by the built-in light meter and is the combination of shutter speed and aperture settings. The following table summarizes three ways you can override the automatic exposure setting.

QUICK REFERENCE: Using Exposure Compensation, Exposure Lock, and Exposure Bracketing

Setting	How It Works	When to Use
Exposure Compensation	You override the camera's automatic setting by manually changing the exposure value	You want to tone down glare from very bright sunlight or to bring out highlights of objects in shade
Auto Exposure Lock	The exposure setting is temporarily changed, usually by using a button on the camera body	Your subject is backlit (at the beach or in front of a large window)
Exposure Bracketing	The camera takes several pictures in sequence and at slightly different exposures	You are not sure the automatic exposure setting will capture the detail you want because the subject is unevenly lit

Exposure Compensation

Sometimes your automatic or semi-automatic exposure setting is not quite right. Your pictures may look overexposed (too light) or underexposed (too dark) even though the camera's light meter is supposedly letting in the correct amount of light. At these times you can use exposure compensation to correct the setting. Exposure compensation is often referred to as the exposure value (EV) adjustment. You might use exposure compensation if you want to tone down glare from very bright sunlight or bring out highlights of objects in the shade.

This picture is too dark because the scene is in a very shady spot.

Setting the exposure compensation value to let in more light resulted in a picture with a balanced exposure for both dark and light areas.

Setting Exposure Compensation

Exposure compensation is usually displayed in the menu or in the smaller LCD as negative and positive numbers. On digital SLRs and some larger compact cameras it can be accessed from a dial and is displayed in the smaller LCD on the top or back of the camera. Choosing a positive number will make a picture lighter and choosing a negative number will make a picture darker.

- Select positive (+) values when large areas of the frame are brightly lit; for example, when the background is much brighter than the main subject or when there is a large expanse of snow or sunlit water. The camera tends to lower the exposure when the scene is very bright, which can make bright subjects look dim.
- Select negative (–) values when large areas of the scene are dark; for example, when photographing in dark shade or when the background is much darker than the main subject. The camera's light meter tends to increase exposure when the scene is very dark, which can make dark subjects appear too bright or washed out.

TIP! Exposure compensation is typically used when you want to reset the exposure for an extended period of time or if you find your camera has a tendency to overexpose or underexpose. It stays set until you manually change it back to normal (0).

Clicking the up arrow of the omni dial activates exposure compensation on this camera. Clicking the right and left arrows change the exposure value settings.

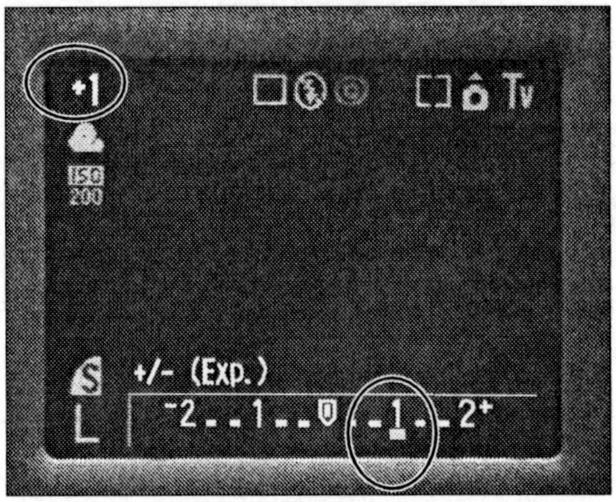

This exposure compensation value is now +1, letting in more light.

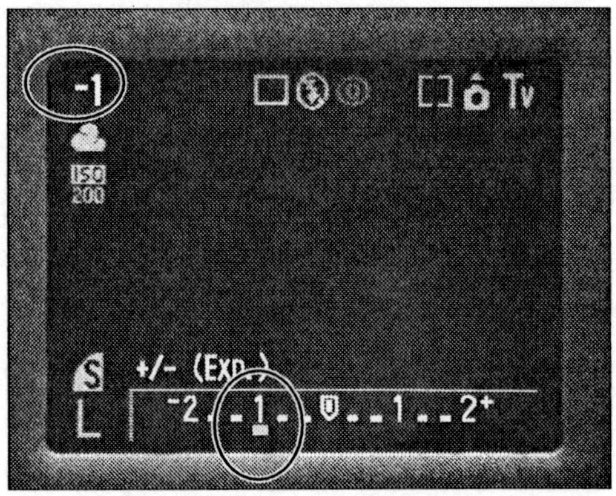

This exposure compensation value is -1, letting in less light.

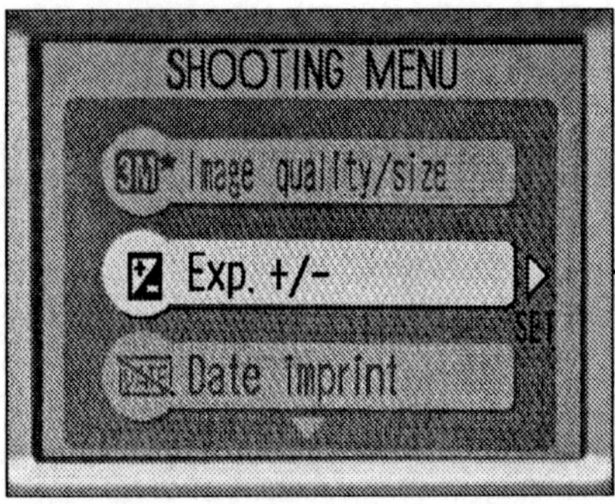

Exposure compensation values are accessed through the menu on this camera.

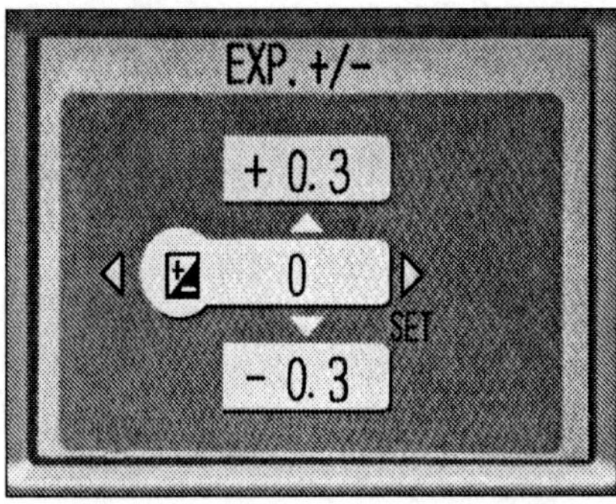

Clicking the up and down arrows of the omni dial changes the exposure values.

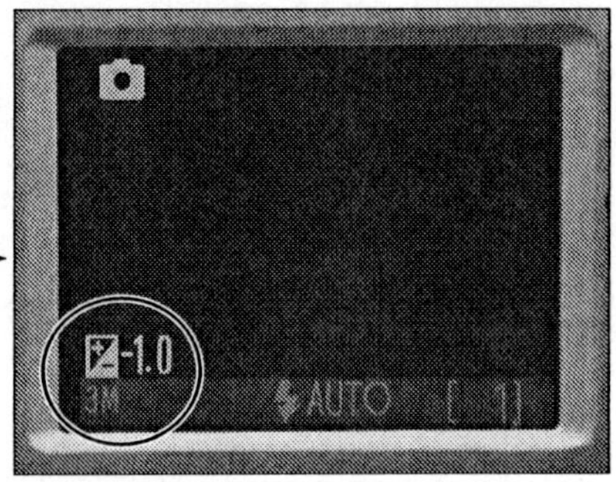

The exposure value is displayed in the LCD until it is deactivated.

TIP! Be sure to reset the exposure value back to the standard setting after you have used exposure compensation or your future pictures may come out underexposed or overexposed!

HANDS-ON 5.4 Use Exposure Compensation

In this exercise, you will find the exposure compensation setting on your camera. Then you will set and use this feature.

1. Look in the index or table of contents of your instruction manual and find the section for exposure compensation.

   This feature has the same name for almost all digital cameras, which makes locating it in your manual very easy.

2. Make sure your camera is set to a shooting mode that supports exposure compensation.

   Exposure compensation may not be available in Automatic mode.

   IMPORTANT! Do *not* change the shooting mode during this exercise. On some cameras, exposure compensation may be reset to zero automatically when you change the shooting mode.

3. Locate how to set exposure compensation and where it is displayed on your camera.

   On some cameras, clicking a button or pressing an arrow on the omni dial activates exposure compensation. On others, you access it via the menu.

4. Set the exposure compensation to -1. On some cameras (like the Canon PowerShot G series) the scene actually becomes darker in the LCD as you move the setting in the minus direction.

   As you set the exposure compensation to a larger negative number, the scene becomes darker and darker.

5. Find a shady area outside, and then compose and take the picture.

6. Set the exposure back to standard (0) and take the same picture.

7. Now set the exposure composition to +1 and take the same picture.

8. Use Playback mode to check the results in the LCD.

   You should now have a series of three pictures: one darker and one lighter than the third. You will be better able to determine which photograph has the correct exposure after you download them.

9. Exit Playback mode, find a very bright scene, and then repeat steps 3–7.

10. Reset your exposure to zero or the standard setting.

    Your camera will not automatically reset the exposure, which could lead to underexposed or overexposed pictures the next time you photograph.

Auto Exposure Lock (AE-Lock)

Auto exposure lock (AE-Lock) is a great and easy way to temporarily change the exposure setting to suit a picture's need. It allows you to lock the exposure at a different place than the point of focus. Once you have locked the exposure you can recompose the shot. This is particularly useful when taking pictures in backlit situations. Suppose your subject is standing in front of a very bright window or on the beach in front of the ocean. If you use the camera's automatic meter, even in a semi-automatic mode, the camera will over factor the bright area and the subject will become a dark silhouette. Instead of using exposure compensation, AE-Lock is a better and easier choice. By aiming the camera at the subject and pressing the AE-Lock button, you can recompose and focus the shot while exposure is calculated from where you locked it. This results in the subject being lightened so that detail is apparent.

AE-Lock dial on camera body

Exposure compensation setting (takes more time to override exposure setting than using the auto exposure dial)

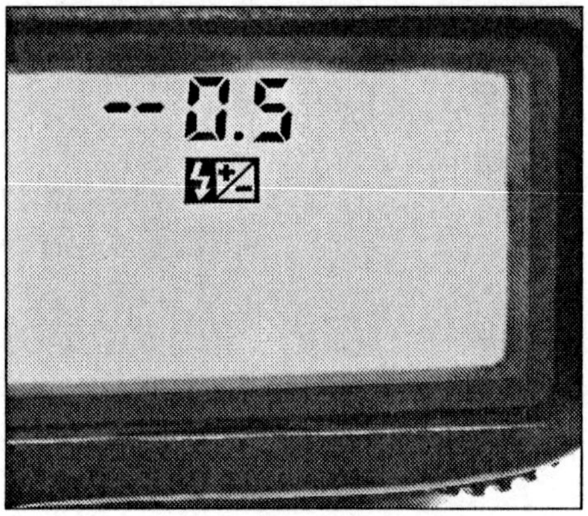

TIP! The great thing about using AE-Lock is that you do not have to reset anything after taking a picture! It automatically returns to the standard exposure after a picture is taken.

What If I Don't Have AE-Lock? Some cameras do not have the AE-Lock feature. However, you can achieve the same effect using exposure compensation to underexpose and overexpose the shot. This can be tedious, but it is a way to compensate for problem lighting situations.

HANDS-ON 5.5 Use Auto Exposure Lock

In this exercise, you will use AE-Lock to bring out detail in a dark area of a backlit scene.

Before You Begin: Check your instruction manual to see if you have to set your camera in a specific shooting mode when using AE-Lock. It may not be available in Automatic mode.

1. Make sure your flash will not fire. Look in your manual for instructions.
2. Find a bright window and place an object or person in front of it. Compose the picture so your focus is on the scene outside, and then take the picture.
3. Look carefully at the picture in Playback mode.

   You should see that the object or person has become a silhouette, while the scene outside is correctly exposed.
4. Take another picture if your subject is not silhouetted (or find a brighter window). Otherwise, continue with the next step.
5. Look in the index or table of contents of your instruction manual for the section on Auto Exposure Lock. This feature may be found under Exposure and referred to as AE-Lock.

   Skip the rest of this exercise if your camera does not support AE-Lock.
6. Make sure your camera is set to a shooting mode that supports AE-Lock.
7. Locate in your manual how to set AE-Lock and where it is displayed on your camera.

   On some cameras all you have to do is aim, press a button, release the button, recompose, and then take the picture. On others you may have to hold a button while you depress the shutter halfway down, and then recompose and take the picture.
8. Now, using the same scene you used in step 1, aim at the subject—not the scene outside—and use AE-Lock to lock the exposure. Then, recompose while aiming at the scene outdoors and take the picture.
9. Review the picture in Playback mode.

   Now the scene outside is washed out, but the subject is lighter and shows detail.

NOTE! You have to make a choice about which is more important, the background or the foreground subject. Unfortunately, you can't get the correct exposure for both.

Exposure Bracketing

Have you ever downloaded your photos to the computer, only to find that the pictures you thought perfectly exposed were too dark or too light? It's difficult to tell from the camera's LCD if the exposure is just right. Exposure bracketing is a process of taking several pictures in sequence and at slightly different exposures: normal, underexposed, and overexposed. You can then look at them later and choose the best. Exposure bracketing settings are set via the menu or with buttons and dials. The most common number of sequential shots is three. On many digital compacts, once the setting is chosen the camera will take three shots in a row as soon as the shutter button is depressed. On other cameras you must press the shutter each time.

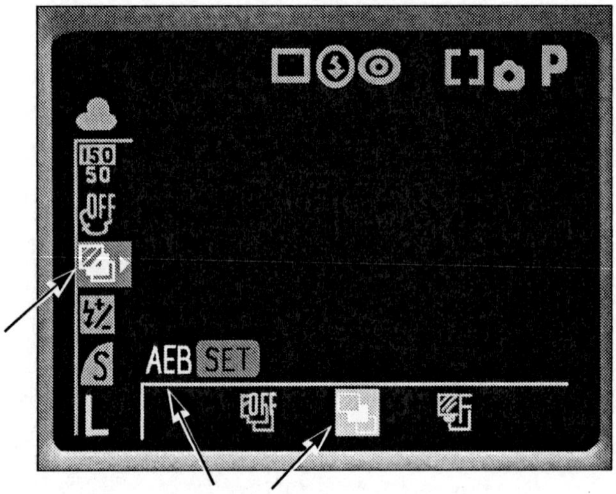

Exposure bracketing settings on Canon G5

Exposure bracketing button on Nikon D100

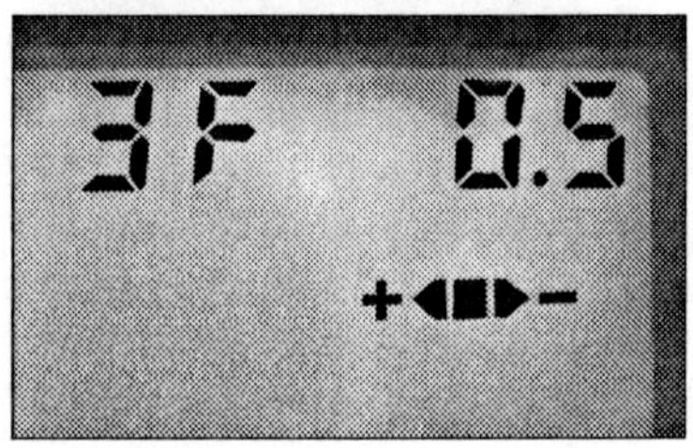

Exposure bracketing setting in LCD on Nikon D100

TIP! The Auto Bracketing setting must be turned off on some cameras after use or it will stay in that mode!

HANDS-ON 5.6A Use Exposure Bracketing (Cameras with Auto Bracketing)

Before You Begin: Check your instruction manual to determine if your camera has the auto bracketing feature, and then decide which exercise to use. This exercise is for cameras that have auto bracketing. Skip to Hands-On 5.6B on page 132 for cameras that do not have the auto bracketing feature.

In this exercise, you will use exposure bracketing to get proper exposure.

1. Look in the index or table of contents of your instruction manual and find the section for Auto Bracketing. Determine if your camera takes multiple pictures automatically (one after the other without stopping) when auto bracketing is activated or whether you must press the shutter release for each bracketed exposure. (You will need this information when you take a picture in step 4.)

   This feature may be found under Exposure as AE-B mode or under Auto Exposure Bracketing.

2. Make sure your camera is set in a mode that supports auto bracketing. (It may not be available in Automatic or Scene Assist modes.)

3. Locate and activate the auto bracketing feature.

   Depending on your camera model, this feature may be found in the menu or accessed through a dial or button on the body of the camera.

4. Use the appropriate step for the way your camera uses auto bracketing:
   - If your camera takes multiple pictures automatically, aim your camera at any subject, indoors or out, and press the shutter.
   - If you must press the shutter for each auto bracket, aim your camera at any subject, indoors or out, and press the shutter. Press the shutter two more times (one for each additional bracket exposure).

   Now you should have at least three photos, each with a different exposure.

5. Go to Playback mode and notice that you have three pictures with different exposures: standard, light, and dark. The sequence may differ from camera to camera.

   Although you will be able to see some differences in the LCD, you really need to look at them on the computer determine which looks best.

6. Deactivate auto bracketing.

   Remember, not all cameras automatically revert back to the standard setting.

Skip the next exercise and continue reading the Working with Sensor Sensitivity section on page 133.

HANDS-ON 5.6B Use Exposure Compensation (Cameras with No Auto Bracketing)

Before You Begin: Check your instruction manual to determine if your camera has the auto bracketing feature, and then decide which exercise to use. This exercise is for cameras that do not have auto bracketing. Go back to Hands-On 5.6A on page 131 for cameras that do have auto bracketing feature.

In this exercise, you will use exposure bracketing to get proper exposure.

Since you already learned how to use exposure compensation in Hands-On 5.4, this exercise will be very easy!

1. Set the exposure compensation to -1 and take a picture of anything inside or outside.

   You have underexposed this picture by changing the setting to -1. This picture will be the darkest.

2. Now set the exposure compensation to +1 and take the same picture you took in step 1.

   You have overexposed the picture and it will be the lightest.

3. Set the exposure compensation back to 0 and take another picture of the same subject.

   Now you have a picture somewhere in the middle of the other two and based on what the camera thinks is the correct exposure.

4. Go to Playback mode and notice that you have three pictures with different exposures: dark, light, and in-between.

   Although you will be able to see differences in the LCD, you really need to look at them once they are downloaded to your computer to make the best choice.

Working with Sensor Sensitivity

How the sensor reacts to light is another important element when calculating exposure. This measurement is called International Organization for Standardization (ISO), which is the name of the group that helped establish how film numbering works. You can buy film anywhere in the world and be assured it will work as you expect based on ISO numbers. An ISO number refers to how sensitive a particular film is to light. When light enters a film camera at the moment of exposure it hits light-sensitive film. When it enters a digital camera it hits a computer chip that acts as a sensor. This sensor is light sensitive and can be adjusted to increase or decrease the camera's sensitivity to light, thereby simulating film speeds.

TIP! ISO on digital cameras is not standardized, so the same number on one camera may not have the same sensitivity as on another camera.

Why Change the ISO?

You change the ISO based on exterior lighting conditions. The lower the ISO number, the more light is needed for correct exposure. You could easily use an ISO setting of 50, 100, or 200 on a bright, sunny day. A higher ISO is recommended in situations with less light, unless you are using a tripod or a flash. An ISO setting of 400 or higher is necessary for indoor pictures, sunset or evening shots, and in very shady areas. The advantage of using a digital camera is that you can change the ISO picture by picture if necessary—as opposed to waiting until you finish a roll of film. ISO numbers usually vary from 50 to 1600, depending on the camera. All you need to know is that the lower the number, the more ambient light is needed and that higher numbers are used in low light conditions.

Effects of High ISO Settings

Higher ISO settings also mean a greater degree of "noise." Noise occurs because the signal from the pixels on the sensor is amplified, resulting in artifacts in the areas of the picture and lower quality images. These artifacts are seen as dots of different colors and show up very strongly when lightening a dark area of the image. This is really not something that can be fixed easily or perhaps at all in an image editing program and they rarely enhance the picture. It is useful to increase the ISO when the conditions warrant it: indoors, shady areas, sunset and night scenes. Remember, however, anything over 400 ISO may adversely affect the quality of the picture. Although you have the option to choose Auto for the ISO setting, it is recommended that you turn off this function and set the ISO manually since it is so important to picture quality.

TIP! Don't hesitate to take the picture because you know a compromise may have to be made between quality and exposure. Incorrect settings often result in happy surprises.

This picture was taken with the ISO set to 100, offering good quality and eliminating noise. It was originally very dark and then lightened in the computer without quality loss.

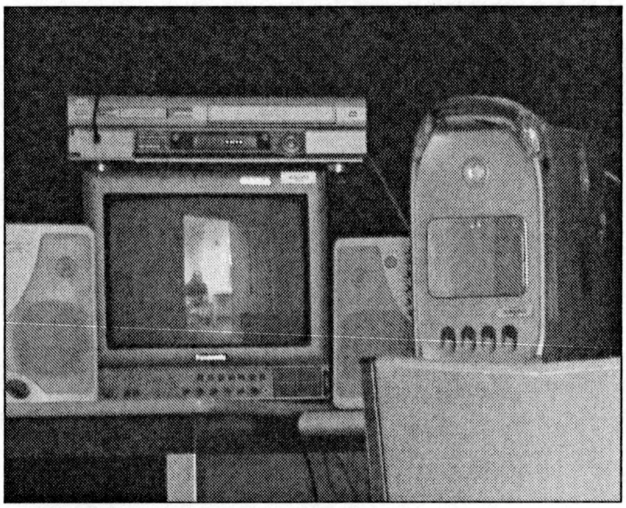

Magnification

This picture was taken with the ISO set to 400. Notice the noise introduced. Noise is even more evident in color photographs. It is often better to use a lower ISO with flash or a tripod.

Magnification

TIP! Remember to reset the ISO when a special setting is no longer needed! Your camera will retain the custom ISO setting until you set it again.

HANDS-ON 5.7 Use ISO Settings

In this exercise, you will find and use the ISO setting on your camera.

NOTE! Make sure your flash is turned off so it will not fire automatically.

1. Look in the index or table of contents of your instruction manual and find the section for ISO. It will be located on a dial on the camera body or in the menu in the LCD.

   This feature may be found under ISO Sensitivity, ISO Speed, or Sensitivity.

2. Find a location indoors that does not have a lot of light but is also not completely dark.

3. Set your camera to Automatic so it will decide the ISO setting, and then compose and take the picture.

   You will compare this picture with those taken in manual ISO mode.

4. Make sure your camera is set in a mode that supports custom ISO settings. (It may not be available if you are in Automatic or Scene Assist modes.)

5. Set your ISO setting to 100 and take the picture, composing it as close as possible to the one you took in step 2.

6. Switch to Playback mode and review your pictures in the LCD. Can you see a difference? Does the picture taken with an ISO of 100 look much darker?

   An ISO of 100 is usually used outdoors in very bright light, where the sensitivity of the sensor to light is not an issue. The result is a picture with virtually no noise.

7. Take three more pictures with the ISO set to 200, 400, and 800 (if available). Compose the picture as close as possible to your previous pictures.

8. Review your pictures in the LCD. Which one most resembles the automatic ISO setting?

   You will now have a pretty good idea of how the ISO is set when in Automatic mode.

9. Download your pictures to the computer and review them for evidence of noise. Magnify your pictures if necessary.

   Although you are able to see differences in the LCD monitor on your camera, you can only check for noise on the computer.

10. Return your ISO setting to 100, 200, or lower.

Remember, your camera will retain the custom ISO setting until you set it again.

NOTE! Noise is most evident when you lighten a dark picture through image adjustments in an image editing program like Photoshop Elements. We will cover this topic in Lesson 8, Exploring Photoshop Elements.

Concepts Review

True/False Questions

			Page number
1. The built-in light meter calculates correct exposures based on lighting conditions.	**true**	**false**	______
2. The two main settings the light meter uses to determine correct exposure are shutter speed and ISO.	**true**	**false**	______
3. The aperture in a lens is fixed to let in a predetermined amount of light.	**true**	**false**	______
4. The f-stop number determines how much light is let in the lens.	**true**	**false**	______
5. Choosing an f-stop setting of f16 will result in a sharply focused scene from front to back.	**true**	**false**	______
6. Depth of field is how much of a scene is sharply focused.	**true**	**false**	______
7. The faster the shutter speed, the larger the fraction of a second.	**true**	**false**	______
8. You use Shutter Speed mode to control how action is portrayed.	**true**	**false**	______
9. AE-Lock allows you to lock the exposure at a place other than the point of focus.	**true**	**false**	______
10. Choosing a positive number when using exposure compensation makes pictures darker because more light is let in.	**true**	**false**	______

Multiple Choice Questions

1. The light meter uses the _______ to calculate correct exposure.

   Page number: ______

   a. length of time the sensor is exposed to light

   b. amount of light in the scene

   c. sensitivity of the sensor

   d. All of the above

2. What is the function of the f-stop number?

   Page number: ______

   a. To control the amount of light entering the camera

   b. To set the ISO

   c. To control how much of the area of the scene is in focus

   d. All of the above

3. When would you use a narrow or small depth of field?

   Page number: ______

   a. When taking portraits

   b. When taking close-ups of flowers

   c. When taking pictures of sports

   d. None of the above

4. Which of the following will result when using a shutter speed setting of 1/500?

   Page number: ______

   a. Blurred action

   b. Frozen action

   c. How the action is portrayed is not affected

   d. None of the above

Skill Builders

SKILL BUILDER 5.1 Compare Aperture Priority and Landscape Mode

In this exercise, you will work with a partner to determine if a Scene Assist mode works the same as using f-stops in landscape pictures.

Before You Begin: If your camera has an aperture priority mode, choose a partner whose camera does not but does have Scene Assist modes. If your camera has only Scene Assist modes, pair up with someone who has an aperture priority mode.

Photographer A has aperture priority. *Photographer B* has Scene Assist modes.

1. Go outside and choose a landscape or cityscape that can be viewed for at least 50 feet.

   This exercise will yield the best results if your landscape or cityscape can be seen very far into the distance.

2. Set the correct f-stop or Scene Assist mode:
   - **Photographer A:** Set your camera to aperture priority and change the f-stop to the largest number available. This will give you the greatest area of sharp focus. Refer to your instruction manual if needed. Remember, shutter speed is set automatically.
   - **Photographer B:** Set your camera to Landscape mode. This will give you the greatest area of sharp focus. Refer to your manual if needed. With this setting, the camera automatically sets the exposure to favor a large f-stop.

3. **Photographers A and B:** Take at least four pictures of the same landscape or cityscape.

   It is important to make sure you are each getting the same amount of the scene. Using the LCD is a great way to check this.

4. Download your pictures to the computer and compare your results. Are the pictures taken with aperture priority the same or similar in areas of sharp focus as the pictures taken in Landscape mode? Check results from other students in your class.

   Zoom in on your pictures to better compare the results.

SKILL BUILDER 5.2 Use Exposure Compensation or Exposure Bracketing

In this exercise, you will work with a partner to see the differences and similarities when using exposure compensation and exposure bracketing.

Before You Begin: If your camera has exposure bracketing, choose a partner who has exposure compensation. If you don't, choose a partner who does.

Photographer A has exposure bracketing. *Photographer B* has exposure compensation.

NOTE! Be sure to turn off the flash, so it doesn't fire automatically.

1. Choose three subjects that are in partial shade or partial light, preferably outdoors.

   Taking pictures outdoors should avoid automatically activating the flash, which will skew the results of this exercise.

2. Set your camera so you are able to choose three different exposures.
   - **Photographer A:** Set your camera to exposure bracketing. Refer to your instructional manual if needed.
   - **Photographer B:** Set your camera to exposure compensation. This will enable you to manually bracket your exposures, simulating exposure bracketing.

3. **Photographers A and B:** Take pictures of each of your three subjects.

   You should end up with three pictures of each subject; each of the three will have a different exposure.

4. Download your pictures to the computer and compare results. Determine the most important part of each picture and choose which exposure is best for this area.

   It is essential to compare the exposures on the computer, rather then on the LCD because it takes close scrutiny to see subtle but important differences.

5. Repeat steps 1–4 but this time use one or more subjects that are evenly lit.

   Take your pictures outdoors for more valid results.

LESSON 6

Exploring Resolution, Compression, and File Formats

High quality prints and properly sized Web and email images depend on correct resolution, compression, and file format settings. Contrary to popular opinion, these settings are not mysterious or difficult to understand and use. The size and quality of prints made from digital camera files is determined by image quality settings in the camera. On a digital camera the number of exposures that can fit on a memory card is also determined by these image quality settings. In this lesson, you will learn about image quality settings, how to set them, and how and why they determine print size and optimal email and Web photographs.

Additional learning resources are available at ***labpub.com/learn/silver/digphoto/***

Case Study

Mary Rose is very excited about making prints from the pictures she has taken with her digital camera. She will be taking family portraits at an upcoming reunion and wants to make 8 × 10 inch prints and send images via email to her family throughout the states. Now that she knows how to capture correctly exposed photographs, she learns how to set image quality settings: resolution, compression, and file formats.

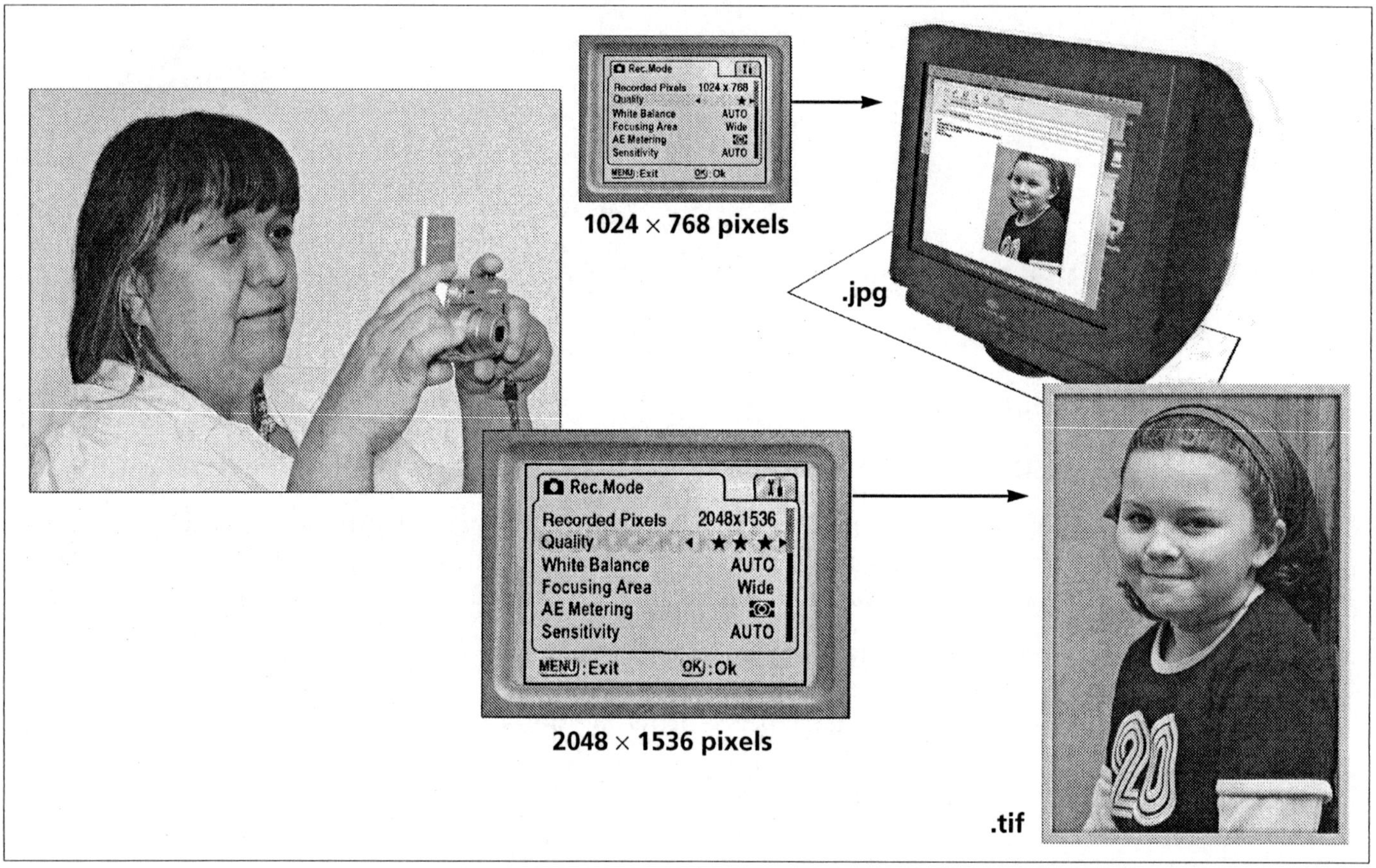

Working with Resolution

Resolution is an image quality setting that affects the size and sharpness of the final image, whether print or Web related. When we think of prints, we typically think of them in measurements of inches. Camera resolution, though, is measured in megapixels. You will also see resolution displayed in as pixel dimensions (such as 1280 × 1024 pixels.) To understand resolution in the digital camera it is important to learn a little about the pixel, which is the measurement system used by both digital cameras and computers. Pixels are arranged in rows and columns to form a grid. Pixel means "picture element." When these pixels are combined to form a grid they become the digital image. The image will be sharper and finer if the pixels are smaller. It follows, then, that as pixels become larger the picture looks blurrier.

TIP! Resolution also has a direct relationship to how large an image can be reproduced in print.

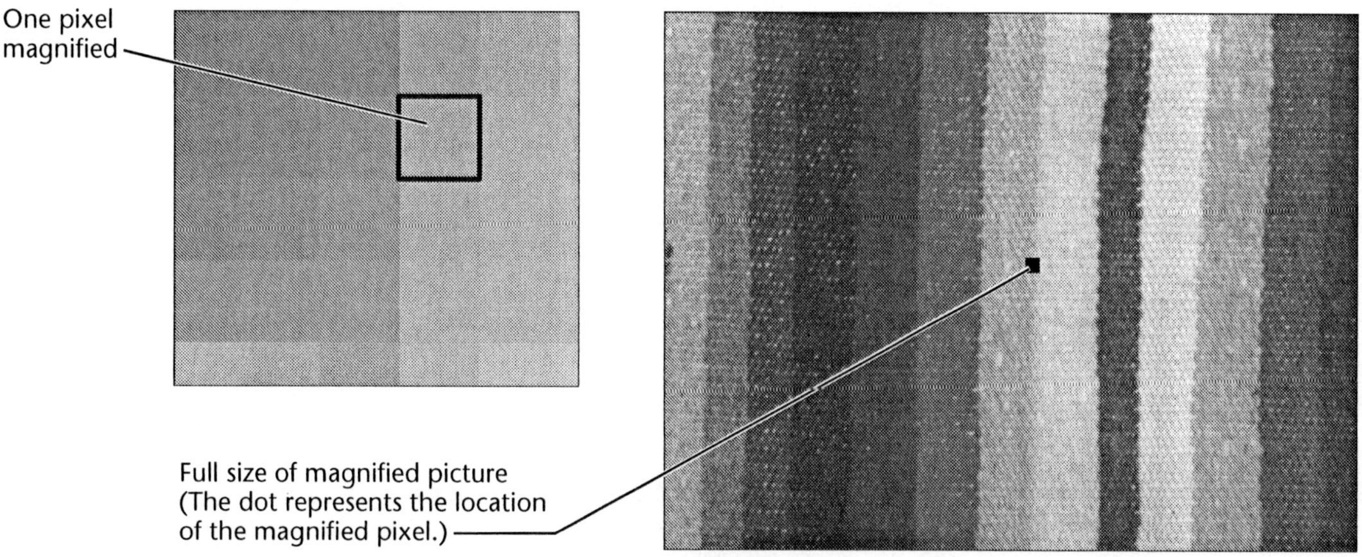

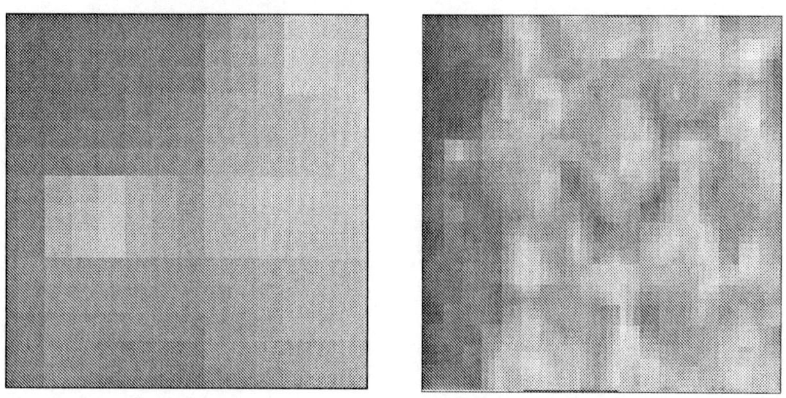

Pixel grids

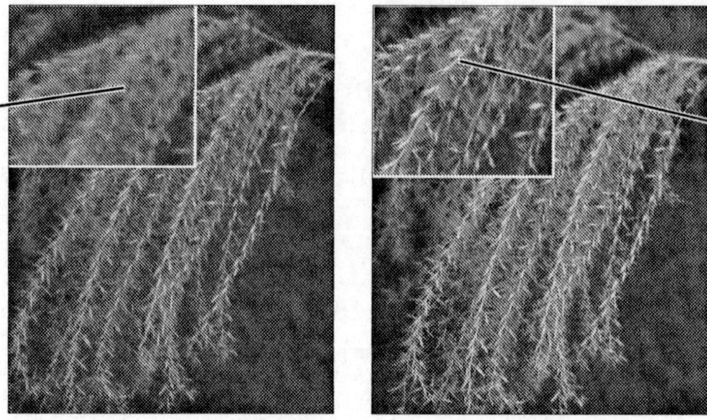

Why Worry About Megapixels?

In Lesson 1, Choosing and Evaluating Digital Cameras, you saw how the imaging sensor (or chip) is composed of pixels. Each camera has a fixed number of pixels on its sensor. The number of these pixels determines how large a print you can make from a photo that will be reproduced in sharp detail. The number of pixels on the sensor is usually in the millions. A million pixels is referred to as a megapixel. The more megapixels, the more information recorded in the image. The term "information" is used to describe detail in a photograph. The more detail captured in a photograph, the better it will represent the subject. Without information (or detail), our photographs would look flat and not very lifelike.

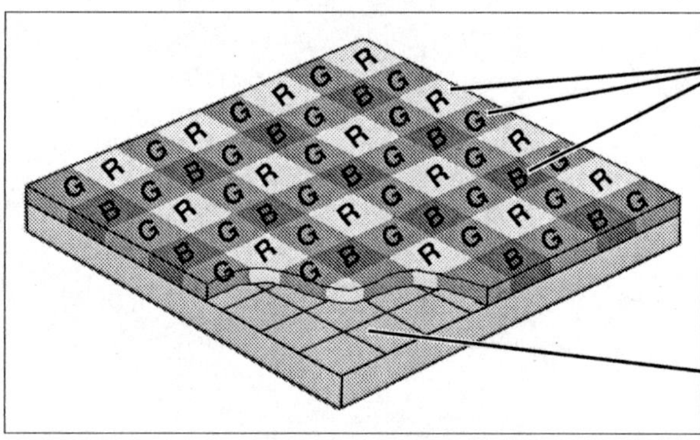

TIP! When you want to improve image quality, start by selecting a larger resolution setting.

QUICK REFERENCE: Defining Megapixels, Resolution, and Approximate Print Size

Resolution in Megapixels	Approximate Resolution in Pixels	Largest Print with High Resolution
6 megapixels	3072 × 2048	13 × 19 inch print
4 megapixels	2272 × 1704	11 × 14 inch print
3 megapixels	2048 × 1536	8.5 × 11 inch print
2 megapixels	1600 × 1200	6 × 8 inch print
1 megapixel	1280 × 960	4 × 6 inch print

Changing the Resolution for Each Picture

You can change the resolution settings to suit the purpose of the image you are about to shoot. If you want a series of pictures to use in a PowerPoint® or other slideshow presentation program, for example, you would change the setting to one megapixel, and then take the pictures of your desired subject. If your next series of pictures are to be used for high quality 8 × 10 inch prints, simply reset your resolution to three megapixels (or higher), and then continue shooting. Because you are using a digital camera, you can even change the setting for each exposure!

Example Mary Rose is on vacation and is becoming concerned about space on her camera's memory card. (She's already filled up her spare card.) Since she intends to simply view the images on her computer and perhaps make a few 4 × 6 inch snapshot-sized prints to share with family and friends, she bumps down the resolution to about one megapixel. This allows her to take about three times as many photos during the remainder of her vacation than if she'd used a three-megapixel setting.

HANDS-ON 6.1 Apply Resolution Settings

In this exercise, you will learn where the resolution settings are on your camera and how to determine which to choose.

Set the Resolution on Your Camera

1. Look in your instruction manual for Image Quality, Image Recording Quality, or Quality. Then, find the section on Image Size, which is the resolution setting.

   Image quality encompasses both resolution and compression. We will cover compression later in this lesson.

2. Follow the instructions for your camera type to locate the image size settings on your camera:
   - **Digital compacts:** Look in the Shooting Menu in the LCD.
   - **SLR digital cameras:** Image size settings are often accessed by buttons and dials on the camera body in addition to the menu in the LCD.

NOTE! You will know you are in the right place when you see settings displayed as pixel dimensions (i.e., 2240 × 1488).

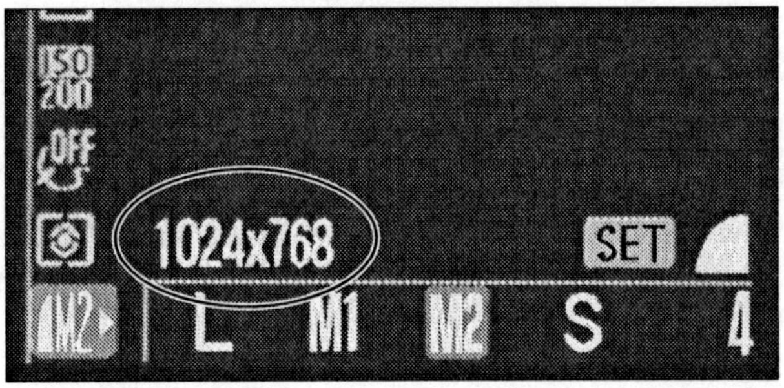

3. Set your camera to the largest image size available.

   You may see it represented as an L, as well as in pixel dimensions (i.e., 2048 × 1536).

4. Check how many exposures are left on your camera. The number of exposures is most often found in the lower-right corner of the LCD or in the smaller LCD on some cameras.

   Choosing a higher resolution results in less remaining exposures; choosing a lower resolution gives you more exposures.

5. Set the image size to the lowest resolution and check how many exposures are left.

   You should now have considerably more exposures.

Choose the Right Resolution

6. Set the appropriate resolution for each of the following print sizes.

   Refer to the Defining Megapixels, Resolution, and Approximate Print Size Quick Reference table on page 145 if necessary. Use the settings that most closely match those on your camera.

   - 8 × 10 inches
   - 4 × 6 inches
   - 11 × 14 inches

7. Set the resolution to match the size print you might typically expect to print or the size you would view on the computer.

   Skill Builder 6.1 guides you through some detailed comparisons of resolution settings, viewing them on the computer screen and in print.

Compressing Image Files

Compression is another way in which you can adjust the number of photos the camera's memory card can hold. Compression enables you to fit more large-dimension photos on the same memory card.

Compression Defined

Compression is more difficult to clearly define than resolution because resolution is finite: once the settings are changed they cannot be altered in the computer without a distinct loss in quality. Compression is more flexible because it is not measured by increasing or decreasing pixel dimensions. Compression actually shrinks file size through processing in the camera. When the image is opened in the computer, it expands to the same size as a non-compressed image. The images have a loss in quality but it often goes unnoticed (especially if you use a minimum amount) when printed and not greatly enlarged.

How Compression Shrinks Files

Compressing a file is really not a mystery or magic although it certainly seems to be—mostly because it's not the easiest concept to understand. Compression works by making assumptions about what should be on a certain pixel according to adjacent pixels. One of the most common examples is a block of the same or similar color, like a blue sky. Suppose there are three pixels of the same color, and the first and the last have the same brightness value. When processed in the camera, the middle pixel will be eliminated but when the image is opened in the computer, the pixel is put back in. However (and this is a *big* however), the pixel added back does not contain image detail: it is just a colored pixel. This could degrade the quality of the picture, depending on the amount of detail and color subtlety in the original picture. It also is affected by the degree of compression used, which will be explained later in this lesson. The loss of quality is most noticeable in enlargements.

Compression and Image Quality

As previously explained, a compressed digital file may result in a distinct loss of quality because bits of the file are discarded during in-camera processing and replaced by colored pixels, not detail. The resulting loss of detail (information) in the picture is determined by the amount of compression chosen and the output choice (Web, print, etc.). Although the resolution setting is also a factor in how many pictures will fit on a card, it does not affect quality unless print size is greater than recommended. When transferred to the computer the image information is intact, complete with all of the detail captured in the camera. Compressed files actually change when opened in the computer. You usually have three choices for setting the amount of compression. The maximum amount of compression is usually acceptable only for display on Web pages because it causes the most amount of file information to be discarded. Using the minimum amount of compression usually yields very good prints and any loss of image quality is often imperceptible.

How Does Compression Differ from Resolution?

Resolution and compression settings determine the quality of your photographs, and they directly affect how many pictures can be stored on a memory card. If you don't know which setting to use, you might be in for a big disappointment when you print an 8 x10 inch picture only to discover that it looks blurry because the compression setting was too small. Resolution and compression work together, but each emphasizes a different aspect of image quality:

- **Resolution** measures the number of pixels in the image and determines the optimum print size that can be made from each digital image.
- **Compression** is the method that makes the digital file smaller so more pictures can fit on a memory card.

Choosing a Compression Setting

Deciding which compression setting to choose is often a compromise between image quality and the number of images you want to fit on a memory card. Compression does what it says: it compresses the file information to fit in a smaller space on the card, thereby getting more pictures per card. When the image file is opened in the computer it is uncompressed. If the compression setting was low, you won't see much loss of detail. If the compression setting was high, you will lose a great deal of detail.

TIP! To make a large print from your image file, remember to set the corresponding resolution setting. No matter how little compression you choose, it will not yield a large print unless resolution is set correctly.

Magnification showing minimum compression (best quality)

Magnification showing maximum compression (least quality)

QUICK REFERENCE: Choosing Compression Settings

Amount of Compression	Quality Level	Camera Brand: Canon	Nikon	Olympus	Panasonic	Sony	Kodak	Used For
Maximum	Least	Normal	Basic	Standard (SQ1 and SQ2)	Standard	Standard	Good	More images on a card
Medium	Average	Fine	Normal	High (HQ)	None available	None available	Better	Normal quality
Minimum	Best	Superfine	Fine	Super High (SHQ)	Fine	Fine	Best	High Quality

Summary It's simple! The more compression (least, normal, basic, standard) the lower the quality and the more images will fit on a memory card. The least compression (best, superfine, fine, Super High) the higher the quality and the fewer images will fit on a memory card.

TIP! You can change the quality settings for each shot. If you are running out of room on your memory card and it's your last one, just lower the quality a little. Aren't digital cameras great?!

HANDS-ON 6.2 Change the Compression Setting

In this exercise, you will locate the compression settings on your camera and practice using each one.

Set the Compression on Your Camera

1. Look in your instruction manual for the section on Image Quality, Image Recording Quality, or Quality.

   Be sure to find the specific section on Quality, which is the compression setting.

2. On your camera, locate how to find and change the compression settings.

   Compression settings are often found in the Shooting Menu in the LCD. Sometimes you access the compression setting via buttons and dials on the camera body.

   TIP! You will know you are in the right place when you see settings displayed as Good, Better, Best; Basic, Normal, Fine, etc. Refer to the Choosing Compression Settings Quick Reference table on page 149 for examples of the words several major brands associate with compression levels.

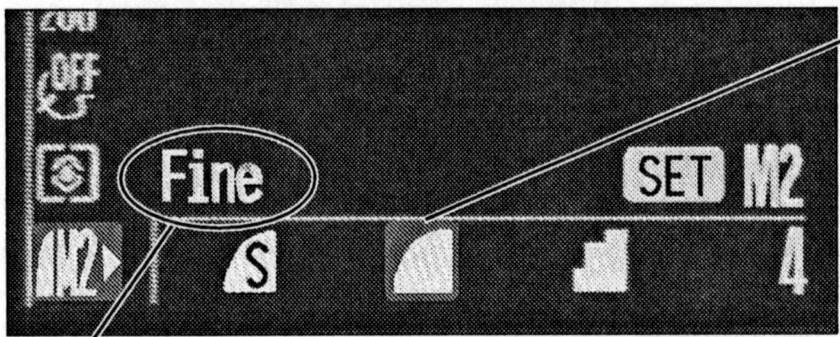

Icon representing the Fine setting

Compression setting on Fine, which indicates medium compression

3. Choose the maximum compression setting, and then check how many exposures are left on your camera.

   You should have many shots on the memory card.

4. Now set the minimum compression setting on your camera.

   The number of shots left on the memory card is significantly reduced.

Set Compression to Attach Pictures to Email

5. Choose a small resolution setting, which will result in a low quality large print but a good quality image for Web use.

   Notice that you have a lot of shots available left in the camera.

6. Choose a compression setting that gives you as many shots as possible (Maximum compression).

   Maximum compression equals low quality prints, but is fine for pictures attached to emails.

7. Choose Normal (Average) compression so you have enough quality for medium to large prints in your remaining shots.

   Skill Builder 6.2 guides you through some detailed comparisons of compression settings on the computer screen and in print.

Working with File Formats

Once you take a picture, the digital camera has to record all of the data to a memory card. (Traditional cameras, on the other hand, record images on the film.) Digital cameras record numbers (the color values of each pixel). These numbers are then translated into images to form a picture from the data collected at the moment of exposure. This data is stored in a standardized form so it can be used with any camera, computer, and software program. We call this standardization a file format. There are many types of file formats for picture files.

Strengths and Weaknesses

Every file format has strengths and weaknesses for accomplishing certain results.

- **Compression:** File formats that enable large pictures to fit on a small amount of space on the memory card
- **Cross Platform:** File formats that work well on both Windows and Macintosh operating systems
- **Web Optimization:** File formats that create images for email attachments and Web pages; they transfer and load quickly
- **Least Loss of Picture Data:** File formats that reproduce digital images most accurately for high-quality prints

- **Quicker Processing of Picture Data to the Memory Card:** File formats that speed up the time it takes to transfer data to the card, thereby shortening the time before you can take the next shot

TIP! File formats are often displayed as extensions at the end of filenames. For example, a JPEG formatted file usually has a .jpg at the end of the filename. Windows normally hides the filename extension.

Macintosh file icons display filename extensions.

Windows' Icon view does not display filename extensions.

Windows' Tiles view displays filename extensions.

Common Digital Camera File Formats

There are three file formats commonly featured with digital cameras: JPEG, TIFF, and RAW. Not all cameras use all three formats; however, virtually all digital cameras can save photos in JPEG format.

JPG or JPEG (Joint Photographic Experts Group) The Joint Photographic Experts Group (JPG or JPEG) is the most commonly used file format for storing digital images. When you save a picture in this format some of the data is lost because of compression. Refer to the Choosing Compression Settings Quick Reference table on page 149 to see the different degrees of compression (best, fine, etc.). When you select a compression setting, you are automatically using a JPEG format. The great thing about this format is that it does quite a good job of preserving all of the visual information our eyes can see in a picture. It is the most commonly used because it saves space and provides good quality images. In addition, almost all image editing software can open and use JPEG files.

WARNING! Pay attention to the compression setting you choose. Initially, you might be happy to see how many pictures you can get on one memory card, but imagine your disappointment when they get blurrier and blurrier as you make larger prints.

TIF or TIFF (Tagged Image File Format) Tagged Image File Format (TIF or TIFF) is only found on some digital cameras. The TIFF format preserves every bit of picture data. Although it sounds great there is a good reason most people do not choose it. The files it stores are huge and take a long time to process. This means you will have a longer wait between shots. Using a high quality JPEG setting might give you about 70 pictures on a memory card, while using the TIF file format will only give you about 10 pictures on the same size card. It is often difficult to see the difference between a TIF image and a high quality JPEG image, which is why TIF is used less often. In addition, many cameras no longer offer this option because high-quality JPEG images are adequate on most compact digital cameras. Advanced compacts and digital SLR cameras use RAW format for higher quality, so they also have no need to offer the TIF format.

RAW The RAW file format name is not an acronym; it describes exactly what it does. Using this file format enables the camera to record the image with totally unprocessed data. In the JPEG and TIFF formats the camera automatically does some color correcting and balancing, and sharpens the image while processing the picture. It will not do this if you choose RAW as your file format. Sounds good, doesn't it?

There are several reasons why RAW is not the ideal format, however. First, as with TIFF, your memory card will only hold a small amount of RAW files compared to JPEG files. Second, you need quite a bit of experience with an image editing program to utilize the best features this file format has to offer, which is that the file comes into the computer unprocessed and you can change settings as if you were taking the picture at that moment. However, you really have to know what you're doing. Finally, you need special software to open these files. RAW format is found most often on advanced compacts and digital SLR cameras. Every camera brand gives the RAW file format a different filename extension but they all can be opened using Photoshop Camera Raw plug-in, which is included with Photoshop Elements.

TIP! RAW file formats are great for experienced Photoshop users who want to reproduce their images as large prints with the best possible quality.

Concepts Review

True/False Questions

			Page number
1. Resolution directly affects print size without negatively affecting image quality.	**true**	**false**	______
2. Once you choose the resolution setting it must remain that way until the memory card is filled up.	**true**	**false**	______
3. The higher the resolution setting, the more pictures will fit on a memory card.	**true**	**false**	______
4. Compression measures the number of pixels in the image.	**true**	**false**	______
5. Maximum compression produces the greatest loss of print quality.	**true**	**false**	______
6. Minimum compression and high resolution yield high-quality, large prints.	**true**	**false**	______
7. More images will fit on a memory card if the compression is set to the maximum setting.	**true**	**false**	______
8. You can set compression and resolution independently.	**true**	**false**	______
9. If you are running out of room on your memory card, lower the image quality setting to create more space.	**true**	**false**	______
10. A standardized file format is important so different cameras, computers, and software can read and display picture data.	**true**	**false**	______

Multiple Choice Questions

1. With maximum compression, you can ________.

   Page number: ______

   a. store more pictures on a memory card
   b. increase the quality of a print
   c. retain picture data without quality loss when the image is opened in the computer
   d. All of the above

2. What does resolution affect?

   Page number: ______

   a. Print size
   b. Sharpness of an image
   c. How many pictures will fit on a memory card
   d. All of the above

3. What file format is available on virtually all digital cameras?

   Page number: ______

   a. JPEG
   b. RAW
   c. TIF or TIFF
   d. All of the above

4. What file formats preserve *all* picture data?

   Page number: ______

   a. JPEG
   b. RAW
   c. TIF or TIFF
   d. None of the above

Skill Builders

SKILL BUILDER 6.1 Compare Resolution Settings

In this exercise, you will take several photos at various resolution settings (but with the same compression setting) and compare them on the computer.

Take Photos at Various Resolutions

1. Set your camera to the maximum resolution. For example, a three megapixel camera would have a maximum resolution of 2048 × 1536.

   The maximum resolution is determined by the maximum megapixels of your camera.

2. Set the compression to a medium (Average) setting, and leave it on this setting for the remainder of this exercise.

3. Set your camera to Automatic or Program shooting mode, and leave it on this setting for the remainder of this exercise.

   Keeping the shooting mode constant will yield more accurate comparisons.

4. Go outside and take pictures of the following scenes, making sure to capture same amount of the picture in each subject:
   - Landscape or cityscape from at least 30 feet
   - Subject located about 6 feet from the camera
   - Subject in motion (something moving in the breeze or a person walking)

5. Now set your camera to a resolution of 1280 × 960, or as close to that setting as possible.

   This setting is the lowest you should use for a high-quality, small print.

6. Repeat steps two and three.

View the Photos on the Computer

Now you will download the photos and view them on the computer.

7. Download your pictures to the computer and look at them in Preview mode.

   Remember, just select all the pictures you want to look at, and then double-click on one to open the built-in preview program in your computer. If you are not successful opening them the first time, take a deep breath and try again.

8. Zoom in at least four times on each picture and compare the same scene captured at high and low resolution. You should be able to see distinct pixels in the picture taken with the lower resolution.

   You will have to zoom in more to see the pixels in the picture with the higher resolution setting.

SKILL BUILDER 6.2 Compare Compression Settings

In this exercise, you will take several photos at various compression settings (but at a single resolution setting) and compare them on the computer.

Take Photos at Various Compression Settings

1. Set your camera to the maximum compression; for example, Standard (SQ1 and SQ2) on an Olympus camera.

   Maximum compression equals lowest quality.

   TIP! Remember, different camera models have different names for compression settings.

2. Set the resolution on your camera to 2048 × 1536.

3. Set your camera to Automatic or Program shooting mode and leave it on this setting for the remainder of this exercise.

   Keeping the shooting mode constant will yield more accurate comparisons.

4. Go outside and take pictures of the following scenes, making sure to capture same amount of the picture in each subject:
   - Landscape or cityscape from at least 30 feet
   - Subject located about 6 feet from the camera
   - Subject in motion (something moving in the breeze or a person walking)

5. Now set your camera to the minimum compression setting; for example, Super High (SHQ) on an Olympus camera.

   A minimum compression setting equals highest quality.

6. Repeat steps 3 and 4.

View the Photos on the Computer

Now you will download the photos and view them on the computer.

7. Download your pictures to the computer and look at them in Preview mode.

   Remember, just select all the pictures you want to look at, and then double-click on one to open the built-in preview program in your computer. If you are not successful opening them the first time, take a deep breath and try again.

8. Zoom in at least four times on each picture and compare the same scene captured at the high and low resolution. Don't worry if you don't see a difference between the pictures.

   Compression settings affect print quality (especially enlargements), not what you see on the computer.

LESSON 7

Adjusting Color with White Balance Settings

Getting the colors in your photographs just the way you want them is of major importance when using a digital camera. Digital cameras can produce beautiful colors if you know how to choose the correct white balance settings.

Have you ever noticed how people look greenish in a picture if the room was lit with fluorescent lights? This is the type of problem that can easily be solved using the flash and correct white balance settings. In this lesson, you will learn what color temperature is and how it affects color in a photograph, what white balance means and why it is important, and how to choose between automatic, preset, and custom white balance settings. You will also learn how to use white balance settings as a creative tool. You will discover that the concept of correcting color in the camera is easy to understand and even easier to accomplish.

Additional learning resources are available at ***labpub.com/learn/silver/digphoto/***

Case Study

Dennis is planning a photo trip in the southwest. He will be visiting places like Arches National Monument and Canon de Chelly. He has taken some pictures in rock and shady areas near his home in preparation for his trip. He discovers that the colors he saw when viewed images in the LCD were not what he saw in the scene. He realizes that in some instances the camera does not capture color very accurately. He does some investigating and finds that there is a setting on digital cameras, called White Balance, which affects how colors are captured. He experiments with different settings and finds that not only can he capture more accurate color he can also make some creative images using the "wrong" white balance setting. He is now confident about getting just the right shots when he takes his trip.

Introducing Color Temperature

When we think of temperature, an image of a thermometer pops into our minds, and we see it measuring heat and cold. Color has temperature, too. The temperature of color, however, has nothing to do with feeling hot or cold. It reflects a visual color as a result of different light sources. Every type of light has individual color characteristics, and these are recorded by the digital camera. So, if you photograph on an overcast day, the light source is different than if you photograph on a bright, sunny day. The camera adjusts for each lighting condition using automatic white balance settings.

Measuring Color Temperature

Color temperature uses a measurement system developed by physicist Lord William Thomas Kelvin. He developed a color measurement scale with units called Kelvins (K). Visual light, whether it is from a light bulb, the sun, candlelight, etc., is described in warm and cool tones. Warm tones are seen as reddish and cool tones are seen as bluish. Remember, we are not talking about the feeling of heat and cold, but instead of a visual representation of warm and cool. The measurement scale for color is the opposite of what we are used to. Instead of the higher number meaning hotter temperatures, the higher number refers to the coolest colors (blues) and the lowest number refers to the warmest colors (reds).

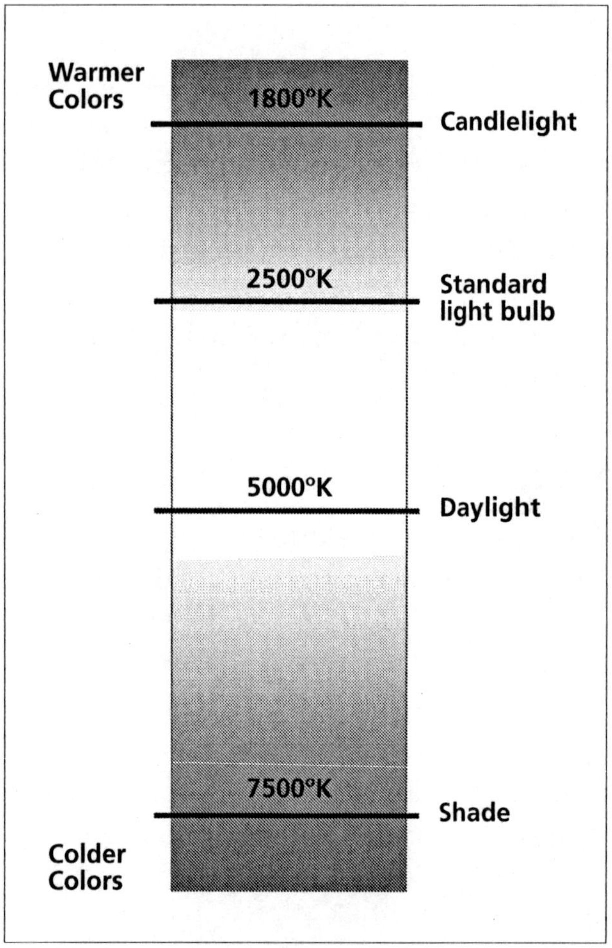

Kelvin Scale

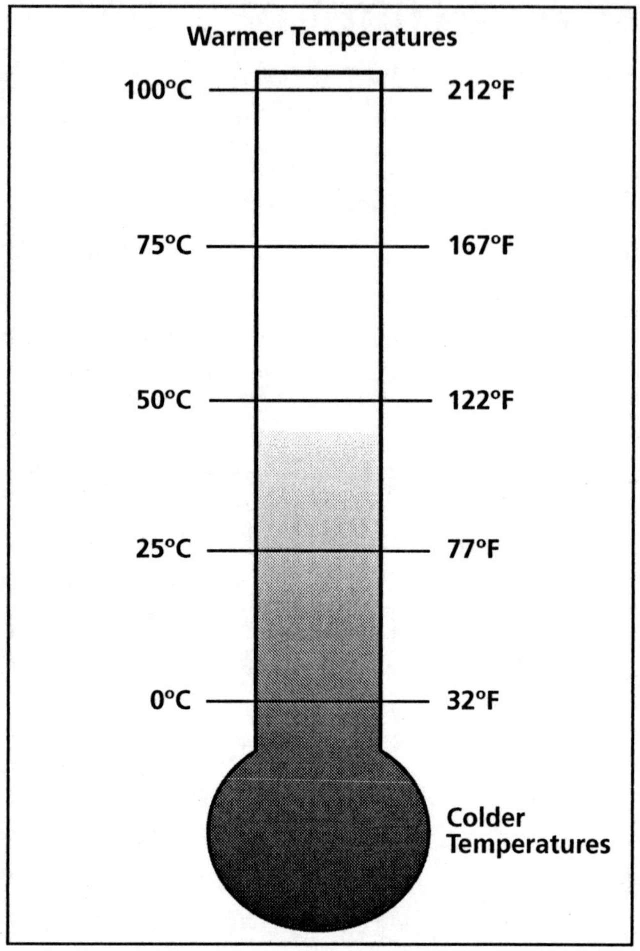

Standard Thermometer

Introducing Color Balance

Color balance refers to rendering colors produced by cameras, computers, and other electronic devices as close as possible to how they are seen by the human eye. Interestingly, our minds and brains balance colors on their own. No matter what color the light source, white appears white, yellow appears yellow, and so on. We can walk in and out of different lighting situations and still register colors accurately. Cameras produce color as affected by the lighting situation. For example, if a picture is taken under fluorescent light and without flash, there will be a distinct yellow-greenish tinge to the picture. This is called a color cast.

Color Casts

An image is said to have a color cast if the colors do not look true (like our eyes see them). This is evident when a predominance of one color is seen in an image. We tend to think of color casts as undesirable because they cause an imbalance in the colors of a photograph. Viewing an image with a color cast is similar to looking at something through colored sunglasses. Think of the phrase "Seeing through rose-tinted glasses." Unlike using the phrase as a metaphor, a camera can actually produce a rose-tinted image if there is a predominance of reddish or pinkish light. This will happen even though we don't see it with our eyes. The camera does not adjust for color casts automatically like our eyes do. Therefore, you need to use special settings to make sure the camera represents color accurately. These are called the white balance settings.

QUICK REFERENCE: Working with Color Temperature, Light Sources, and Color Casts

Approximate Color Temperature	Light Source	Color Cast
1000–2000K	Candlelight, firelight	Very red
2000K	Sunrise, sunset	Less red, more orange
2500K	Incandescent bulbs, standard light bulbs	Less red
3300K	Studio lights	Tinge of red
5000K	Standard daylight	None, neutral
6500K	Bright sun, clear skies	Tinge of blue
6000–7000K	Somewhat overcast skies	Bluer
9000K	Shade	More blue
10,000K	Very overcast	Very blue

HANDS-ON 7.1 View Photos with Different Light Sources

In this exercise, you view the same picture under different lighting conditions to compare the color cast from each light source.

1. Launch your Web browser and type **`labpub.com/learn/silver/digphoto/`** in the address bar.

Macintosh OS X

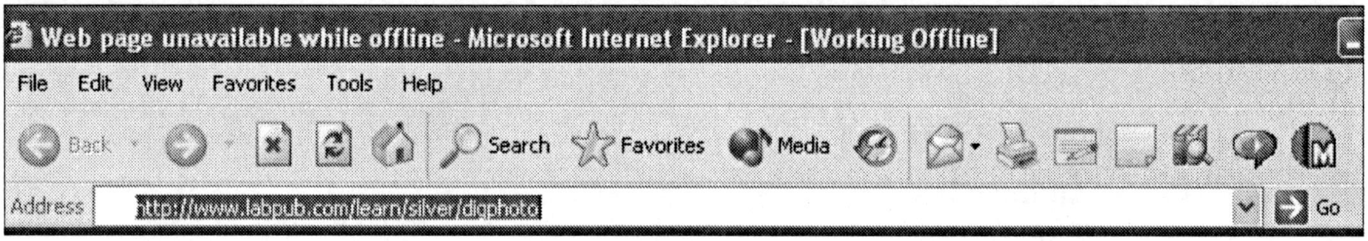

Windows XP

2. Click the White Balance Gallery link.
3. Click the Light Sources link on the White Balance Gallery Page.
   An online gallery appears, displaying examples of the same photo under different light sources.
4. Use the Fluorescent button to simulate how the subject looks under fluorescent light, click the Overcast button to simulate how it looks on an overcast day, and then click the Daylight button to view how the subject would appear in daylight conditions.
5. Click the Back to the Main Book Page link and continue reading the next topic when you are finished.
   Leave the browser window open since you will view another gallery later in this lesson.

Choosing and Using White Balance Settings

It can be very disappointing when colors seen through the LCD look all wrong compared to what you saw in the original scene. Don't despair; your knowledge of white balance settings will come to the rescue! Read on and find out how simple it is to achieve natural looking and correct colors.

Why Is It Called White Balance?

Our eyes see white objects as white in any lighting situation. This is not so with the camera. The camera captures any reflected color and will represent whites with a cast of whatever color is present as ambient light or as color dominant in a scene (for example, a red wall). So, what the camera is doing (and what can also be done later in the computer) is choosing white as a neutral standard color. The balancing part is done by filtering the light with the opposite color cast to make the white look white. Not only are these corrective settings a built-in feature of digital cameras, but you also have immediate color feedback when you view your pictures in Playback mode.

TIP! To correct color casts with film camera, you must attach different color filters to the lens. You won't know if it worked until the film is processed. Another great reason for choosing a digital camera!

Example If you take a picture in the shade, the camera will record the color temperature as cool. The resulting picture will be bluish. However, the camera's automatic white balance feature will add a filter containing a warm color (orange) to neutralize or balance the picture. To mimic this effect you could hold an orange transparency over a blue transparency, all on top of a white piece of paper. The filter effect is like the transparency and the camera, when set on automatic white balance, knows which filter to use to balance the colors so white appears white in the picture. A photographer using a film camera actually uses a filter over the lens to compensate for any color cast. The filters come in shades of blue, orange, and red with different degrees of density. Also, some film is made to work in specific lighting situations. The beauty of digital cameras is that compensating for color casts is simple.

White Balance Settings on Your Camera

On some digital SLRs, the white balance can be changed using a dial and the small LCD on the top or back of the camera. On compacts, the setting is accessed through a button or dial on the camera in combination with the menu on the LCD, or it will only be found in the LCD.

TIP! Some cameras may require a specific shooting mode to use white balance settings.

Pressing the down (WB) arrow displays the white balance menu on this camera.

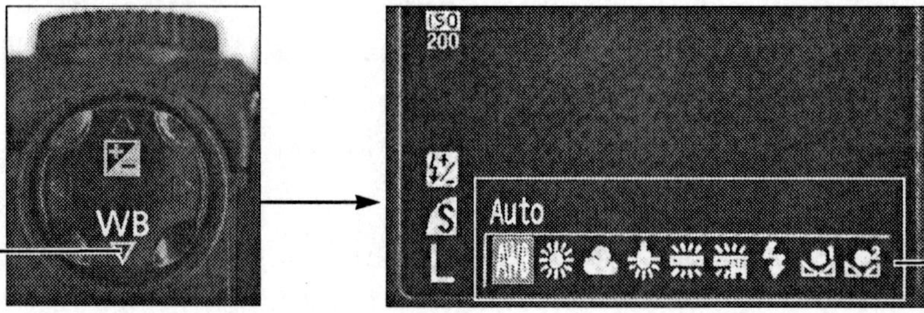

These are the white balance settings.

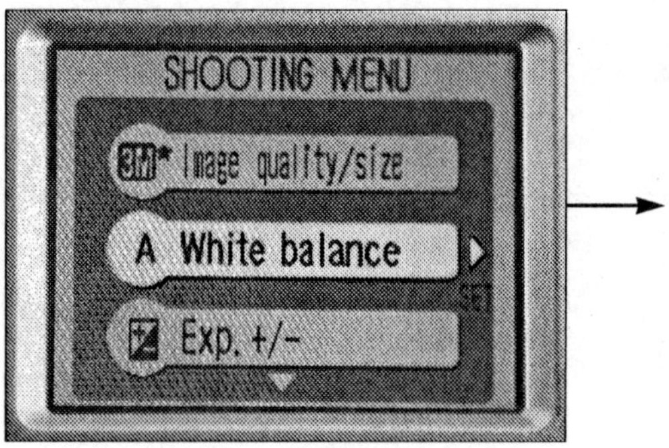

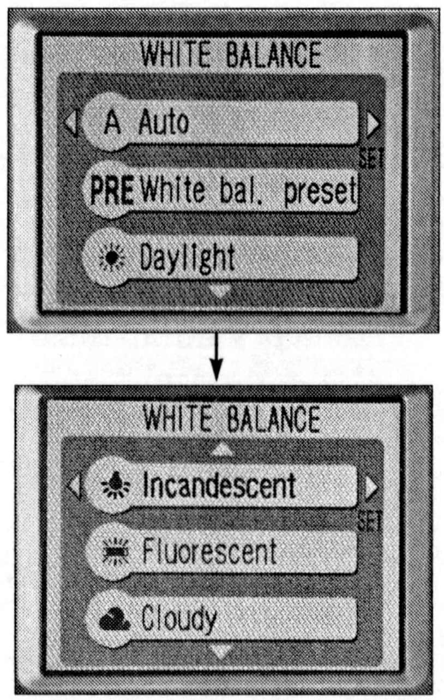

White Balance settings on this camera are made solely in the menu.

Automatic White Balance Adjustment

Automatic white balance setting is the default on digital cameras. The camera chooses what it thinks is the right correction for the ambient light conditions based on how it sees a white object. Most of the time the automatic white balance setting does a very good job.

Preset White Balance Adjustments

Preset white balance settings are available, and you can set them manually when the automatic setting does not give desired results.

NOTE! If you use white balance presets be sure to change your camera back to automatic before photographing in different lighting conditions or your next pictures may not be the right colors.

QUICK REFERENCE: Defining Common White Balance Settings

White Balance Icon	Lighting Condition	When to Use
A AWB	Auto	You want the camera to calculate the white balance; use this setting most of the time
	Daylight	You want to prevent a bluish cast when photographing outdoors on a bright day
	Cloudy (overcast)	You want to reduce a blue cast when photographing under overcast or cloudy skies
	Shade	You are photographing in deep shade (under a tree, among rocks, etc.)
	Tungsten (Indoors or Incandescent)	You are photographing indoors under standard light bulbs
	Fluorescent	You are photographing in fluorescent light
	Flash	You are photographing with the flash

HANDS-ON 7.2 Use White Balance Settings

In this exercise, you will learn where the default white balance settings are on your camera, how to set them, and how to compare what each setting does.

Set White Balance

1. Look in your instruction manual for White Balance. Determine if you need to be in a specific shooting mode. If so, set your camera to that mode.
2. Follow the directions for the type of camera you have to locate the white balance settings on your camera:
   - **Digital compacts:** Look in the menu in the LCD.
   - **SLR digital cameras:** White balance settings are often accessed by buttons and dials on the camera body in addition to the menu in the LCD.
3. Set the white balance to Automatic, if necessary.

Use White Balance Settings

You will only be using the default white balance settings (all except Preset). Refer to the Defining Common White Balance Settings Quick Reference table on page 167 for a review of these settings.

4. Choose a scene that has a lot of different colors, like flowers, colorful material, or patterned clothes. In addition:
   - Choose a scene with only one light source; if you can, go outside.
   - Make sure your scene is no more than six feet from the camera.

   You will be using this same scene for the rest of this exercise.
5. Compose and take a picture using the Automatic White Balance setting.

   This picture will be the normal, or standard, with which you will compare the other settings.
6. Now, take the same picture you took in step 5 using each default white balance setting except Preset. Write down the name and sequence of the setting used for each.

   Using the Custom Preset mode is not required for this exercise because you are only comparing the default settings. Your written notes will be helpful when you view the photos on the computer.
7. When you are finished, reset your white balance setting to Automatic.

   Your camera will stay in the last white balance setting that was used, which could lead to unwanted colors in future photographs. Automatic White Balance works great in almost all instances.

View the Pictures on the Computer

You will now download your pictures and compare the different settings.

8. Download your pictures from the memory card to your computer. Store them in your file storage location in a new folder named **`White Balance`**.

9. Open the White Balance folder, and then follow the instruction for your computer:

   - **Windows XP:** Click the View icon and choose Filmstrip so that all your pictures are displayed.

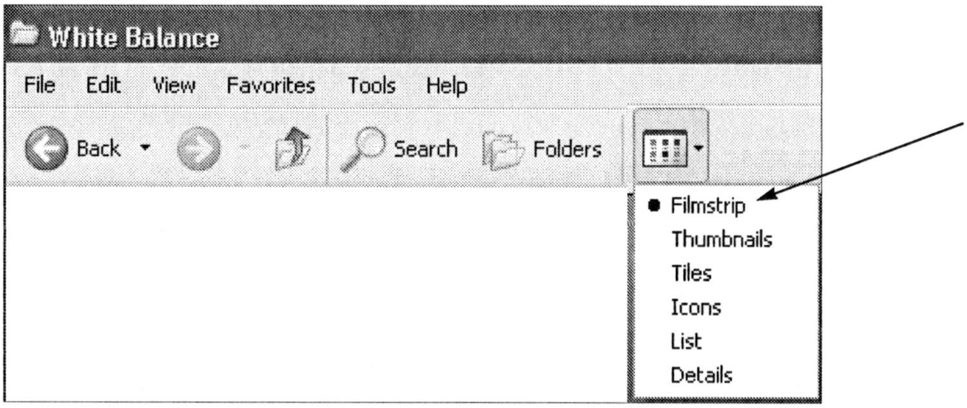

   - **Macintosh OS X:** Use Edit→Select All from the menu bar to select all of the photos. Double-click on any of the selected pictures. Remember, if they all don't open, go back a step and try again. Be patient with yourself. Adjust your view in the preview window according to the following steps:

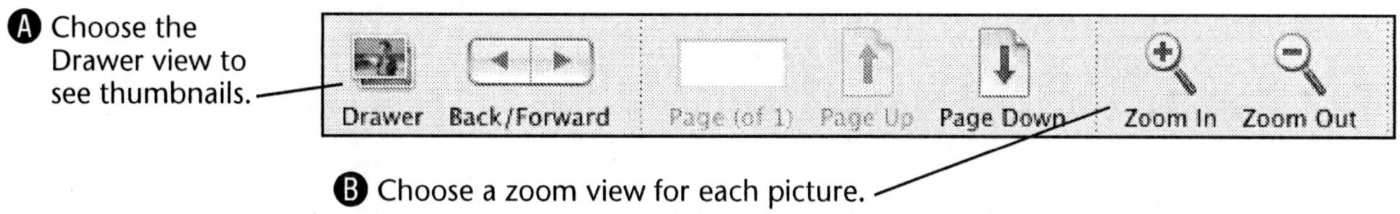

10. Scroll through the thumbnails. Compare each picture and note how the color changes with each white balance setting.

11. Determine which (if any) setting most accurately reflects the true colors in the scene. Compare your results with other members of your class.

12. Keep these notes and the folder of pictures as a reference on how your specific camera uses the white balance settings.

Working with Custom White Balance

You can usually determine in Playback mode if the color is correct in your photo. When automatic and preset settings do not give you the correct colors, however, you have a manual option.

Example

Dennis is taking pictures indoors and the scene is illuminated by daylight and fluorescent lights. Because of the mixed lighting sources, his colors are slightly off and cannot be corrected using white balance presets. He creates his own white balance setting by choosing a white object and, using the custom white balance feature, creating his own white balance preset.

Basically, to create a custom white balance setting, you photograph a white object (piece of white paper, a white t-shirt, etc.) using normal exposure in the current lighting conditions and make this as your preset white balance setting. The camera will keep your custom setting until you change it by photographing a white object in different lighting conditions. Each camera model has its own way of setting a custom white balance preset, so refer to the directions for your specific camera. The good news is that white balance is easy to find in your instruction manual because all camera manuals refer to it as the same thing—white balance!

Cameras Without Custom White Balance

Not all digital cameras have the custom white balance feature. If yours doesn't, you can use the setting that most closely matches what you perceive as the correct colors. You can fix it later in the computer using an image editing program.

NOTE! Setting a custom white balance setting is an advanced feature. Automatic and preset white balance settings should work in almost all instances.

Using White Balance as a Creative Tool

Now that you have learned what white balance settings do, it's time to have some fun! If you were using a film camera you could add filters for special effects: create a special mood by enhancing colors to make skies look bluer or even orange and red, or just experiment to see what happens. This is very easy to do. You simply use any of the presets in other lighting conditions than the ones they are specifically set up for.

HANDS-ON 7.3 View Photos Using White Balance as a Creative Tool

In this exercise, you will view pictures that have been altered using white balance settings to enhance and change the natural colors.

1. If necessary, launch your Web browser and type **`labpub.com/learn/silver/digphoto/`** in the address bar.
2. Click the White Balance as a Creative Tool link.

   An online gallery appears, displaying examples creative uses of the white balance feature.
3. Browse through the examples.

   These examples demonstrate the creative effects you can obtain with White Balance settings.
4. Close the Web browser when you are finished.

Concepts Review

True/False Questions

			Page number
1. The bluest colors on the Kelvin scale have the highest numbers.	**true**	**false**	______
2. A color cast is similar to looking through different color sunglass lenses.	**true**	**false**	______
3. White balance is called that because it uses a while filter to correct color casts.	**true**	**false**	______
4. Checking a picture in Playback mode lets you immediately see if the color is correct.	**true**	**false**	______
5. Using white balance settings may require a specific shooting mode.	**true**	**false**	______
6. Color is balanced on digital cameras by filtering light with the opposite color cast.	**true**	**false**	______
7. When colors are filtered using the opposite color cast, white appears white, which is why the term White Balance is used.	**true**	**false**	______
8. Film cameras require external filters to correct color casts. Digital cameras do not.	**true**	**false**	______
9. Per the Kelvin scale, a standard light bulb has a higher temperature than candlelight.	**true**	**false**	______
10. The camera records objects under fluorescent light as greenish-yellow unless the appropriate white balance setting is used.	**true**	**false**	______

Multiple Choice Questions

1. What can you do with the white balance settings?

   Page number: ______

   a. Use them as a creative tool

   b. Use them to correct color casts

   c. Remove an unwanted predominant color tint

   d. All of the above

2. Why do we see white as white as in any lighting situation?

   Page number: ______

   a. White always appears white in any light

   b. Our eyes automatically adjust for color casts

   c. White is a neutral color

   d. None of the above

3. Each type of light has _______.

   Page number: ______

   a. individual color characteristics

   b. a cool or warm tone

   c. an opposite color to correct a color cast

   d. All of the above

4. In which way is the Kelvin measurement scale different than a standard thermometer?

   Page number: ______

   a. It does not use degrees as a measurement system.

   b. It has the opposite meaning of high and low numbers on the scale.

   c. It does not use warm and cool as descriptive terms.

   d. None of the above

Skill Builders

SKILL BUILDER 7.1 Practice Setting White Balance

In this exercise, you will take photos using correct and incorrect white balance settings. Then you will compare the results on the computer.

Before You Begin: Following the instructions in you manual, turn off the flash. The flash will skew the results of this exercise.

Take Photos Indoors

1. Switch on a light in a room. With your camera set to Automatic White Balance, take a photograph of a scene or object in the room, and then review it in Playback mode.

   Set the camera on something like a table to steady it and take another photo if the picture looks blurry when you check it in Playback mode.

   There may not be enough light to take the picture without steadying it and keep it from blurring.

2. Make a white balance setting in your camera appropriate to that light source and photograph the same scene or object.

3. Change the white balance setting in the camera for a different light source. (For example, choose Incandescent when the light source is really fluorescent lighting or vice versa.) Photograph the same scene or object.

Take Photos Outdoors

4. Set your camera's white balance back to Automatic. Go outdoors, choose a scene, and then photograph it.

5. Choose a white balance setting appropriate to the lighting conditions of the scene, and then photograph it again.

6. Choose a white balance setting for a different lighting condition. (For example, choose Shade when the lighting is Bright Sunlight and vice versa.) Photograph the same scene one more time.

Review the Photos

7. Download your photos to your file storage location a new folder named **`Skill Builder 7.1`**.

8. Open the folder and preview your photos in a large thumbnail mode.

TIP! Repeat the instructions in step 9 of Hands-On 7.2 on page 168 if you don't recall how to do this.

9. Compare the results of each setting. Did one white balance setting work equally well in more then one light source? What would happen if you chose a particular white balance setting, and then forgot to reset it to Automatic as you continued taking photographs under different lighting conditions?

SKILL BUILDER 7.2 Use White Balance Settings as a Creative Tool

In this exercise, you will use white balance settings to create unusual and artistic effects on some of your photographs.

Take the Photos

1. Set your camera's white balance to Fluorescent. Go outdoors. Choose a scene that is very colorful and take a picture.

   In this and the next step, you will deliberately use an "incorrect" white balance setting. The fluorescent setting will give a yellowish-green color cast to the photo, and could look pretty awful...or quite intriguing.

2. Continue taking pictures of the same scene from different angles, getting very close and getting further away until you have at least ten pictures.

   Leave the white balance setting on Fluorescent for all of these additional photos.

3. Change the white balance setting to Shade, Cloudy, or Overcast if it is a sunny day. Change it to Daylight if it is an overcast or cloudy day or if you are in the shade.

   The scene should have an orange cast if Shade, Cloudy, or Overcast is used on a sunny day. Using the Daylight setting in the shade will give the picture a bluish tint.

4. Repeat step 2, taking another ten pictures with the white balance on the new setting.

Review the Photos

5. Download your photos to your file storage location in a new folder named **`Skill Builder 7.2`**.

6. Open the new folder and preview your photos in a large thumbnail mode.

7. Compare the results of each set of pictures. Did changing the view and distance make a difference in the effect you created? Which pictures are the most successful? Why?

   You may find that the effect was stronger at specific angles and more pronounced in close-ups. It really depends on your subject and lighting conditions.

8. Look at other students' pictures to see their results and discuss the pictures you thought were particularly successful. See if you can tell why.

LESSON 8

Exploring Photoshop Elements

Many of the pictures you take will look quite good, but most photos can look even better with the enhancements that a good image editing program can provide. One of the best entry-level image editing programs available is Adobe Photoshop Elements. In this lesson, you will use Photoshop Elements to practice some basic image editing tasks. Just as on your digital camera, Photoshop Elements offers automatic and manual controls. In this lesson, you will learn how to open and save your image files and how to use automated settings and tools in Photoshop Elements to adjust contrast, color, and brightness to enhance your digital photos.

Additional learning resources are available at ***labpub.com/learn/silver/digphoto/***

Case Study

Chris is very excited about the photos he took of his daughter, Anna, with his digital camera. Her expressions came out just right and he likes the setting, but the contrast was too dull and there are distracting elements around her. He wishes he had gotten closer. Using Adobe Photoshop Elements, Chris is able to improve his photos. The basic tools, commands, and automated dialogue boxes in the program allow Chris to make his photos better match his original vision. Photoshop Elements gives him the tools necessary to transform his pictures from good to great!

Editing Photos

By now you have gained a great deal of skill with your camera and have learned quite a bit about taking better pictures. However, every photo may not turn out exactly as you intend. Perhaps a little cropping or a change in the contrast or adjustment of color will make a good photograph great! These tasks are exactly what image editing programs are designed to do. The subject of this lesson, Photoshop Elements, is a great tool for correcting and editing pictures. It's also fun to use, and easy to learn. Think of editing your photographs as fine-tuning, another useful digital skill to compliment your use of a digital camera.

What You Can Fix

Photoshop Elements (PE) has a tool or command that can fix almost anything, but showing you that would take a whole book of its own! In this lesson, you will use basic tools and commands to fix some common problems found in photographs, such as:

- Overexposed and underexposed photographs
- Unnecessary elements
- Improper color
- Blah photographs that need contrast

Overexposed Photographs An overexposed picture is one in which everything is too light. Incorrect exposure, too much light hitting the sensor, is the cause. Even though you learned to use exposure lock, exposure compensation, and exposure bracketing in Lesson 5, Exploring Exposure, you will have the occasional photograph that needs fixing because it is too light and looks washed out.

Underexposed Photographs If an overexposed photograph is too light, then, as you might surmise, an underexposed photo is too dark. This problem is also caused by an exposure error; not enough light has reached the sensor, causing the picture to be too dark.

Cropping Out Elements Sometimes you will look at a picture you took and wish you had gotten a little closer and filled more of the frame with the subject. This is an easily remedied problem. Cropping is like cutting a photograph with scissors, but you do it in the computer. Most of the time, you can enlarge the cropped part of the picture without losing quality.

Color Adjustments You probably noticed that using white balance settings works most, but not all, of the time to remove a color cast. You can fine tune photographs needing more color adjustment using the appropriate tools in Photoshop Elements.

Adding Contrast to Blah Photos Have you ever taken a picture and really liked how the subject was framed, but noticed that there was no "punch" in it? This is usually because there is not enough contrast. Taking pictures in overcast weather can cause this because the light is dull and even, so the picture also looks dull. Contrast refers to the emphasis of dark and light tonal values in a picture. There is a great auto adjustment in PE that can fix this problem and turn blah images into bright and beautiful photographs.

Introducing Photoshop Elements

Photoshop Elements takes many of the features of Adobe Photoshop, the premier image editing program, and puts them into an easy-to-use application for all levels of computer users. PE is the perfect tool for fine tuning and altering photographs you have taken with your digital camera. There are versions of PE for Windows and Macintosh systems.

The Welcome Window

When you first launch PE, a Welcome window opens. This window will open every time you start PE if you check the box on the lower-left corner of the window (Macintosh) or choose Welcome Window from the drop-down menu on the bottom bar of the window (Windows). The Welcome window is helpful and easy to use. It also happens to be one of the few features that look different on Windows and Macintosh systems, as you can see in the following illustrations. The Welcome Window is a convenient way of choosing major tasks in PE, including opening images for editing, acquiring images from your camera, creating a new image, and many others.

Macintosh Welcome Window

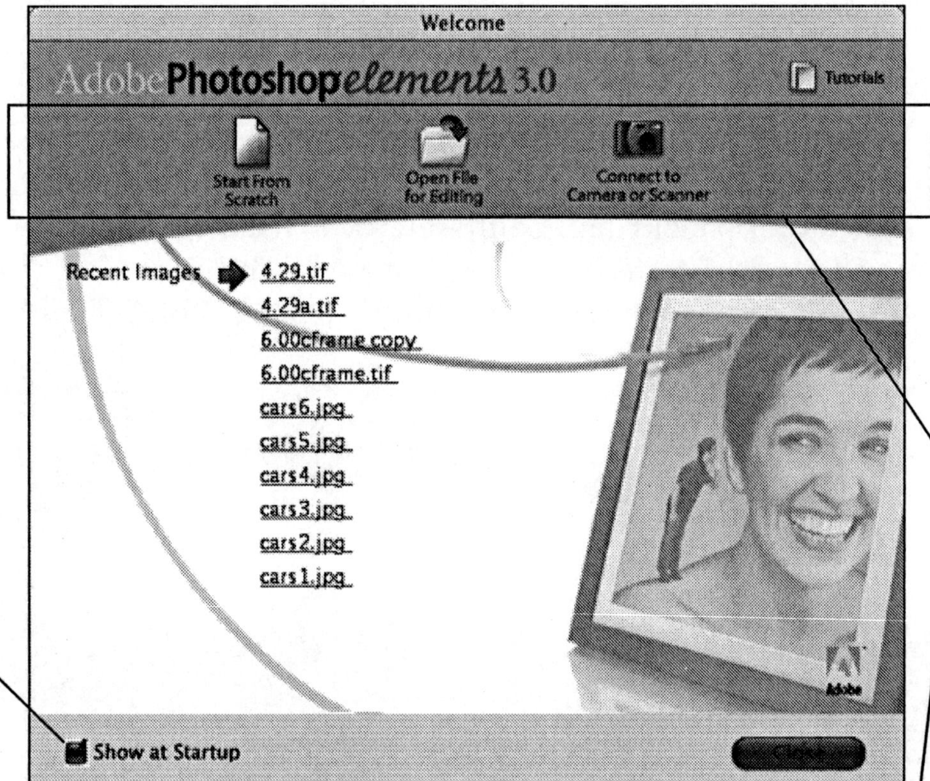

Check here if you want the Welcome window to open when PE opens. You will be able to access it again if you close it.

The Welcome window displays commonly performed photo editing tasks.

Windows Welcome Window

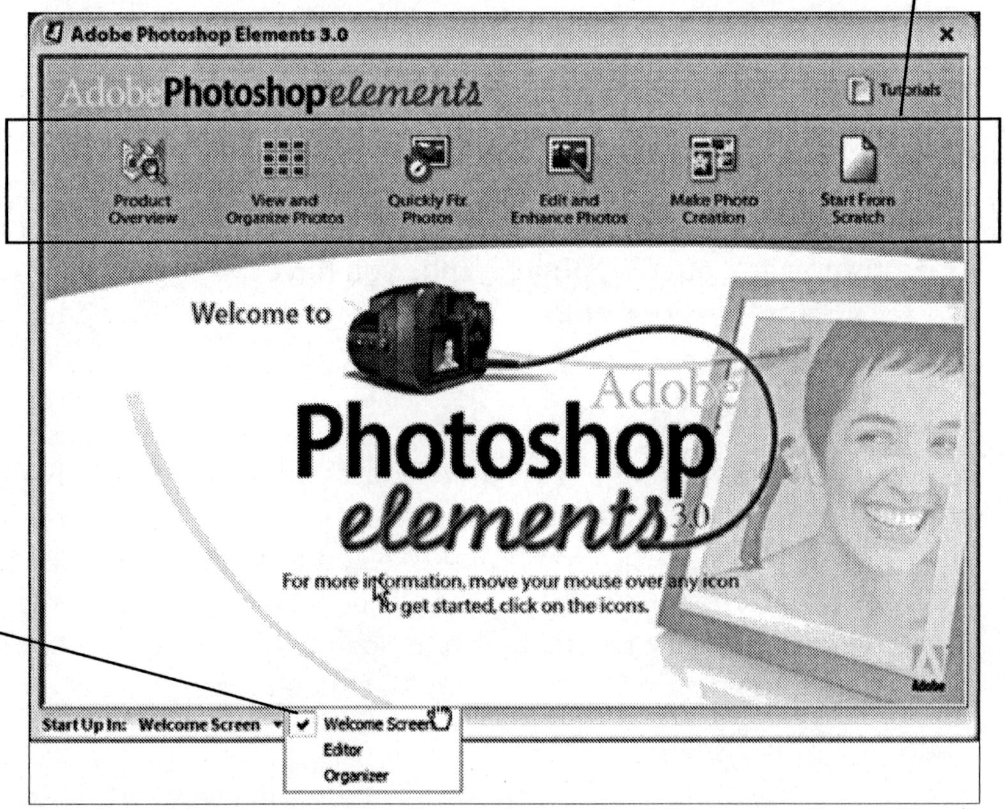

Choose from this drop-down menu how you want PE to open.

The Photoshop Elements Work Area

The work area opens automatically in Windows when you choose Edit and Enhance a Photograph in the Welcome window. It opens automatically on the Macintosh system when you close the Welcome window. Once the work area window is open, you have the choice of using one of two workspaces to edit your photos: Quick Fix or Standard Edit. A workspace is the way the work area window is set up for you to perform your tasks. It's similar to the way you would set up your desk when you sit down to work.

- The Quick Fix workspace has many of the basic tools for correcting color and lighting. It is a great place to begin fixing your photos, especially if you are new to image editing, because the tasks are automated in a step-by-step process.
- The Standard Edit workspace has tools to correct color problems, create special effects, and enhance photos. Using this workspace requires more experience with the program because the tasks are not as automated as those in the Quick Fix workspace.

Shortcuts Bar
Menu Bar
Toolbar
Editing Space
Quick Fix Button
Quick Fix Panel
Photoshop Elements File Edit Image Enhance Layer Select Filter View Window Help
Sun 8:15 AM
Type a question for help
Quick Fix
Standard Edit
Actual Pixels
Fit On Screen
Print Size
After
Reset
General Fixes
Rotate:
Smart Fix:
Auto
Amount
Lighting
Levels:
Contrast:
Lighten Shadows
Darken Highlights
Midtone Contrast
Color
Color:
Saturation
Hue
Temperature
Tint
Sharpen
Sharpen:
Amount
View: After Only
Photo Bin
More
8.00c.tif
1 file in bin
Photo Bin
Before/After View

The Quick Fix Workspace

The Quick Fix workspace guides you step by step through the photo editing process. You will use this feature for many of the exercises in this lesson. In this section, you will learn about some of the prominent features in the Quick Fix workspace.

Menu Bar The menu bar contains menus for performing specific tasks. The menus are organized by topic; for example, the Enhance menu contains commands for working with photo enhancements, like improving color.

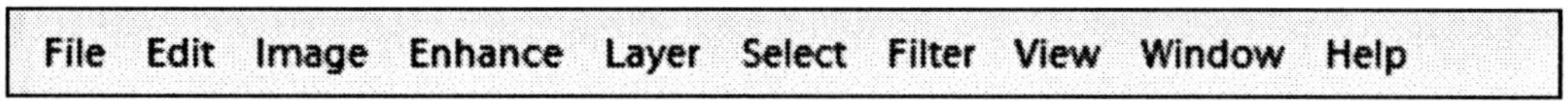

Windows Photoshop Elements Menu Bar

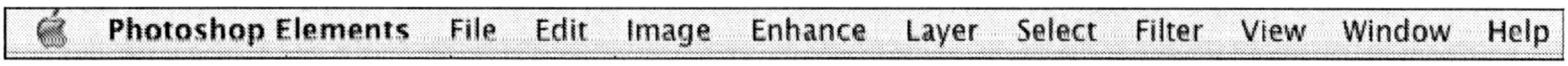

Macintosh Photoshop Elements Menu Bar

Shortcuts Bar The shortcuts bar displays buttons for implementing commands also found in the menu bar. For instance the File→Open command is found in both the menu bar and the shortcuts bars. To see the name of a button, hover the pointer over the button to make a ToolTip appears.

Click the Help Contents button in the shortcuts bar to open the Photoshop Elements Help system. Here, you can find answers to questions and instructions for completing common tasks.

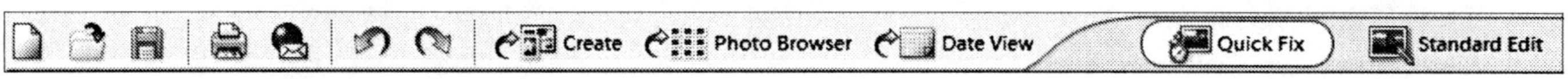

Windows Shortcuts Bar

Macintosh Shortcuts Bar

Toolbox The toolbox is small but it holds important tools helpful for editing images. The zoom tool, for example, allows you to zoom in and out of the picture you are working on so you can see parts of it more clearly.

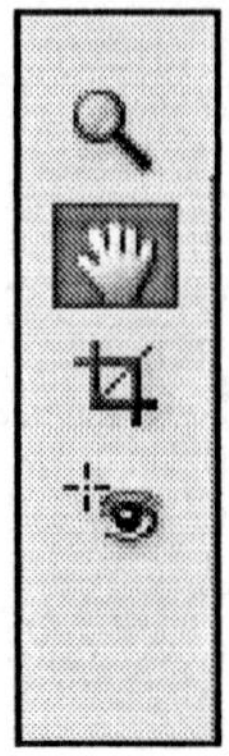

Palettes The palettes, located on the right side of the workspace, contain commands to edit and modify pictures. These commands are also found in the menu bar but they are more easily accessed through palettes. Through palettes you can, for example, rotate a picture. The palettes are grouped for easy access and workspace management.

Palettes in the Quick Fix workspace

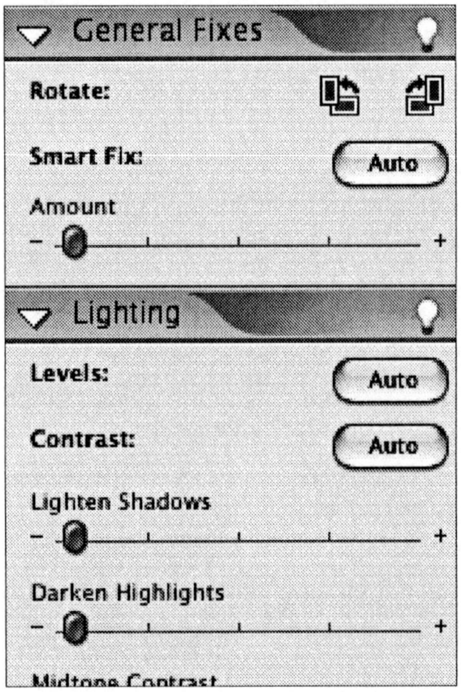

Palettes in the Standard Edit workspace

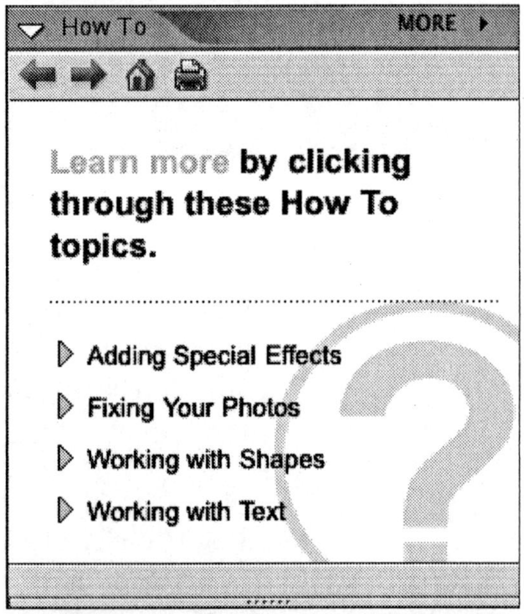

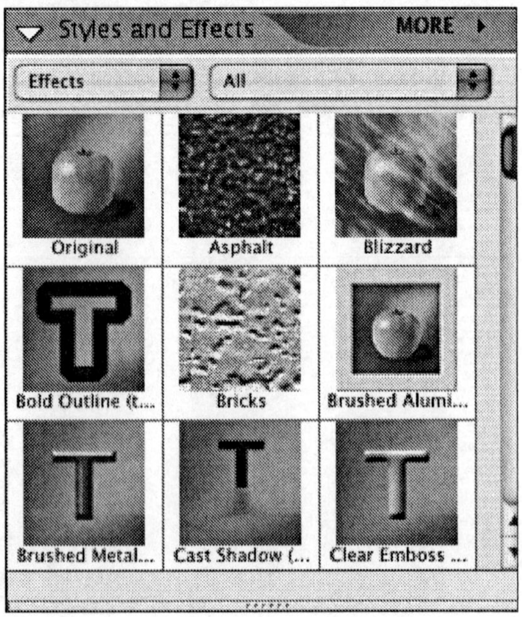

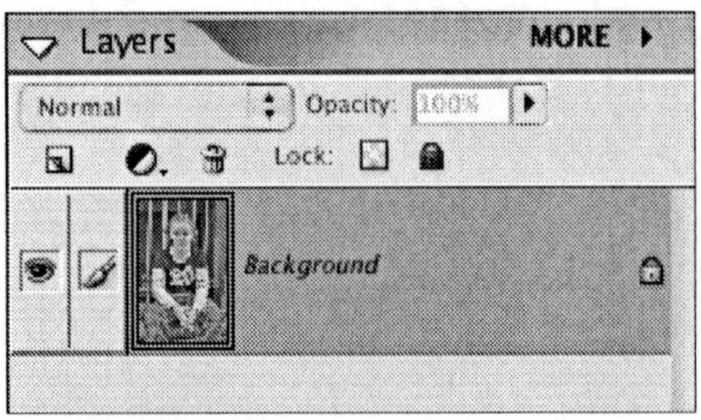

Palette Bin The palette bin helps you organize the palettes in your work area. It is a storage area for keeping palettes easy to find and use.

Photo Bin The photo bin, located at the bottom of the Standard Edit and Quick Fix workspaces, displays thumbnails of opened images. This feature keeps track of the images you have opened, thus allowing you to easily find and edit them. The photo bin includes controls that let you open and close, hide, duplicate, and rotate images.

HANDS-ON 8.1A Open a Photo (Windows XP)

Before You Begin: If you are using Windows XP, follow this exercise. If you are running Macintosh OS X, skip to Hands-On 8.1B on page 188.

In this exercise, you will download a photo from a Web page, and then load it into Photoshop Elements for editing.

Download a Photo

1. Launch your Web browser and navigate to labpub.com/learn/silver/digphoto/.
2. Right-click the Download a Photo link and choose Save Target As or Save Link As from the pop-up context menu according to the following examples.

Internet Explorer

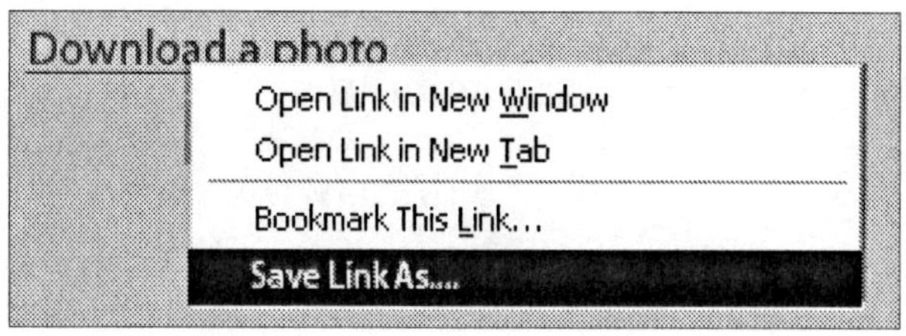

Firefox

Your browser may prompt you for a filename and location to save the file.

3. Save the file to the Desktop. Choose Yes if you are prompted to replace an existing version of the file. (If your browser does not prompt you for a save location, it most likely will save the file to the Desktop.)
4. Close the browser window.

Launch Photoshop Elements

5. Choose Start→All Programs→Adobe Photoshop Elements. (The name may vary slightly according to the version of the program installed on your computer.)

   Windows launches the program. Depending on how it is configured, a Welcome window may appear.

6. Choose the Edit and Enhance Photos option if the Welcome window is visible. Otherwise, continue to step 7.

7. Click the Open  button on the toolbar.

8. Click the Desktop button on the right side of the Open window, and then double-click the Anna010 image file.

   PE displays the file in the editing area of the program window.

Skip the next exercise and continue reading Editing Your Photographs section on page 190.

HANDS-ON 8.1B Open a Photo (Macintosh OS X)

Before You Begin: If you are using Macintosh OS X, follow this exercise. If you are running Windows XP, go back to Hands-On 8.1A on page 187.

In this exercise, you will download a photo from a Web page, and then load it into Photoshop Elements for editing.

Download a Photo

1. Launch your Web browser and navigate to labpub.com/learn/silver/digphoto/.

2. To display the pop-up menu, use [Ctrl]+click on the Download a Photo link. Then, choose Download Linked File As.

Your browser may prompt you for a filename and location to save the file.

3. Save the file to the Desktop. (If your browser does not prompt you for a save location, it most likely will save the file to the Desktop.)

   The Downloads window may be displayed while the file is saved to the Desktop. This may take a few minutes.

4. Close the Downloads and the browser windows.

Launch Photoshop Elements

5. Choose Go→Applications in the Finder's menu bar, and then follow these steps to open Photoshop Elements:

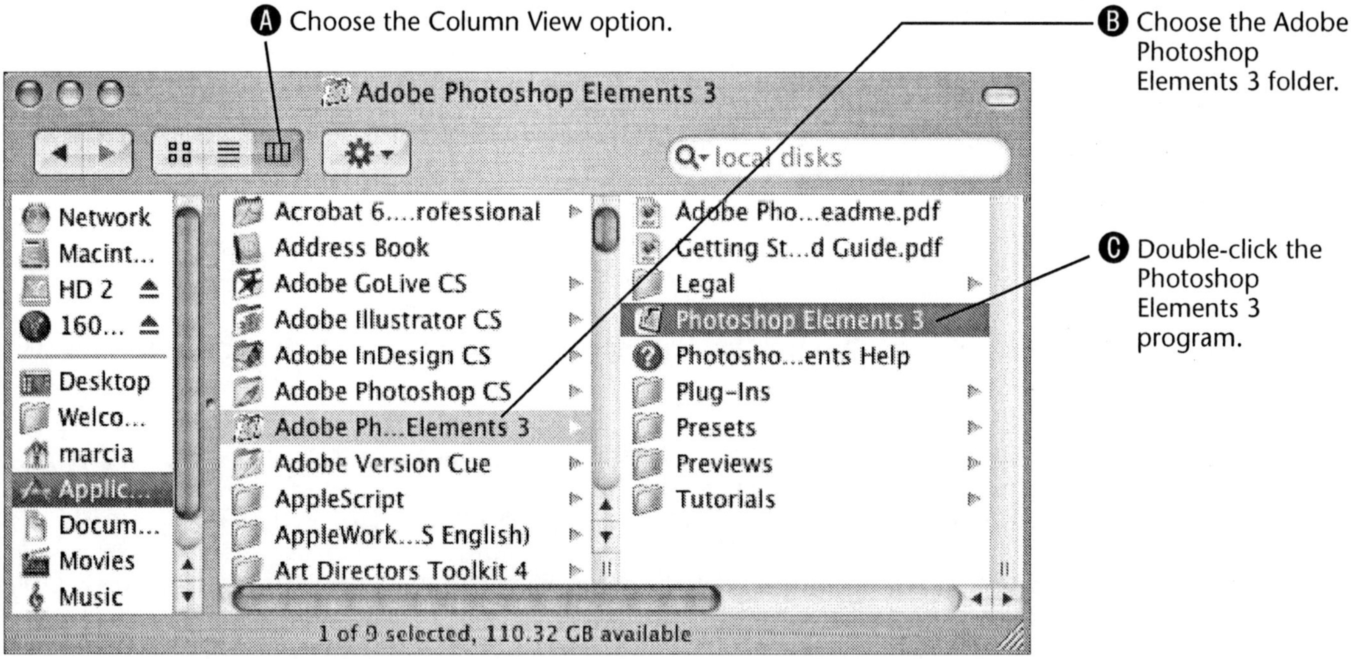

The PE program window appears. Depending on how the program is configured, you may see a Welcome window.

6. Close the Welcome window if it is visible.

7. Click the Open button on the shortcut bar.

   The Open window appears.

8. Navigate to the Desktop, and then double-click the Anna010 image file.

   PE displays the file in the editing area of the program window.

Editing Your Photographs

Photoshop Elements offers a tremendous variety of commands, tools, and settings to adjust color and brightness, crop photos, create special effects, and much more. It is Photoshop's little brother (or sister). It contains all of the features needed for editing photos and leaves out features that only professional photographers would use. You have the option of using the features in automatic modes (Quick Fix workspace) or manual controls (Standard Edit workspace). Sounds a lot like a digital camera, doesn't it?

Editing a Photo

The first step in the editing process is to choose which photos you want to correct and enhance. Organizing and managing your image files are important parts of the editing process. Try the following tasks before working on individual pictures in PE:

- Locate the photographs you are considering editing and display them in Preview on the computer.
- Scroll through the images and, without thinking, jot down the names of the ones that grab you.
- Save the ones you picked in a new folder named Picks.
- Open the Picks folder in Preview and choose a photo to edit.
- Analyze it for what you think it needs to make it a better photograph: Does it need cropping? Is it too light or dark? Does it have a color cast?

TIP! You will be much more informed and prepared for the next step in the editing process if you take time to analyze your pictures for editing needs before beginning your work.

Common Editing Tasks

There is a suggested sequence of tasks that works best for editing pictures because one part of the editing process builds on the next. If you follow this sequence, you will not have to repeat a task and your photographs will look more natural. For instance, if you do the last task first (sharpening), you will cause the defects (dust spots, unwanted areas) to become larger and darker, and it will take more time to fix than if you had corrected them before sharpening.

The following Editing Tasks: When and Why to Use Them Quick Reference table gives recommendations for the effective flow of editing tasks.

The Quick Fix Panel

The Quick Fix Panel is a group of four palettes located on the right side of the Quick Fix workspace. Each palette contains automatic and semi-automatic commands for different aspects of the editing tasks. It is a convenient and easy way to begin using the editing features of PE. There are four palettes, and each contains subtopics and controls for editing photos. The first palette is used for general editing commands: rotating a picture and automatically adjusting the overall color balance and contrast.

NOTE! These are not rules about how or when to complete an editing task, only suggestions.

QUICK REFERENCE: Editing Tasks: When and Why to Use Them

Task (in order of sequence)	When to Use	Quick Fix Workspace Tool or Command
Analyze your picture for cropping, contrast, color, and sharpness	You first choose a photograph for editing	None (use your eyes, brain, and intuition)
Rotate the photo	You want to work with the photo in another orientation	Quick Fix→General Fixes→Rotate
Save a copy of the original photo	You think you might want to go back to it if you don't like what you did in the editing process	File→Save As (name the file Name.original)
Crop the photo	You would like to remove distracting or excess parts of the picture	Crop Tool
Adjust the Contrast	The picture does not have strong enough dark or light tones, or you would like the picture to have more "punch"	QuickFix→Lighting→ Levels /Contrast
Correct Color	There is an unwanted color cast or the colors are not exactly what you want	Quick Fix→Color
Sharpen the photo	You want the picture to look sharper and more focused	Quick Fix→Sharpen

Before and After View

Photoshop Elements has a fabulous feature in both the Standard and Quick Fix workspaces called Before and After view. It's located (almost hidden) right above the photo bin and below the open image. Choosing Before and After view lets you see how the photograph changes as you make corrections and enhancements.

Rotating a Photo

A picture opened in the workspace may come in with the incorrect orientation, depending on how the camera was held when the picture was taken. If you take a picture of someone and hold the camera vertically (Portrait mode) it looks right in the camera, but the review processes in the camera and the computer show everything horizontally (Landscape mode). Some cameras do have a feature for rotating photos in the camera, but that takes extra time. PE has a Rotate command in both the Quick Fix and Standard Edit workspaces.

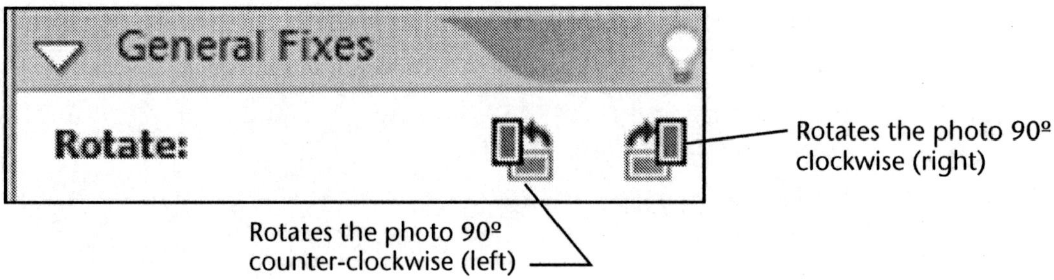

Cropping a Photo

Cropping is a great way to emphasize a subject by cutting away distracting or unnecessary elements from a picture. Even though you might pay attention to this when reviewing your pictures in the camera, deciding where to crop will be easier to see once the photo is viewed in Photoshop Elements. How much you can enlarge the cropped area depends on resolution and compression (image quality) choices made at the time of exposure.

Cropping allows you to cut away unnecessary elements of a photo.

QUICK REFERENCE: Cropping and Rotating Photos

Task	Procedure
Rotate a Photo	• Open the photo. • Choose Image→Rotate→[desired rotation] from the menu bar. • Choose Edit→Undo, if necessary.
Crop a Photo	• Open the photo. • Display the Quick Fix panel. • Choose the Cropping tool from the palette. • Drag a selection around the portion of the photo you wish to keep. • Double-click inside the selection or tap Enter or Return to complete the crop command. • Choose Edit→Undo, if necessary.

HANDS-ON 8.2 Edit a Photo

In this exercise, you will crop the photo and use the Quick Fix panel to perform some automated color correction.

Before You Begin: The Anna010 file should still be open.

NOTE! Because PE functions so similarly on both Windows and Macintosh computers, there is only one version of this exercise.

Use the Quick Fix Panel

PE groups many of the most useful editing commands (including image rotate) in the Quick Fix panel.

1. Click the Quick Fix tab on the top-right side of the PE window.

PE displays the Quick Fix panel and its commands. This panel displays settings for brightness/contrast, color, and sharpness (focus). It is very useful because you can choose a combination of automated and semi-automated commands to edit your photos. PE also allows you to set a before and after comparison view and describes what each command does as you choose them so you can clearly see the effect of each adjustment.

TIP! Adjustment controls are also found in the Enhance menu.

2. Set the View option at the bottom-left corner of the Window to Before and After (Portrait).

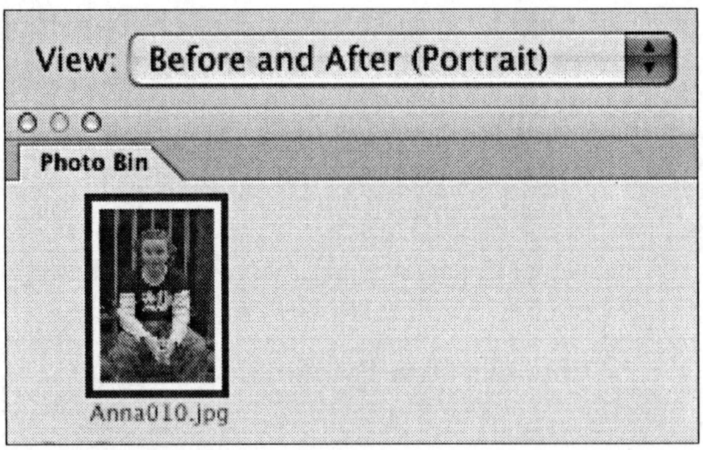

PE displays the two photos side by side. This makes it easy to compare your edited version with the original.

Crop the Photo

Now you will crop some unnecessary portions of the photo.

3. Follow these steps to crop the photo:

Ⓐ Click the Fit On Screen button near the top-left corner of the PE window to resize the photos to the proper proportion.

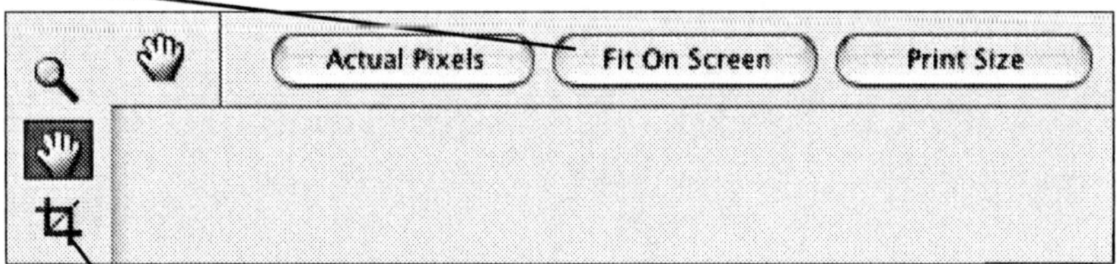

Ⓑ Choose the Crop tool.

Ⓒ In After (not Before) view, drag a selection box around the subject of the photo.

Ⓓ Double-click anywhere within the selection to complete the crop command.

PE cuts away the unselected portion of the photo.

Use Smart Fix

PE includes some highly automated quick fix commands. The most automatic fix is the Smart Fix button near the top of the Quick Fix panel.

4. Click the Auto button for Smart Fix.

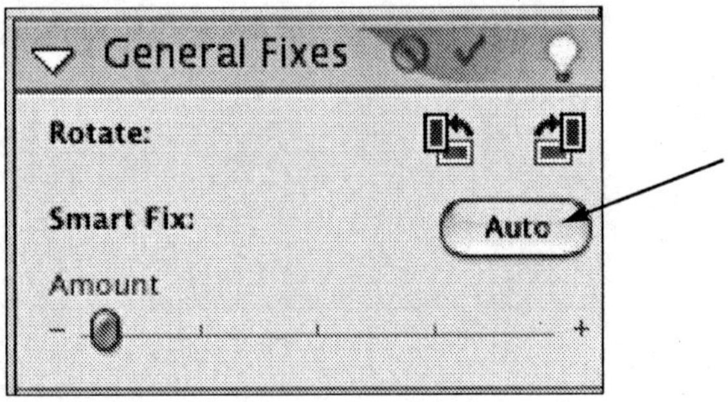

PE applies various fixes to the photo. This is quick and highly automatic but not necessarily the optimal adjustment for the photo. In the next exercise, you will learn how to apply individual fixes for an even better result.

5. Click the Undo button on the toolbar.

PE undoes the Smart Fix command.

Making Basic Photo Adjustments

Once you have brought your photos into Photoshop Elements you have several choices for correcting and enhancing the lighting, color, and sharpness. You may apply these adjustments automatically by pressing one button or use the sliders in each adjustment to control the amount of adjustment.

About Auto Adjustments

PE has several fully automatic and semi-automatic lighting and color correction commands. Choosing fully automatic lets the program make the best correction, not unlike using auto adjustments in the camera. Much of the time the fully automatic adjustments work quite well, and are very helpful for beginners.

Lighting Adjustments

Lighting adjustments refer to correcting and enhancing contrast in a photo. The Lighting palette in the Quick Fix panel contains five automatic and semi-automatic controls you can use to change the contrast of a picture:

- **Levels:** Try this command for correcting a color cast or to add more contrast. Moving a slider increases or decreases the amount of this adjustment.
- **Contrast:** This adjustment affects contrast but not color. Use this control when your colors are good but you want to increase the contrast (darks darker, lights lighter).
- **Lighten Shadows:** Dragging the slider lightens the dark areas of your photo without affecting the highlights or pure blacks.
- **Darken Highlights:** Dragging the slider darkens the lightest areas of your photo without affecting the shadows or pure white areas.
- **Midtone Contrast:** Dragging the slider adjusts the contrast of the tonal values that are about halfway between pure white and pure black (midtones).

Color Adjustments

Color adjustments are used to correct and alter the color in a photograph, from slight changes for correction purposes to extreme color shifts for creative endeavors. There are five adjustments within the Color palette:

- **Color:** The slider adjusts the overall color and contrast of an image, reducing color casts and color imbalance.
- **Saturation:** This control makes colors more vivid or more muted.
- **Hue:** This control actually shifts colors to an entirely different color.
- **Temperature:** This control makes colors warmer (red) or cooler (blue) and is very useful for reducing color casts.
- **Tint:** This control makes color more green or magenta and is used to fine tune the colors after using the Temperature control.

Sharpening Photos

It would be wonderful if we could take an out-of-focus picture and miraculously make it sharp and in focus. However, the sharpening feature in PE does not actually sharpen. Instead, it chooses edges of high contrast within the photograph and darkens the dark pixels on the edge and lightens the light pixels on the edge. This gives the illusion that the picture is sharper and more in focus. How many pixels are chosen and how much they are "sharpened" can be controlled with the slider that is part of the control.

The Auto Sharpen control sharpens photos to give them the appearance of being more in focus. Be careful not to overdo this control. It shows up more in print than in the computer, so what looks good on the monitor might be too much in print.

TIP! This lesson can only scratch the surface of what Photoshop Elements can do. To learn more editing techniques and creative controls available in PE find a book or enroll in a class in the Credit or Continuing Education department of your local community college.

QUICK REFERENCE: Applying Photo Adjustments

Task	Procedure
Manually Adjust a Photo	• Open the photo. • Display the Quick Fix panel. • Set the view to Before/After. • Use the Auto buttons or make manual adjustments as desired. • Choose File→Save As from the menu bar. • Change the filename.

HANDS-ON 8.3 Adjust a Photo Manually

In this exercise, you will manually edit the contrast and color of your photograph.

Before You Begin: The Anna010 file should be open. The Quick Fix tab should be displayed and the View set to Before and After (Portrait).

Adjust the Lighting

First you will adjust the lighting levels of the photo.

1. In the Lighting section, click the Auto button for Contrast.

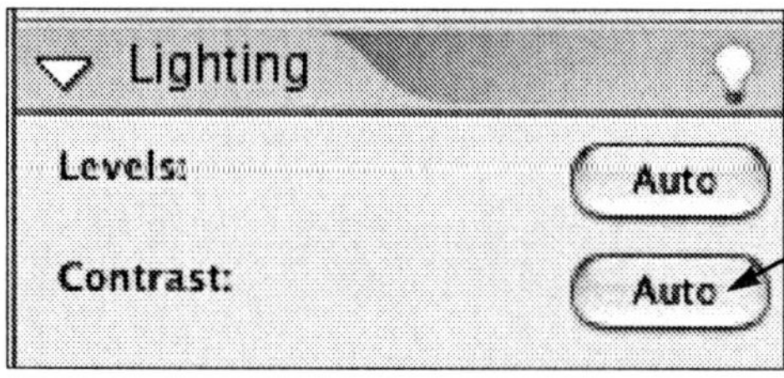

This adjustment automatically gives more contrast to your picture. The darks get darker and the lights get lighter. However, the color of the picture is unaffected.

TIP! Start with Lighting (contrast) correction before making any other adjustment.

2. Click the Undo button if you did not like the result of the Auto Contrast command.

   Unlike the slider controls, the standard Undo button works for the various Auto buttons in the Quick Fix panel.

3. Click the Auto button for Levels. Click the Undo button if you don't like the results.

   Auto levels adjust contrast and may also affect color.

4. Click the Help Contents button for the Lighting section.

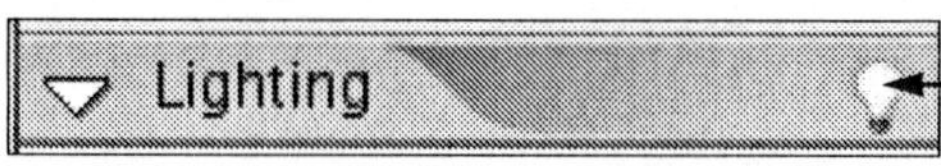

PE displays a Help window directly related to the adjustments you can make in the Quick Fix panel.

5. Read the descriptions for the Lighten Shadows, Darken Highlights, and Midtone Contrast settings, and then close the Help window.

6. Try moving the sliders in the Lighting section to see how these adjustments affect the picture. Click the Cancel button after each slider move if you don't like the results.

   These adjustments affect various ranges of the image brightness. You control the amount. It is recommended for slight adjustment.

Adjust the Color

7. Follow these steps to adjust the color automatically:

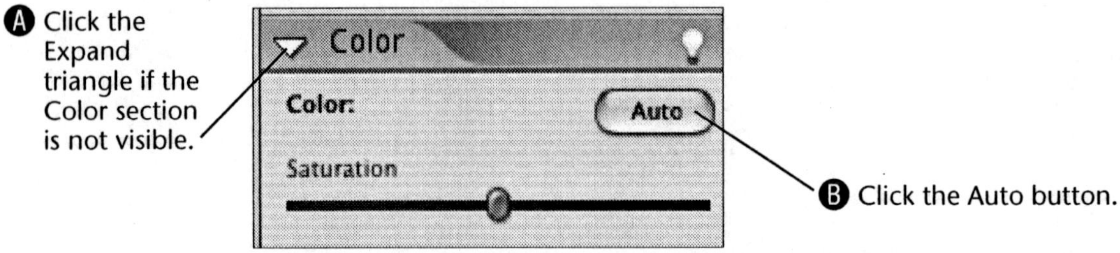

PE analyzes the picture and fixes color problems that may have not been corrected in the digital camera.

In the next two steps, you will manually adjust the vividness (saturation) and color (hue). Unlike automatic adjustments, you control the amount of change in the photo.

8. Follow these steps to manually adjust the Saturation setting:

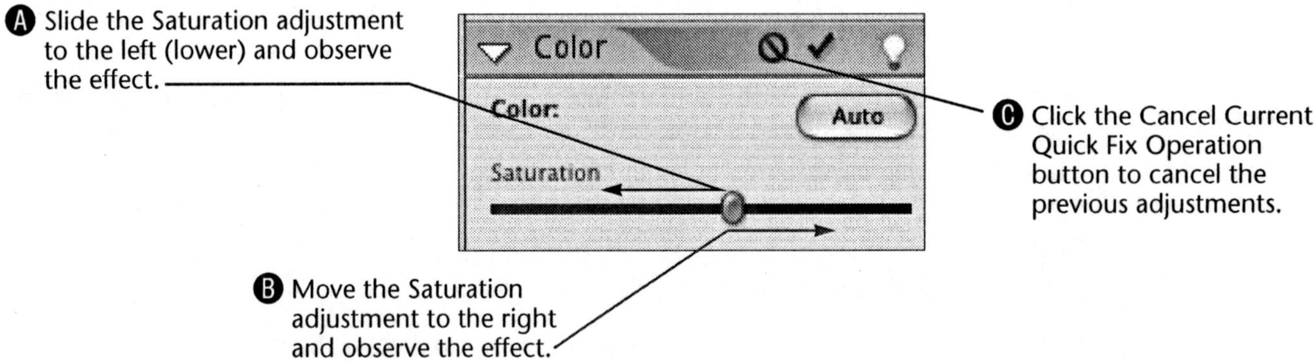

You should use the Cancel button on the Quick Fix panel rather than the Undo button on the toolbar to cancel manual adjustments in this panel.

9. Drag the Saturation adjustment slider to a setting that looks good to you.
10. Drag the Hue adjustment to the right and left, and then leave it at a setting that looks good to you.
11. Experiment with settings for Temperature and Tint.
12. Click the Commit Current Quick Fix button.

    PE resets the slider controls to the center but keeps the manual adjustments you've applied thus far.

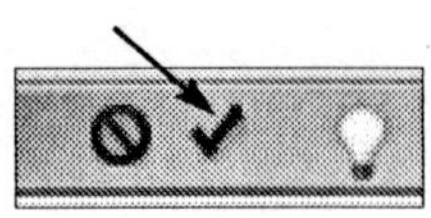

Adjust the Sharpness and Save Your Edits

13. Click the Auto button for Sharpness near the bottom of the Quick Fix panel.

    This setting sharpens details in your photo to make the picture look more in focus.

14. Follow the step for your computer:

    - **Windows XP:** Click the Save button on the toolbar.
    - **Macintosh OS X:** Choose File→Save As in the menu bar.

    PE displays various options for saving your picture. In this case, you will save your edits as a copy.

15. Follow these steps to save a copy of the picture:

A Place a checkmark in the As a Copy box.

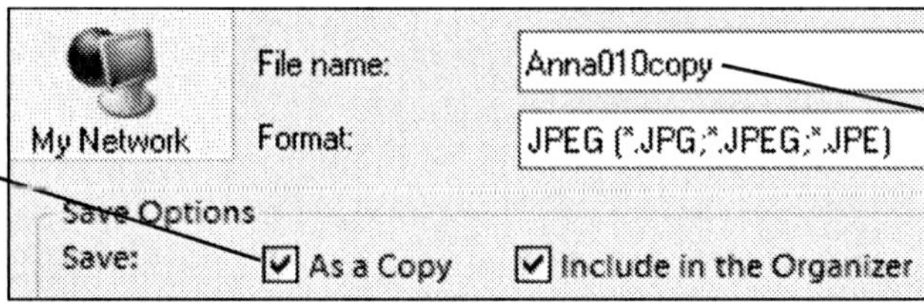

B Notice that PE automatically adds the word "copy" to the end of the filename. This leaves the original version of the photo intact.

16. Click the Save button.

    PE displays options to save the picture in its JPEG format. In this case, you will leave the default settings as is. In Lesson 9, Outputting to Printers and the Web, you will adjust settings such as Quality to reduce the size of the picture for attaching to email.

17. Click OK to save the picture with the default settings.

    PE saves the edited file to the Desktop.

NOTE! At this point, you should move the Anna photos you have been working with in this lesson from the Desktop to your file storage location. This will ensure that you do not lose track of them.

Concepts Review

True/False Questions

			Page number
1. An overexposed photograph is a result of not enough light hitting the sensor.	**true**	**false**	_______
2. Using color adjustments in PE can fine tune white balance adjustments in the camera.	**true**	**false**	_______
3. The palettes in the Quick Fix workspace are identical to palettes in the Standard Edit workspace.	**true**	**false**	_______
4. Using the Standard Edit and Quick Fix workspaces is similar to using manual and automatic controls on your camera.	**true**	**false**	_______
5. You cannot rotate a picture using the Quick Fix panel.	**true**	**false**	_______
6. You have some control over the adjustments in the Quick Fix panel.	**true**	**false**	_______
7. Once you have made an adjustment in the Quick Fix Panel you cannot undo it.	**true**	**false**	_______
8. The Sharpening control will make an out-of-focus picture sharp and in focus.	**true**	**false**	_______
9. An underexposed photograph is a result of not enough light hitting the sensor.	**true**	**false**	_______
10. You cannot fix a photo that has incorrect exposure.	**true**	**false**	_______

Multiple Choice Questions

1. Which of the following can you fix in Photoshop Elements?

   Page number: ______

   a. A picture that is too light

   b. A dull looking picture

   c. A picture with a color cast

   d. All of the above

2. The first step in the editing process is to ________.

   Page number: ______

   a. crop

   b. analyze the photograph to determine what needs editing

   c. choose a photograph

   d. None of the above

3. What do lighting adjustments in the Quick Fix Panel correct?

   Page number: ______

   a. A picture that is too dark

   b. Color cast

   c. A picture is dull looking

   d. All of the above

4. Cropping is a great way to ________.

   Page number: ______

   a. emphasize a subject

   b. increase resolution

   c. remove distracting elements

   d. All of the above

Skill Builders

SKILL BUILDER 8.1 Open and Edit a Photo

In this exercise, you will manually edit the contrast and color of your photograph.

Open the Photo

1. Start Photoshop Elements.
2. Follow the step for the computer you are using:
   - **Windows XP:** Choose Quickly Fix Photos if the Welcome window is visible.
   - **Macintosh OS X:** Close the Welcome window if it is visible.
3. Click the Open button on the toolbar, navigate to your file storage location, and then open one of your photos.
4. Make sure that the Quick Fix mode is chosen, and then choose Before and After (Portrait) in the View box near the bottom of the PE window.

   The Before and After view will already be displayed if it was left this way the last time a photo was edited.

Experiment with Various Quick Fixes

5. Follow these steps to use the General Fixes adjustments:

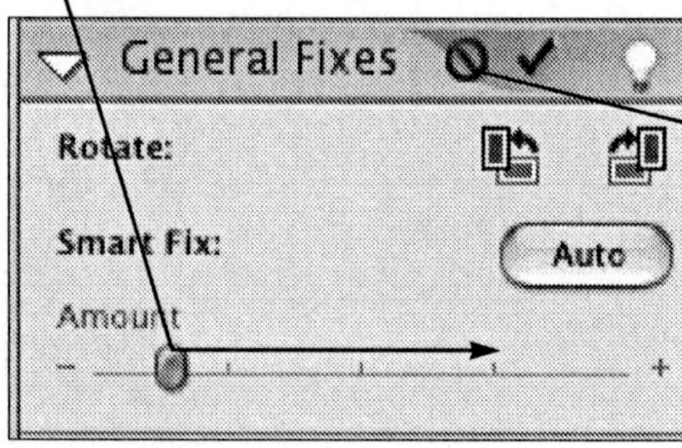

6. Use the slider controls on the Color section to experiment with various effects:
   - Use the Cancel button to cancel a specific effect.
   - Use the Reset button just above the After photo if you want to cancel all of the effects after using the Cancel button in one of the Adjustment palettes.
7. Click the Reset button after clicking the Cancel button in one of the palettes.

   PE cancels all of the effects you've tried so far.

Adjust the Lighting

8. Use the three slider controls in the Lighting section to observe the effects of each.

9. Click the Commit Current Quick Fix Operation button when you find settings that look good.

   PE adjusts the photo to your current settings. All future adjustments will use this version of the photo as the starting point.

10. Drag the Smart Fix slider to the right and notice that the effects of this control differ from what you observed in step 5.

    The new lighting adjustments you committed in step 9 alter the effects of the Smart Fix adjustments.

Save a Black and White Version of the Picture

11. Drag the Saturation slider control in the Color section all the way to the left.

    A minimum color saturation setting converts the picture to black and white.

12. Follow the step for your computer:

    - **Windows XP:** Click the Save button on the toolbar.
    - **Macintosh OS X:** Choose File→Save As in the menu bar.

13. Now follow these steps to save a copy of the picture with a new name:

Ⓐ Place a checkmark in the As a Copy box.

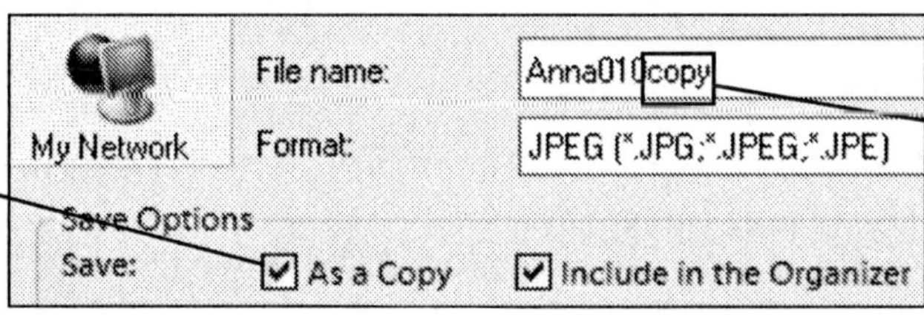

Ⓑ Type **-bw** in place of the word "copy."

14. Click the Save button.

    PE displays options to save the picture.

15. Make sure that the image quality is set to Maximum, and then click OK to finish saving the picture. (You will learn about setting quality settings in Lesson 9, Outputting to Printers and the Web.)

    PE saves the edited file.

16. Choose File→Close from the menu bar.

    PE prompts whether you wish to save the edited version of the photo.

17. Follow the step for your computer:
    - **Windows XP:** Choose No to preserve the original (unedited) version of the photo.
    - **Macintosh OS X:** Choose Don't Save to preserve the original (unedited) version of the photo.

    PE closes the file without saving any of your edits.

SKILL BUILDER 8.2 Crop a Photo

In this exercise, you will reopen and crop the photo you edited in Skill Builder 8.1.

1. Choose File→Open Recently Edited File from the menu bar.

    PE displays a list of the files you've recently opened in the program.
2. Choose the file you edited in Skill Builder 8.1 if it is visible. Otherwise, choose another file from the list or use the normal File→Open command.
3. Make sure PE is in Quick Fix mode and that the View box is set to Before and After (Portrait).
4. Choose the Cropping tool from the toolbox on the left side of the program window.
5. Drag a selection box around an area of interest in the picture.

    PE displays a marquee (marching ants) around your selection and darkens the area of the photo that will be cropped.
6. Double-click within the selection to complete the crop command.

    PE cuts out the area outside your selection.

Save the Cropped Version of the Photo

7. Follow the step for your computer:
    - **Windows XP:** Click the Save button on the toolbar.
    - **Macintosh OS X:** Choose File→Save As in the menu bar.
8. Place a checkmark in the As a Copy box, then change the end of the filename to read: **`-cropped`**
9. Click the Save button, and then click OK.
10. Choose File→Close from the menu bar. Choose No when PE asks if you wish to save the edited version.

    PE closes the file without your edit.

SKILL BUILDER 8.3 Apply a Filter

In this exercise, you will reopen the photo you edited in Skill Builder 8.1 and experiment with various PE filters. Then you will save a copy of the photo with one of the filter effects applied to it.

1. Choose File→Open Recently Edited File from the menu bar.

   PE displays a list of the files you've recently opened in the program.

2. Choose the file you edited in Skill Builder 8.1 (not the cropped version from Skill Builder 8.2) if it is visible. Otherwise, choose another file from the list or use the normal File→Open command.

3. Choose Filter→Filter Gallery... from the menu bar.

   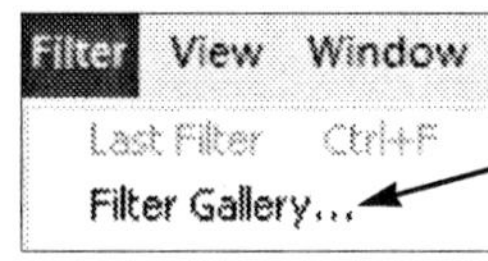

   PE opens a new window displaying the various filter categories and a preview of your photo applying the most recently used filter. Depending on your photo and the portion of it that is visible, you may not see much difference.

4. Follow these steps to arrange your photo in the gallery window:

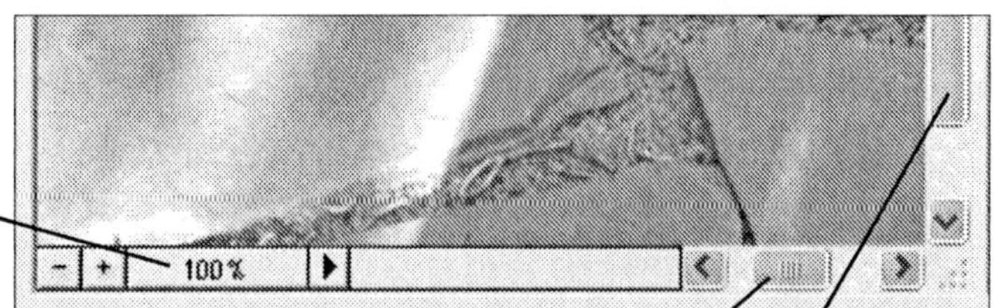

When you are finished, a recognizable and interesting region of your photo should be visible. You can change the zoom and view it later if you wish to focus on the filter's effect on a particular region.

Apply a Filter

Now that you've adjusted the view, you are ready to try a filter. The effect of a filter depends a great deal on the nature of your photo, so this initial filter may not have a visible or very profound effect.

5. Follow these steps to apply the Photocopy filter:

Ⓐ Scroll down the category list and, if necessary, click the Expand button beside the Sketch category so the various filters are visible.

Ⓑ Choose the Photocopy filter.

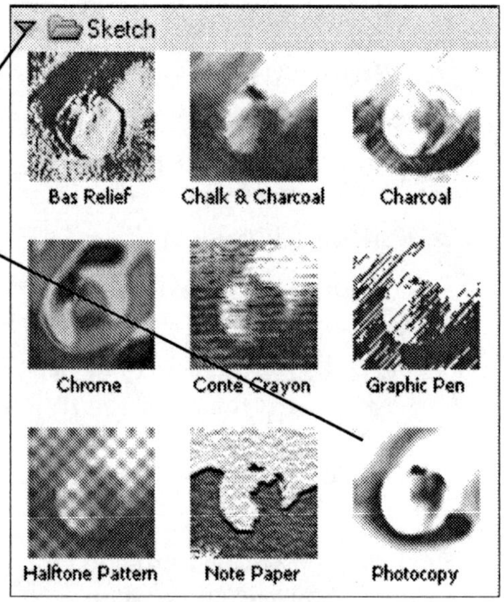

PE displays a preview of the filter on your photo. Every filter has custom settings you can adjust to vary its application. The two for this filter appear in the rightmost column of the window.

6. Follow these steps to adjust the settings of the filter:

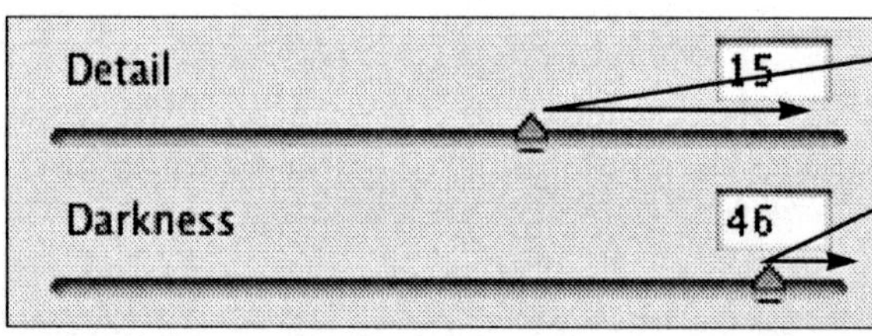

Ⓐ Drag the Detail slider control near the rightmost (high) setting.

Ⓑ Drag the Darkness slider control near the rightmost setting.

These high settings may exaggerate the effect of the filter much more than you like.

7. Experiment with various slider settings until you find a setting that creates an interesting and attractive effect.

Apply Other Filters and Save the Photo

8. Expand other filter categories in the center column of the window, and then choose and adjust another filter.
9. Click OK when you have found a filter and settings you would like to save.
   Photoshop displays the photo with its filter effect beside the Before version of the photo.
10. Follow the step for your computer:
    - **Windows XP:** Click the Save button, place a checkmark in the As a Copy box, and then add the name of the filter to the filename. For example: Mantle – Photocopy filter.
    - **Macintosh OS X:** Choose File→Save As, place a checkmark in the As a Copy box, and then add the name of the filter to the filename. For example: Mantle – Photocopy filter.
11. Click Save, and then click OK.
12. Follow the step for your computer:
    - **Windows XP:** Choose File→Close from the menu bar. Choose No when PE asks if you wish to save changes to the original version of the photo.
    - **Macintosh OS X:** Choose File→Close from the menu bar. Choose Don't Save when PE asks if you wish to save changes to the original version of the photo.

LESSON 9

Outputting to Printers and the Web

There are many output options available for digital photographers, and the number of them is growing by leaps and bounds. When digital cameras first emerged for consumer use, print options were limited: either print it yourself or find a lab that handled digital processing. Today's scene is very different. Self-service digital print kiosks are found in photo labs, photo stores, drug stores, supermarkets, discount stores, and other locations. If you don't like using the self-service kiosk, many locations also offer over-the-counter service, at which, just like at traditional film labs, you drop off a memory card or CD and come back later for prints. Online labs are another option, in which you electronically send your digital files, order prints, and create albums for others to view via the internet—all without leaving your home. Reasonably priced printing systems are available for you to use at home, without a computer. Sending digital photos to friends and family via email and using these images for Web pages is extremely popular. However, knowing how to optimize these digital photos is important for successful delivery. In this lesson, you will learn about the types of print and Web options, how they work, and how to best utilize them for successful prints and Web and email images.

Additional learning resources are available at ***labpub.com/learn/silver/digphoto/***

Case Study

Eleanor has some wonderful photos she took while traveling and is excited about having prints made so she can share them with her friends over the Internet. She discovers a neighborhood digital photo processing lab right in her favorite drug store! She also realizes that even as she travels, she can get prints made in nearby towns. Eleanor learns how to use the self-service digital kiosk and the convenience of dropping off her memory card and coming back to pick up prints.

Eleanor also has a new inkjet printer, and by consulting the instruction booklet that came with the printer, she learns the best settings to use for different paper types and how to get photo-quality prints. She then attends a workshop about resizing photos for the Web and learns how to create high-quality images that will quickly download to her friends' computers. Once she feels knowledgeable about printing and emailing photos, she decides to try online photo labs. Eleanor soon discovers the convenience of this valuable service, not only for ordering prints but also for sharing her photos with friends and family—all done at home with her personal computer.

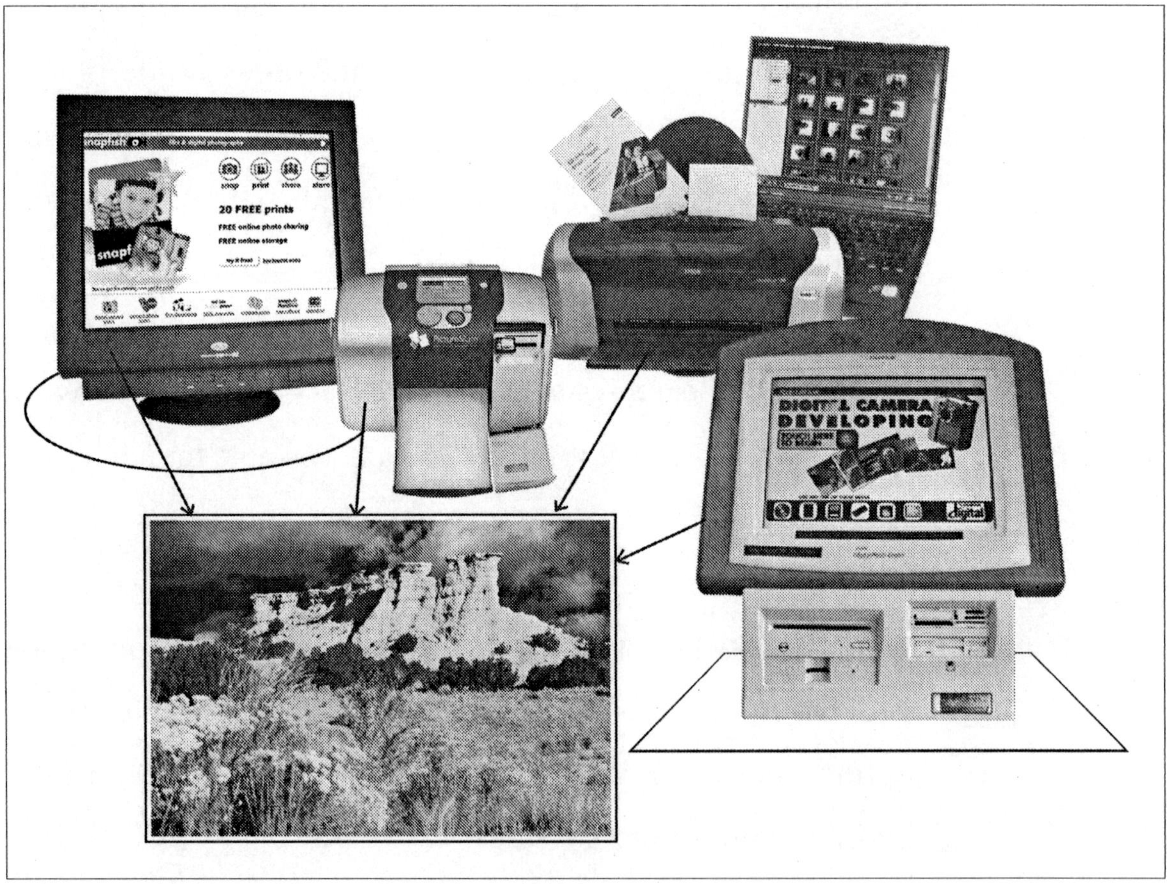

Printing Your Digital Photos

How do you know which print option is right for you? Usually, trying them yourself or reviewing a friend's pictures is a great way to determine which to choose. An important factor in making your decision is how much computer and image editing experience you have. There are pros and cons for each print system. Look at the following table and choose the features that best suit your needs.

QUICK REFERENCE: Working with Print Options

Print Option	Equipment and Supplies Needed	Experience Needed	Approximate Cost per 4 × 6 Print	Advantages	Disadvantages
Personal inkjet printer	Computer, inkjet printer, paper, ink	Computer skills, image-editing software knowledge	Variable	• You can customize and enhance your photos • You don't have to leave your home	• Cost of equipment and supplies • Need computer and software skills
Printers that do not need a computer	Printer, paper, ink	None	29 cents or less	• No other equipment is needed • You can print directly from a memory card or disc	• Paper size limitation on some • Cost of equipment and supplies
Self-service kiosks	None	None. (The lab technician can help you get to know the system or you can use the step-by-step instructions in the kiosk.)	19–29 cents	• No equipment or computer skills necessary • You can easily enhance and correct pictures with the kiosk software	• Less control than if you print yourself with an inkjet printer
Photo Labs (Over-the-counter service)	None	None	29 cents to $1.00	• Familiar: it is just like bringing a roll of film in to be processed	• Picture adjustments may not be available
Online Labs	Computer and internet connection.	Basic computer and web navigation skills.	10–29 cents	• Convenient • Many labs to choose from • Offers a place to store and share your photos	• Need a computer • May be a slow process if you have a slow Internet connection

Personal Inkjet Printers

You can buy a personal inkjet printer for $5,000, $500, or even $50. Some only print 4 × 6 inch prints while others print 24 inches, 36 inches, and larger. You can choose the type of paper you use (glossy, matte, canvas, watercolor, and many more). Inkjet printers are getting larger and less expensive every year.

The quality of early inkjet prints did not match the quality of photographic prints. It was easy to spot an inkjet print because of its graininess. Today that is no longer true. Inkjet print technology has advanced quickly and we can now make photographic-like prints in the comfort of our own homes. So, why doesn't everyone get an inkjet printer and print their own photographs?

- Initial cost of the printer, and even more significant, the continuing cost of ink and paper. These supplies must be replaced frequently if you do a lot of printing, and often it takes more than one try to get the print the way you want it.
- You need some expertise in computer and image editing skills to best utilize the printer technology.
- As in film photography, many photographers are only interested in taking pictures and would rather leave the processing to someone else.

An affordable inkjet printer makes up to 8 × 10 prints.

This more expensive model makes 13 × 19 archival prints.

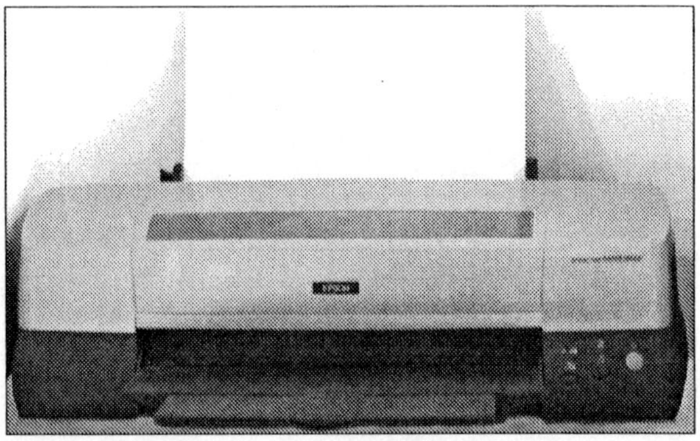

Tips for Buying and Using an Inkjet Printer Consider the following points as you shop for an inkjet printer. Take time to do some research, just as you did when you shopped for your digital camera.

- Choose a printer based on the largest size print you think you will want. If you know your only want 4 × 6 inch prints, then there is no need for a machine that prints larger. However, it's probably a good idea to get one that will print 8 × 10 inch prints so you have that option.

- Printers that come with individual color cartridges are more economical than those with only one large color cartridge (with all the colors) and one smaller black cartridge. With in individual cartridges, you don't have to replace the entire cartridge just because one color is used up—you simply replace that one color cartridge.
- The variety of papers for inkjet printers is almost endless. Generally, it is best to use papers made by the same company that made your printer. However, there are a number of interesting papers worth trying.

TIP! If you are getting poor results from your printer, it might be caused by the type and brand of paper.

- Selecting correct print settings is important for making good quality prints. Read the section in your printer guide (just like reading your camera's instruction manual!) pertaining to print settings and quality.

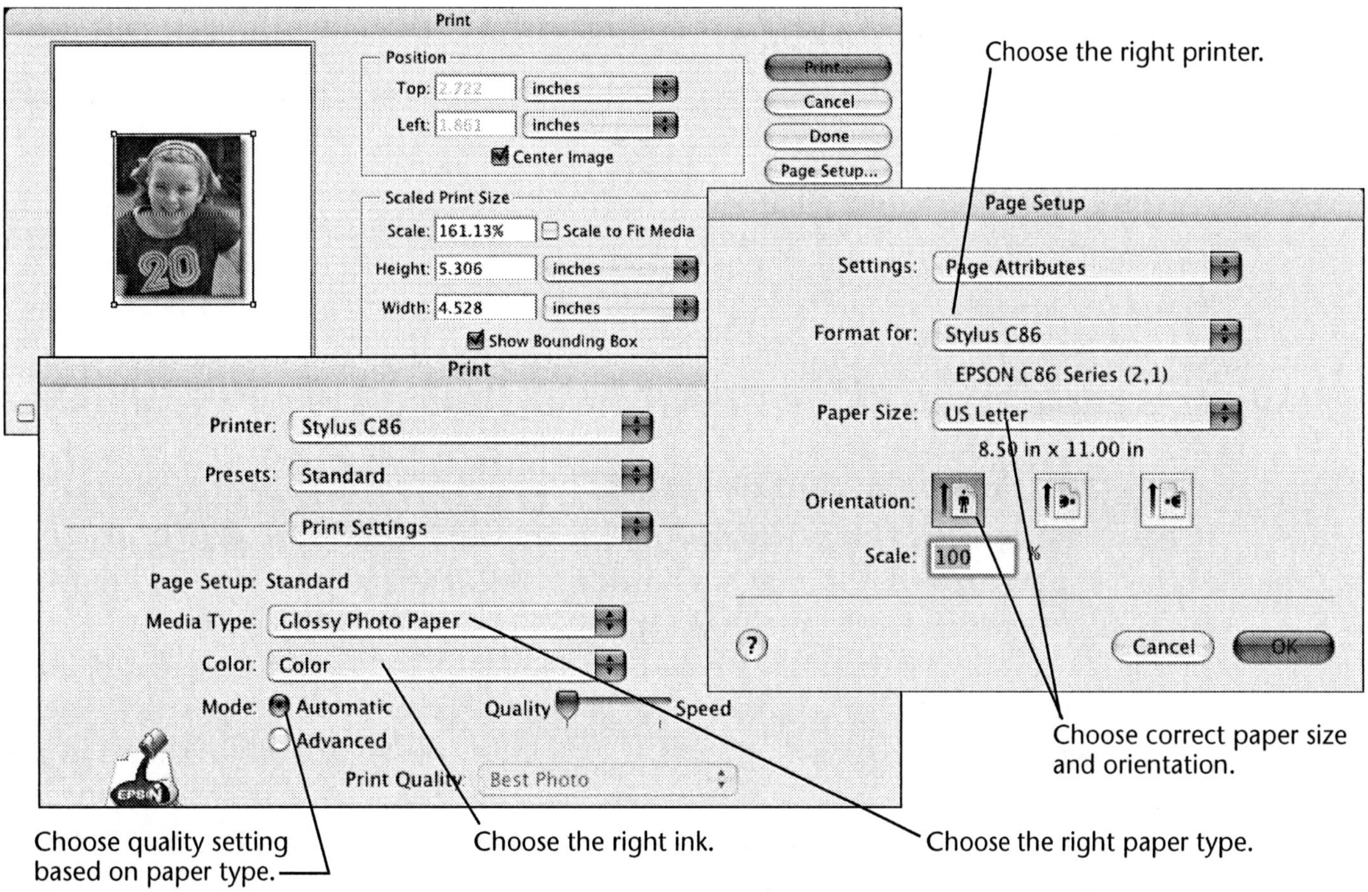

Print dialog boxes for an Epson inkjet printer. Although these settings may not match your printer, they serve as a guide for what to look for.

Printers That Do Not Need Computers

There are many printers on the market that do not require the use of a computer. These are very convenient and a great option if you don't own a computer or if you would rather not learn new software. Basically, you put a memory card in the slot provided on the printer, press a button, and print! Some printers also come with a small LCD and offer image adjusting features. The largest print you can make with this type of printer is 8 × 10 inches, but the majority print only 4 × 6 inch pictures. This printing method is becoming more and more popular and, as technology improves, the cost goes down.

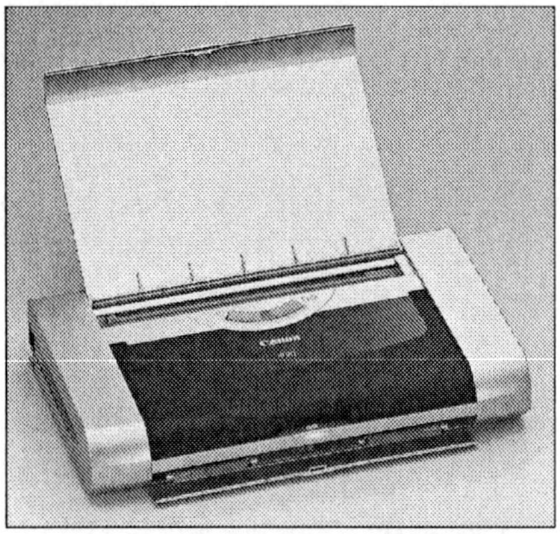

A typical example of a small and easy-to-use printer that does not need a computer.

The Kodak Easy Share system works directly from the camera to the printer.

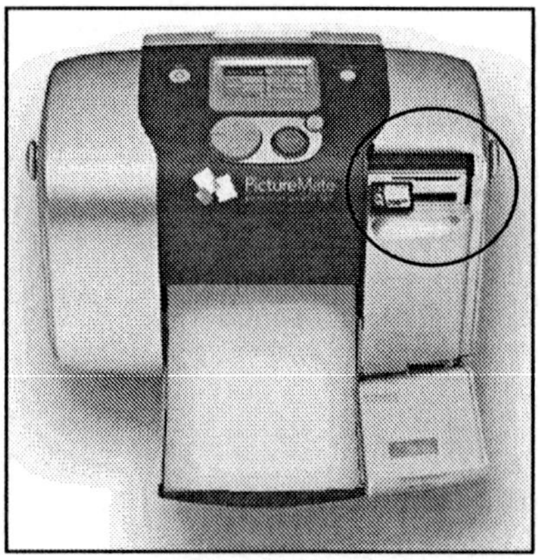

Epson Picture Mate prints directly from memory cards. Notice the slots for memory cards.

TIP! Make sure the printer you buy will accept your type of memory card!

Self-Service Photo Kiosks

The self-service kiosk has brought the ease of film processing to digital photographers. Not only has it made it simple to have your digital "film" developed; it has become self-service! This was not possible with film processing. These kiosks are in many familiar locations: grocery stores, drug stores, discount stores, photo labs, and photo stores—and the list grows daily as more businesses include them in their line of services (not unlike ATMs, which are found practically everywhere). You can choose from a variety of print sizes and also purchase a CD with your images. This provides an easy way to keep back ups of your photos.

How They Work The first time you use a self-service kiosk might be a little confusing because there are many steps in the process. Directions are provided by touching the screen and following directions displayed. You are able to go back or cancel and exit anytime throughout the process. Don't be afraid to ask for assistance from a store assistant. Most kiosks work essentially the same so once you have the general practice done, you should be able to use one anywhere you go. Some kiosk systems print your photos as you wait; others print a receipt and you come back for your pictures.

The following are basic steps for all self-serve kiosks:

- Touch the Welcome screen and you will be given a prompt to select the type of media you are using (CompactFlash card, Memory Stick, CD, etc.).
- Insert the media when prompted.
- Preview your pictures after they have loaded.
- Select the images you want printed.
- Select a print size.
- When prompted, remove the media.

Other options are available as you step through the process. Prompts will be displayed at intervals showing what else is available. Some options include:

- Cropping
- Adjusting Colors
- Adjusting Contrast
- Adding Text
- Using special templates to frame your image
- Changing a color picture to black and white or sepia
- Making a CD of your images

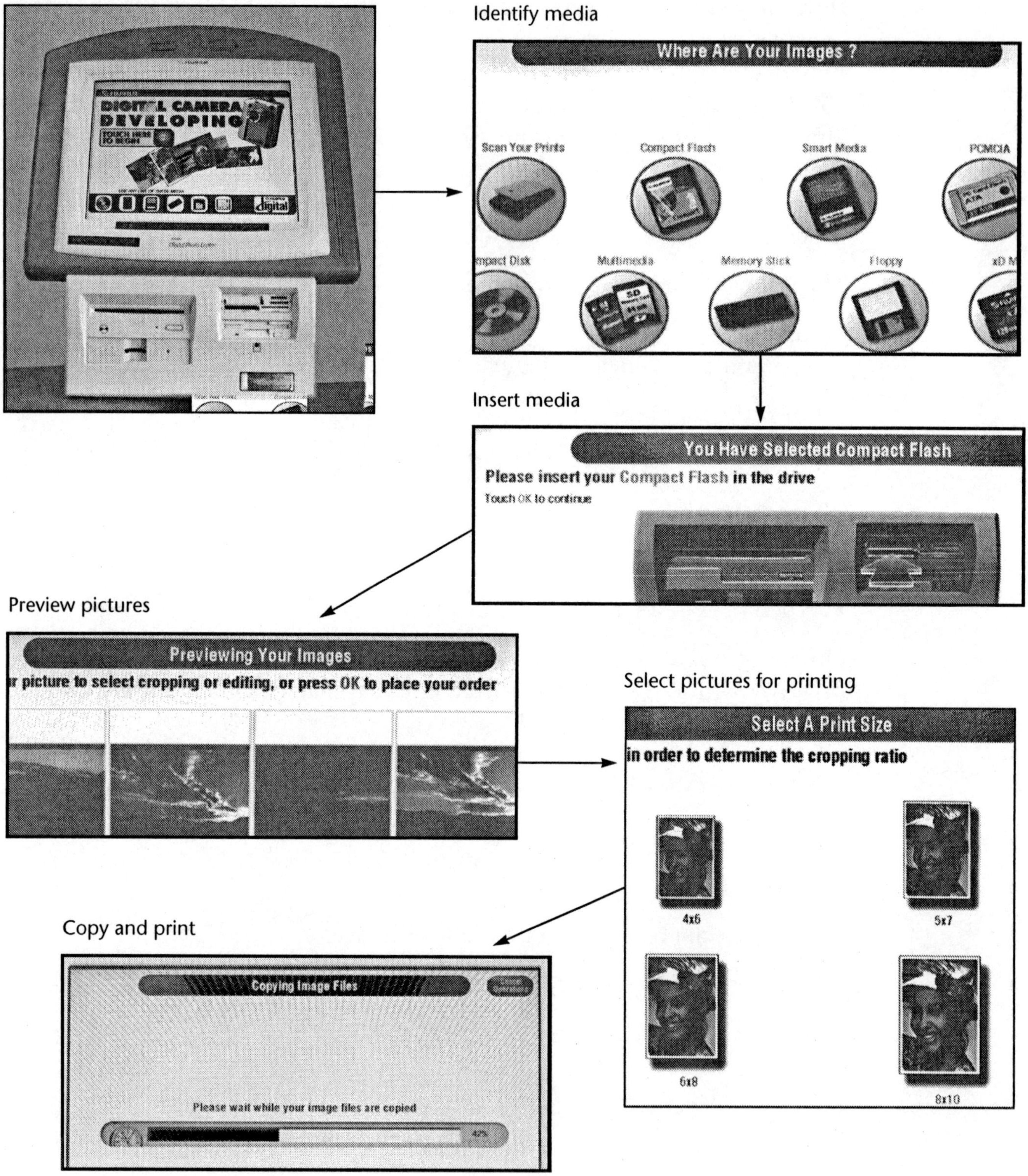

TIP! Be prepared to spend some time at a self-serve kiosk, especially as you first learn to use them. Also, not all machines give the same results (even those of the same type and brand) so if you are not satisfied, try another store.

Photo Labs (Over-the-Counter Service)

Photo labs are a great option if you want to leave the entire print processing to someone else. It's simple! Bring your memory card or CD-ROM to a photo lab, either professional or those found in drug stores, grocery stores, discount stores, etc. They will download and print your pictures, and you come back and pick them up—just like film processing. If you are not satisfied with the results, the lab can reprocess the photos, correcting color and lightness/darkness. The cost is usually comparable to self-service kiosks but you don't have to spend the time making the prints. Instead, you can use that time to take more pictures!

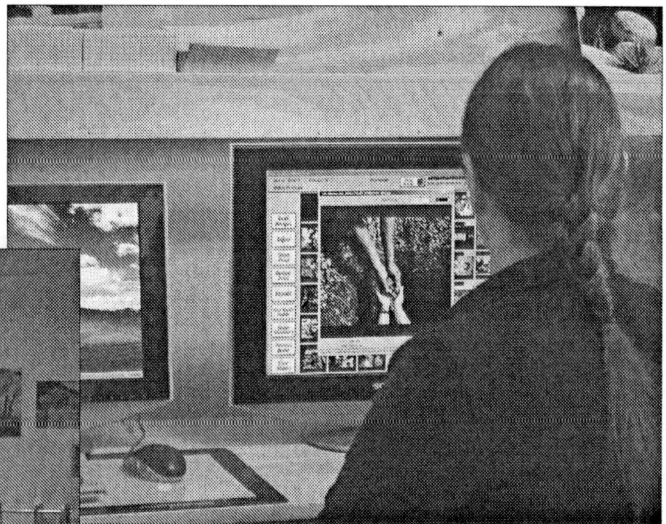

Great service from Our Color Photo Lab in Santa Fe, NM

TIP! Different photo labs produce different results, just like self-service kiosks. If you are not satisfied with one, try another.

Online Labs

Another alternative for printing your photos is to use an online photo lab. What could be easier? You do need to know how to use the Internet, but that's the only skill required. You simply upload (transfer your digital pictures) files to the lab's Web site where you can order prints that will be sent to you, create online photo albums that are available to your friends and family, have photos sent to others, and have others order prints themselves. Imagine going to a family reunion or wedding and being able to share your pictures immediately, without having to email each individual or send prints via the post office. More and more companies are offering this service.

Saving Files for the Web and Email

Have you ever received an email with a photo attached that was so large the nose covered the entire screen? Or, has an attachment taken so long to download that it tied up your computer for 10 minutes or even an hour? Both of these situations happen frequently and are a result of not knowing how to properly save images for email and Web purposes. In this section, you will be guided through the process of saving images for the Web using Photoshop Elements' Save for Web feature. It's really pretty easy and very rewarding. (Other software programs offer similar features and also produce excellent results.)

QUICK REFERENCE: Optimizing Images for the Web

Optimum download time	30 seconds or less
Optimum height in pixels	768 pixels or less
Optimum file size dimensions	1024 × 768 pixels or less
Optimum file size	100 Kilobytes or less (300 K is acceptable but smaller is better)

The Save for Web Window

PE's Save for Web window offers many options you can use to find the optimal balance between file size and image quality. The following figure displays many key settings on this window.

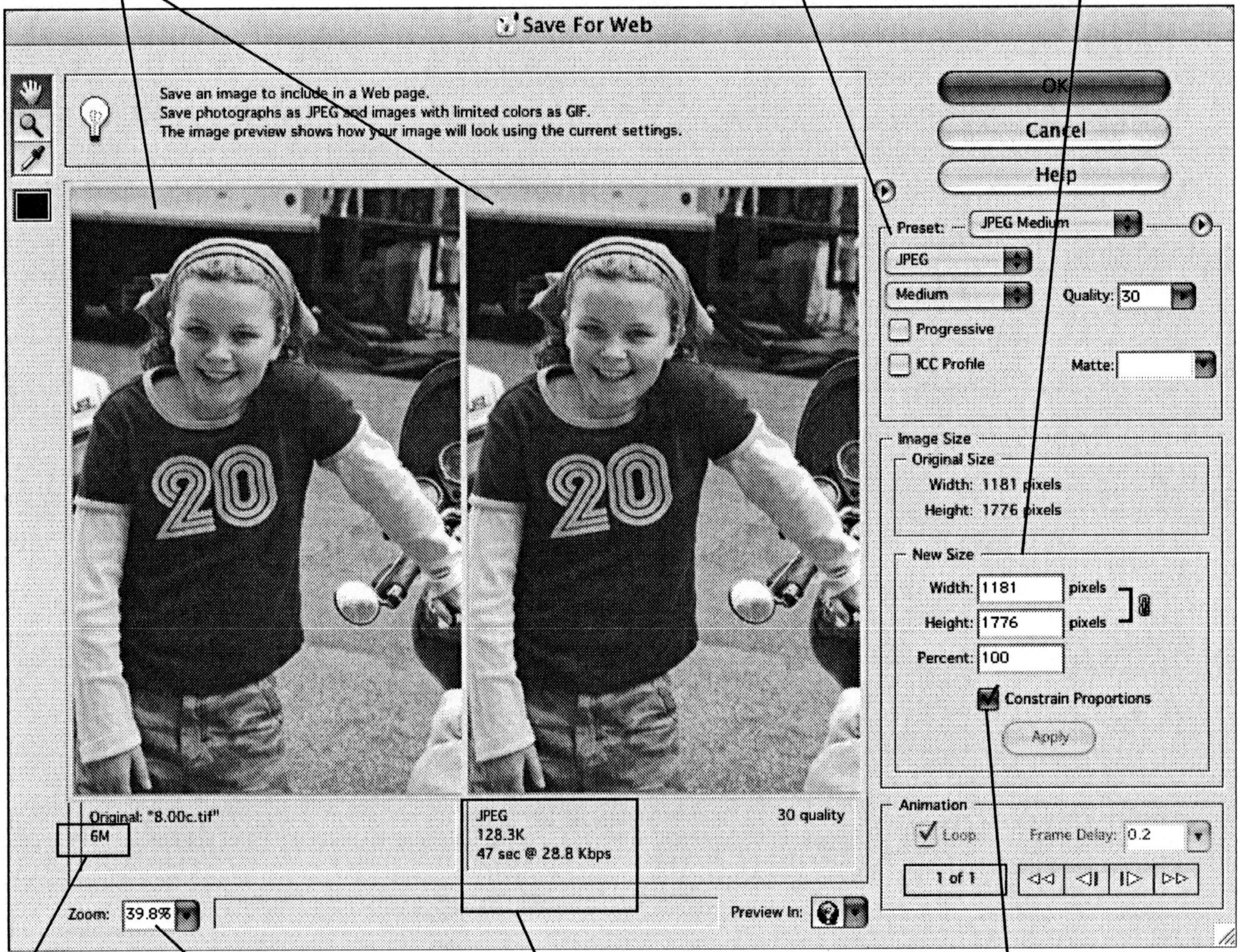

HANDS-ON 9.1 Save a Photo for the Web

In this exercise, you will open a photo and use PE to save a version of it with a reduced file size.

Before You Begin: You will use the Anna10 photo used in Lesson 8, Exploring Photoshop Elements. Follow steps 1–4 in the appropriate version of Hands-On 8.1 to download the photo if it is not available on your computer.

Launch Photoshop Elements and Open the Photo

1. Launch Photoshop Elements.

   Depending on how the program is configured, a Welcome window may appear.

2. Follow the step for your computer if PE displays the Welcome window:

   - **Windows XP:** Choose the Edit and Enhance Photos option.
   - **Macintosh OS X:** Click the Close button.

3. Choose File→Open from the menu bar, navigate to your file storage location, and open the file.

4. Choose File→Save for Web from the menu bar.

   PE opens the Save for Web window. The original photo is on the left and the version you will save is on the right.

Change the Image Settings

5. Choose JPEG Medium from the Presets list, if necessary.

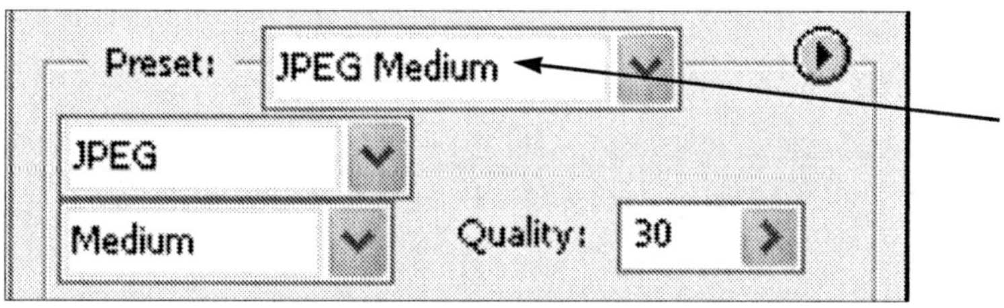

PE displays the file size and estimated download time for the photo at this setting below the After version. (Depending on previous edits to the photo, the numbers you see will differ from the example shown.)

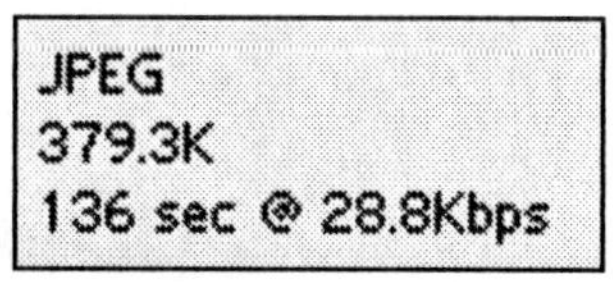

6. Choose the GIF 32 No Dither setting from the Preset box.

   PE displays a preview of the photo with the new setting. Notice how the GIF format changes the appearance of the photo—and not for the better. The JPEG format not only saves file size, it makes the photo look better too.

7. Choose JPEG High from the Preset box.

   The photo looks much better and is about the same size as the GIF version.

8. Choose JPEG Low from the Preset box.

   Depending on your monitor settings, the photo may not appear to change very much.

9. Choose JPEG Medium from the Preset box.

   This setting appears to create a good combination of quality and file size.

Change the Image Size

Another way to reduce the file size of an image is to change its dimensions.

10. Follow these steps to change the size of the image:

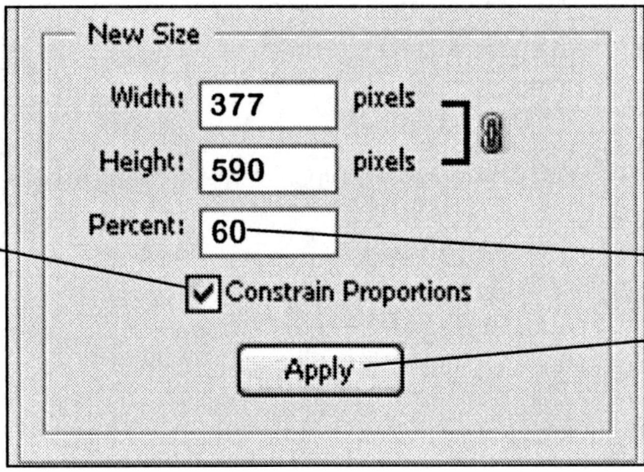

PE resizes the photo to 60% of its original size. Notice the current file size and download time indicated. Reducing the size of a photo can greatly reduce its file size.

11. Type 500 in the Width box, and then click Apply.

PE alters the size of the photo again. Notice that the height also changed because the Constrain Proportions setting keeps the proportions constant.

Save the Photo

12. Click the OK button at the top-right corner of the window.

PE displays the Save As window, where you can give the modified photo a new name.

13. **Macintosh only:** Click the arrow to the right of the filename to expand the Save As window if it is not already expanded.

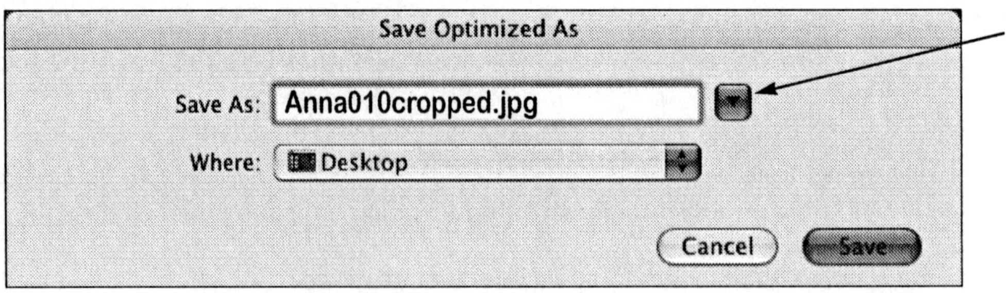

14. Rename the file `Anna010-web` and save it to your file storage location.

PE saves the photo with the new name and returns you to the original version of the photo.

15. Follow the step for your computer:

- **Windows XP:** Choose File→Exit from the menu bar. Choose No if PE asks if you wish to save any changes to the photo.
- **Macintosh OS X:** Choose Photoshop Elements→Quit from the menu bar. Choose Don't Save if PE asks if you wish to save any changes to the photo.

PE closes the program window. Your newly saved file should be visible on the Desktop.

Attaching Photos to Email Messages

There are many ways to send a picture with an email message, and all are very effective. You can add the photo file directly from an image editing program like PE, using a built-in operating system feature, or right in your email message window.

Attaching is the term used for including the picture in your message so the recipient will have access to it. The attachment symbol is often a paperclip located in the shortcut bar in the email message window. It looks slightly different in each email program. If you don't see a button, you can usually find the attachment command on the Insert or Edit menu on the menu bar.

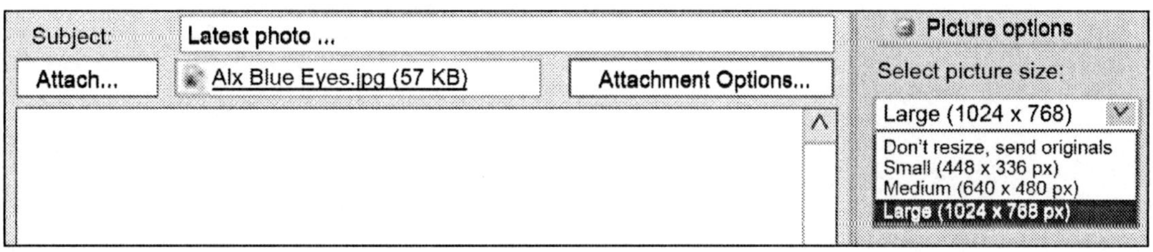

Outlook 2003 has a picture size option that conveniently allows you to reduce the size of photos without modifying them in an image editing program.

QUICK REFERENCE: Attaching Photos to Email Messages

Task	Procedure
Prepare the photo for attachment	• Make sure the photo is in a compressed file format (usually JPEG). • Use the Save for Web command in PE (or a similar command in another program) to optimize the photo for transmission. • Consider adjusting the dimensions of the photo to a smaller size, such as 1024 × 768 or 800 × 600. • (Optional) Adjust the compression of a JPEG file to Medium.
Attach a photo to an email message	• Begin composing a new email message or a reply to a previously received message. • Click the Attach File button on the message window. • Navigate to the folder containing the photo(s) to be attached. • Use the Ctrl and Shift (Windows) or ⌘ and Shift (Macintosh) keys to select multiple files. • Click the Attach button to complete the command. • (Outlook 2003 Only) Choose a size setting from the attachment menu if you wish to use Outlook's image sizing capability.

Concepts Review

True/False Questions

				Page number
1.	Choosing correct print settings is an important factor when printing pictures.	**true**	**false**	______
2.	You may only be able to create 4 × 6 inch prints on printers that work without computers.	**true**	**false**	______
3.	An important factor to consider before using an online photo lab is the speed of your Internet connection.	**true**	**false**	______
4.	Generally, it is best to use photo paper made by your printer manufacturer.	**true**	**false**	______
5.	Before you buy a printer that does not need a computer, make sure it accepts your type of memory card.	**true**	**false**	______
6.	The disadvantage of using online labs is that you cannot get prints.	**true**	**false**	______
7.	The Save for Web feature in PE is completely automatic so you have no control over the settings.	**true**	**false**	______
8.	The main reason to use the Save for Web feature is to make smaller image files.	**true**	**false**	______
9.	To send a picture to a friend via email, you must attach it to the email message.	**true**	**false**	______
10.	It is okay to use a TIFF file format on images you send via email.	**true**	**false**	______

Multiple Choice Questions

1. You do not need a computer if you choose a(n) _______.

   Page number: ______

   a. over-the-counter photo lab

   b. online photo lab

   c. self-service Kiosk

   d. All of the above

2. Which of the following services do online photo labs offer?

   Page number: ______

   a. Make prints

   b. Create albums

   c. Send photos to others

   d. All of the above

3. A disadvantage of printing your own pictures is _______.

   Page number: ______

   a. paper size limitation

   b. cost

   c. quality is not as good as labs

   d. None of the above

4. Which of the following can you do using a self-service kiosk?

   Page number: ______

   a. Make different size prints

   b. Add type to your photo

   c. Remove distracting elements

   d. All of the above

Skill Builders

SKILL BUILDER 9.1 Compare Prints from Different Self-Service Kiosks

In this exercise, you will take the same image to several self-service kiosks to compare the quality of each.

Make Prints

1. Choose two pictures on your memory card. Use photos that have a lot of different colors (the subject does not matter).

   Some colors are more difficult to print than others. Choose a picture with many different colors for a good test.

2. Locate at least two businesses that have self-service kiosks.

   Contact large discount stores, grocery stores, drug stores, and photo labs.

3. Complete the following at each location:
   - Print one 4 × 6 inch picture of each image with no adjustments.
   - Print one 4 × 6 inch picture of each image using the same color adjustment.

   For example, add more green to the pictures. Being consistent is very important to get valid results, so use the same or similar adjustment at each kiosk.

4. Mount your pictures on a piece of poster board and label them with the following:
   - Name of store
   - Cost per print
   - Time to make prints (if delivered directly from the kiosk)
   - Time to receive prints (if not delivered directly from the kiosk)
   - Level of service (one to ten, ten is best)
   - Staff knowledge

Share Results with the Class

Now you will bring your board to class and compare results with other students.

5. Put the boards around the room and take some time for everyone to look at them.
6. Spend some time listening to each person's experience as you are shown his pictures.
   - Did the subject matter make any difference? Were certain colors easier to reproduce?
   - Did anyone go to the same place as you, but got different results?
7. Save your board as future reference. You might want to repeat this exercise in a month or so to see if conditions have changed.

APPENDIX A

Using File Storage Media

This appendix contains instructions about using this book with various file storage media.

In This Appendix

The following topics are addressed in this appendix:

Working with File Storage Locations

New technologies continue to expand the variety of available computer storage media. The 3½ inch floppy diskette has been around since 1983. That's incredibly ancient in the fast-moving field of computers. It's easy to use other storage media with this book. Potential alternative storage locations include:

- The My Pictures folder (Windows XP)
- The Pictures folder (Macintosh OS X)
- A USB flash drive
- A folder on your local hard drive
- A folder on a network drive

You can also store your files on a CD-R. For more information, see the Backing Up Your Digital Photos section of Lesson 3.

Using the My Pictures Folder (Windows XP)

Windows creates a unique My Documents folder for each login, and within this folder is a subfolder called My Pictures. The My Documents folder resides on the main system drive (usually the C: drive).

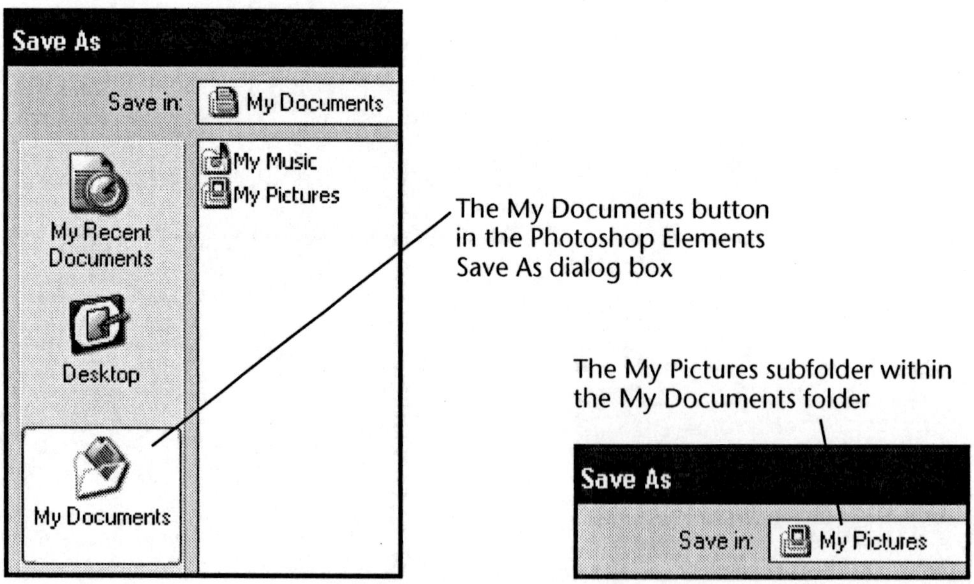

Using the Pictures Folder (Macintosh OS X)

Macintosh OS X creates a unique user folder for each login name, and within this folder is a subfolder called Pictures. The user folder resides on the main system drive (Macintosh HD).

The Pictures button in the left pane of any open window.

Using a USB Flash Drive (Windows XP)

A USB flash drive stores your data on a flash memory chip. You simply plug it into a USB port on any computer and Windows and the Macintosh immediately recognize it as an additional disk drive. USB flash drives typically are able to store 32 megabytes (MB) or more of your data files. Large capacity USB flash drives can store 512 MB or more. The Macintosh displays the flash drive on the Desktop like another disk drive. Windows assigns the flash drive a new drive letter (see next topic).

Most USB flash drives are about the size of your thumb and plug into any available USB port on your computer.

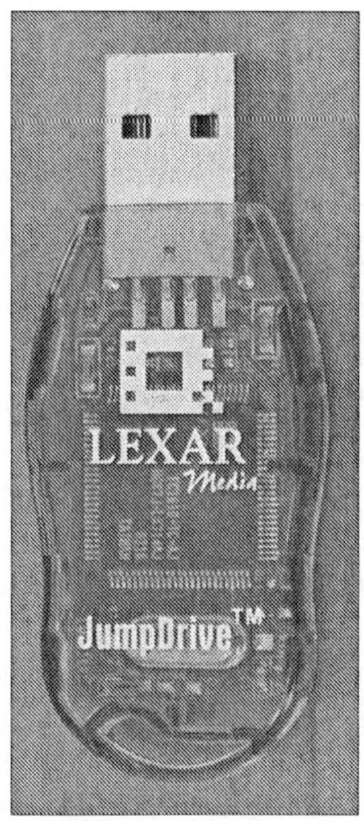

USB Flash Drive Letter

When you plug in a USB flash drive to a Windows computer, Windows automatically assigns it the next available drive letter. Windows uses drive letters to identify each drive connected to the computer. For example, the primary part of the hard drive is always identified as the C: drive. The CD/DVD drive is typically the D: or E: drive.

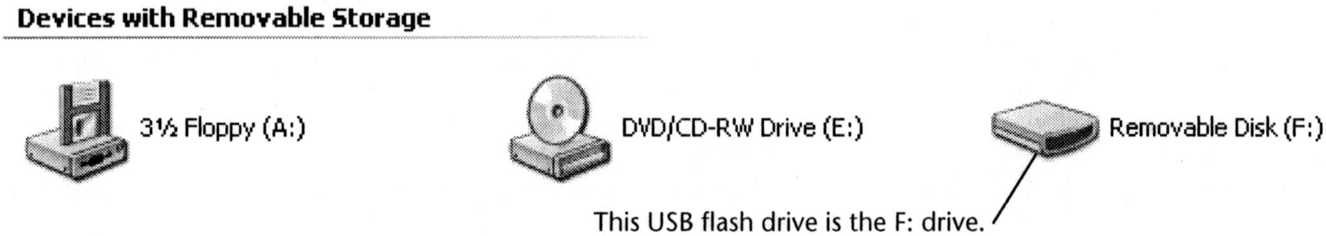

TIP! Your USB flash drive may receive a different drive letter on different computers. This does not affect any files stored on the hard drive.

Using a USB Flash Drive (Macintosh OS X)

When you plug in a USB flash drive to a Macintosh computer, Macintosh automatically displays it on the Desktop. Macintosh will use the name already given to the drive or, if no name has been given, will use the default designation No Name.

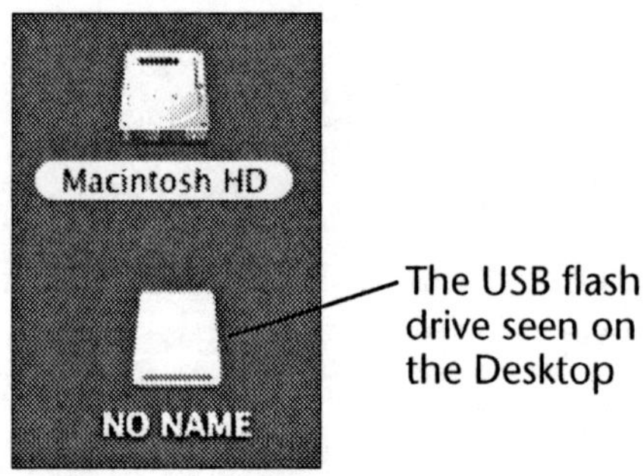

HANDS-ON A.1A Rename Your USB Flash Drive (Windows XP)

Note to Windows Users: You may find it convenient to rename your USB flash drive to make it easier to recognize when you save or open files.

TIP! Some Windows systems may not give you renaming privileges for drives.

1. Plug the USB flash drive into an available USB port.
2. Open a My Computer window.
3. Right-click your USB flash drive and choose Rename from the context menu.

NOTE! In the next step, Windows may display a prompt that you cannot rename this flash drive. You have not done anything wrong! You can use the drive with its current name. You may also want to try renaming it later using a different login.

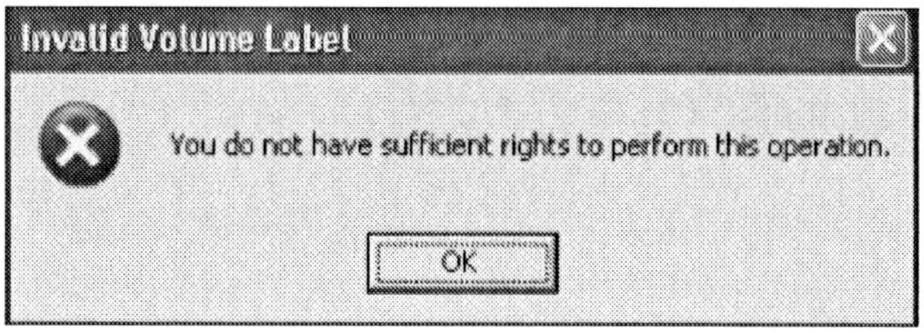

4. Type **`FlashDrive`** as the new drive name and tap [Enter]. Click OK if you receive a prompt that you do not have sufficient rights to perform this operation.

   If you were unable to rename the flash drive, don't worry. Renaming the flash drive is a convenience for recognition and has no other effect.

HANDS-ON A.1B Rename Your USB Flash Drive (Macintosh OS X)

Note to Mac Users: You may find it convenient to rename your USB flash drive to make it easier to recognize when you save or open files.

1. Plug the USB flash drive into an available USB port.
2. Single-click on the name of the USB flash drive shown on the Desktop.

   Be sure not to double-click on the name or the flash drive will open.

3. Type **`FlashDrive`** as the new drive name and tap [Return].

Using the Hard Drive

If you will routinely work with this course on the same computer, you can store the exercise files in a folder on the hard drive. Windows users may wish to create a folder in the My Documents folder. Macintosh users should use the Documents folder.

Using a Network Drive Folder

You may use a system connected to a network. There may be a folder on a network computer in another location that is dedicated to storing your work. Windows users should look for this folder within the My Network Places folder. You may have to navigate deeper into the network drive to locate your personal network drive folder.

Macintosh users should look for this folder by choosing Network in the left pane of the window that opens when you double-click on the hard drive (or any folder on the Desktop.)

Macintosh only

Glossary

Alkaline battery A non-rechargeable battery that puts out less and less power until maximized; most common and least expensive battery (*See also* page 13)

Example: The batteries in your TV remote

Aperture The opening in a lens that admits the light that strikes the sensor in a digital camera (*See also* page 113)

Aperture Priority mode A semi-automatic setting used to set a specific f-stop while the camera sets the corresponding shutter speed (*See also* page 117)

Attaching The process of including an image file in an email message so the recipient can access it; typically indicated by a paperclip icon (*See also* page 225)

Auto exposure lock (AE-Lock) A feature that enables you to lock the exposure at a location other than the point of focus (*See also* page 128)

Automatic mode A digital camera feature in which the camera chooses all the settings (*See also* page 89)

Bracketing (Exposure) A process of taking several pictures in a sequence, each at slightly different exposures (normal, underexposed, overexposed) (*See also* page 130)

Buffer Where images are stored before being transferred to a memory card (*See also* page 102)

Burn The process of saving files to a CD-R, CD-RW, or DVD (*See also* page 71)

Byte A single character of data (*See also* page 28)

Example: A, B, C, %, 4.

CCD (charge-coupled device) A small plate covered with a grid of light sensors used by digital cameras to record images (*See also* page 3)

CD-R A disc onto which you can burn images in multiple sessions; once images are burned to a CD-R, they cannot be deleted (*See also* page 72)

CD-RW A disc onto which you can burn images in multiple sessions; images burned to a CD-RW can be deleted and new ones can be burned onto it; CD-RWs are not as stable as CD-Rs (*See also* page 72)

Color balance Refers to rendering colors produced by cameras, computers, and other electronic devices as close as possible to how they are seen by the human eye (*See also* page 162)

Color cast A predominance (usually unwanted) of one color in an image; can cause an imbalance in the colors of a photograph (*See also* page 163)

CompactFlash The most widely used memory card; sturdy and not very susceptible to damage from handling (*See also* page 14)

Composition Describes how elements in a photographed are placed and framed (*See also* page 35)

Compression The process of making digital files smaller so more pictures can fit on a memory card (*See also* page 147)

Continuous Drive mode Also called Burst mode; allows you to take several pictures, one after the other, without a pause between shots (*See also* page 102)

Depth of field How much of a scene is in focus (*See also* page 116)

Digital viewfinder Also called electronic viewfinder; means of looking through a camera to compose a shot; a digitized version of what the camera sees (*See also* page 5)

Digital zoom A feature that allows you to go beyond the optical zoom capability by selecting a group of pixels in the scene and process them to look larger; results in a magnified, but blurry, enlarged image (*See also* page 10)

Docking station A feature of some digital cameras that allows you to transfer images from the camera to the computer, recharge batteries, and print images (*See also* page 54)

Downloading Also called transferring, the process of moving images from a memory card to the computer; creating a backup of your photographs (*See also* page 54)

Electronic (digital) viewfinder Also called digital viewfinder; means of looking through a camera to compose a shot; a digitized version of what the camera sees (*See also* page 5)

Exposure compensation Also called Exposure Value (EV); feature that allows you to correct exposure setting to tone down glare from bright sunlight or to bring out highlights of shaded objects (*See also* page 124)

Exposure value (EV) *See* Exposure compensation

File format A standardized form of storing data understood by all types of digital cameras, computers, and peripheral devices (*See also* page 151)

Fill Flash mode A flash mode that fills in the dark area of a scene with light so the subject is not a dark silhouette; often used when the subject is in shade or is in front of a bright background (*See also* page 97)

Focus lock Feature that enables you to point the camera at a subject and lock the focus, making sure the subject is sharp and clear (*See also* page 33)

Format (a memory card) The process of erasing all images on a memory card before using it in another camera or completely erasing all pictures on a card (*See also* page 27)

F-stop Indicates how large or small the diameter of the aperture opens or closes (*See also* page 113)

Index In the back of your instruction manual, a list of terms and topics discussed in the manual; use the index to locate specific topics that will answer your questions (*See also* page 25)

Information Term used to describe detail in a photograph (*See also* page 144)

JPEG (JPG) Joint Photographic Experts Group; the most commonly used file format for storing digital images in the camera (*See also* page 152)

Kelvin (K) Unit in the color measurement scale, which measures color temperature (*See also* page 161)

Kiosk A self-service photo processing unit found in drug stores, discount stores, grocery stores, and photo labs (*See also* page 216)

Liquid crystal display (LCD) The small monitor on the back of some digital cameras; allows you to accurately see the picture you are taking (*See also* page 3)

Lithium-ion battery A rechargeable battery; camera specific, so you must get a battery that fits with your camera; lasts longer than alkaline batteries but are more expensive (*See also* page 13)

LCD *See* Liquid crystal display (LCD)

Megabyte (MB) Approximately one million *bytes* of data (*See also* page 28)

Example: One 3 inch, high resolution color photograph

MB *See* Megabyte (MB)

Megapixel (MP) Approximately one million pixels (*See also* page 8)

Example: One 4 x 6 inch, high resolution color photograph

Memory (in batteries) Used to describe a battery's tendency to remember at what stage it is recharged (*See also* page 14)

Example: If you recharge your battery while it is two-thirds full, it will always need to be recharged when two-thirds full and will only take a two-third charge

Memory card The "film" of digital cameras (where pictures are stored); can be used over and over; camera specific (*See also* page 14)

Memory card reader Any variety of inexpensive devices used to download images to the computer; may include multiple slots to accommodate different card types (universal or 6-in-one card readers) (*See also* page 54)

Memory Stick (Memory Stick PRO) A memory card used exclusively by Sony cameras; longer and thinner than the other types of storage media (*See also* page 14)

Monitor hood A rubber or plastic device that attaches directly to the LCD; provides shade so the display can be viewed under bright light (*See also* page 49)

MultiMedia A very small memory card (*See also* page 14)

Nickel Cadmium (NiCad) battery A rechargeable battery; must be completely drained before being recharged (develops memory); economical (*See also* page 14)

NiCad battery *See* Nickel Cadmium (NiCad) battery

Nickel Metal Hydride (NMH) battery A rechargeable battery that can be recharged at any time without developing memory; more powerful and more expensive than NiCad batteries (*See also* page 14)

NMH battery See Nickel Metal Hydride (NMH) battery

Noise Term that describes artifacts in the areas of an image due to amplified pixel signals on the camera's sensor; results in lower- quality images (*See also* page 133)

Optical zoom Moves the lens around to magnify a image without quality loss (*See also* page 10)

Overexposed Term used to describe a photograph in which all elements are too light (*See also* page 179)

Peripheral Any standalone device used in conjunction with your computer (*See also* page 72)

Example: CD burner, printer, scanner keyboard, mouse

Pixel A picture element; many pixels make up a picture (*See also* page 3)

Program mode A digital camera feature in which the camera assigns certain settings and the user assigns others (*See also* page 89)

RAW A file format that enables the camera to record the image with totally unprocessed data (*See also* page 153)

Red-eye Occurs when the subject's eyes become dilated when the flash is fired; results in an eerie red color in the pupil of the eye (*See also* page 98)

Replaying (Reviewing) Using the LCD, the process of viewing photos one at a time, in index mode, as a slide show, or magnified (*See also* page 49)

Resolution Measures the number of pixels in an image and determines the optimum print size that can be made accordingly (*See also* page 143)

Scene Assist mode A digital camera feature in which settings are made according to subject matter (*See also* page 90)

Secure Digital The newest form of MultiMedia memory cards (*See also* page 14)

Session Refers to each time you add (burn) files on a CD-R that already contains saved files (*See also* page 72)

Shutter speed Controls how long the aperture stays open; determines how motion will be captured (*See also* page 120)

Shutter Speed Priority mode A semi-automatic setting that allows you to choose the shutter speed and the camera selects a corresponding f-stop (*See also* page 121)

Shutter lag The time it takes to charge the sensor and perform exposure and focus operations before the shutter fires (*See also* page 11)

Single Drive mode The drive mode used most often; the camera takes and processes pictures one at a time (*See also* page 102)

Single lens reflex (SLR) When you look through the optical viewfinder you are seeing what the camera sees via a mirror reflecting the image into the viewfinder (*See also* page 5)

SLR *See* Single lens reflex (SLR)

SmartMedia A memory card; because the card is so light and thin and contacts are exposed (vulnerable to damage), these cards require great care (*See also* page 14)

Storage capacity In regards to memory cards, the amount of available space (measured in megabytes) on which to store images (*See also* page 28)

Table of Contents In the front of your instruction manual, a list of chapters and sub-chapters (*See also* page 25)

TIFF (TIF) A file format that preserves every bit of picture data (*See also* page 152)

Transferring *See* Downloading

Underexposed Everything in the photograph is too dark (*See also* page 180)

Usenet The world's largest online bulletin board; search Usenet to find information on just about any topic (*See also* page 16)

Wallet A device that holds and organizes multiple memory cards when not in use (*See also* page 29)

White balance settings Special settings that automatically adjust for color casts; simulates what the human eye does (*See also* page 165)

Workspace In PE, refers to the setup of the work area window (*See also* page 183)

xD Picture A memory card used exclusively by Fuji and Olympus cameras; more expensive than CompactFlash and Memory Stick cards (*See also* page 14)

Zoom factor Indicated amount of zoom possible with a specific lens (*See also* page 10)

Example: A 3X zoom means the subject will appear three times closer when the zoom lens is fully extended

Index